Environmental Decision Making for Engineering and Business Managers

Other Environmental Engineering Books from McGraw-Hill

American Water Works Association
WATER QUALITY AND TREATMENT

Baker and Herson
BIOREMEDIATION

Chopey
ENVIRONMENTAL ENGINEERING FOR THE CHEMICAL PROCESS INDUSTRIES ✓

Corbitt
STANDARD HANDBOOK OF ENVIRONMENTAL ENGINEERING

Freeman
HAZARDOUS WASTE MINIMIZATION

Freeman
STANDARD HANDBOOK OF HAZARDOUS WASTE TREATMENT AND DISPOSAL

Jain
ENVIRONMENTAL IMPACT ASSESSMENT

Levin and Gealt
BIOTREATMENT OF INDUSTRIAL AND HAZARDOUS WASTE

McKenna and Cunneo
PESTICIDE REGULATION HANDBOOK

Majumdar
REGULATORY REQUIREMENTS OF HAZARDOUS MATERIALS

Nanney
ENVIRONMENTAL RISKS IN REAL ESTATE TRANSACTIONS

Waldo and Hines
CHEMICAL HAZARD COMMUNICATION GUIDEBOOK

Environmental Decision Making for Engineering and Business Managers

Betty J. Seldner
Environmental Consultant
Santa Clarita, California

Joseph P. Cothrel
Communications Consultant
Chicago, Illinois

McGraw-Hill, Inc.

New York   San Francisco   Washington, D.C.   Auckland   Bogotá
Caracas   Lisbon   London   Madrid   Mexico City   Milan
Montreal   New Delhi   San Juan   Singapore
Sydney   Tokyo   Toronto

Library of Congress Cataloging-in-Publication Data

Seldner, Betty J.
    Environmental decision making for engineering and business
  managers / Betty J. Seldner, Joseph P. Cothrel.
        p.   cm.
    ISBN 0-07-056141-9
    1. Industry—Environmental aspects.   2. Environmental engineering—
  Decision making.   3. Industrial management—Decision making.
    I. Cothrel, Joseph P.   II. Title.
    TD194.S45   1994
    658.4'08—dc20   93-38881
                                                                        CIP

1 2 3 4 5 6 7 8 9 0   DOC/DOC   9 0 9 8 7 6 5 4

ISBN 0-07-056141-9

*The sponsoring editor for this book was Gail F. Nalven, the editing supervisor
was Joseph Bertuna, and the production supervisor was Suzanne W. Babeuf. It
was set in Palatino by McGraw-Hill's Professional Book Group composition
unit.*

Printed and bound by R. R. Donnelley & Sons Company.

Contents

3. Environmental Liability and Reducing Corporate Exposure   33

4. Inspections and the Enforcement Process   49

5. The Role and Function of the United States Environmental Protection Agency   61

Contributors

Mark G. Busch *Senior Environmental Control Engineer, Northrop Aircraft Division.* (CHAP. 9)

John Cornelison *Senior Project Manager, Manager of Safety, America North, Inc.* (CHAP. 10)

Paul B. Duff *Director, Environmental Affairs, Textron Inc.* (CHAP. 2)

John Gunderson *Major, United States Air Force.* (CHAP. 16)

Glenn Heyman *Environmental Scientist, U.S. Environmental Protection Agency, Region IX.* (CHAP. 5)

Stephen T. Holzer, Esq. *Principal, Parker, Milliken, Clark, O'Hara & Samuelian.* (CHAP. 3)

Steven J. Jones *Supervising Air Quality Inspector, South Coast Air Quality Management District.* (CHAP. 4)

Hank Martin   *Manager, McLaren-Hart.* (CHAP. 11)

Gary A. Meyer, Esq.   *Principal, Parker, Milliken, Clark, O'Hara & Samuelian.* (CHAP. 3)

John E. Mullane   *Vice President and Director, Division of Scientific, Technical and Environmental Affairs, Hill and Knowlton, Inc.* (CHAP. 13)

Edward O. Raynolds   *Senior Vice President, Hill and Knowlton, Inc.* (CHAP. 13)

Kenneth M. Ries   *Director, Environment and Energy, The Dial Corp.* (CHAP. 1)

Kraig H. Scheyer   *Manager, Safety, Health, and Environmental Affairs, TRW.* (CHAP. 7)

Richard Varenchik   *Public Information Officer, State of California Environmental Protection Agency.* (CHAP. 14)

Norman L. Weiss   *Compliance Manager, EMCON Associates.* (CHAP. 6)

W. Gordon Wood   *Vice President, Finance (CFO), Facilities Division, Fortune 100 Company.* (CHAP. 15)

Cathie Wright   *The Hon. California State Senate.* (CHAP. 12)

Robert Young   *Manager, Environmental Services (Retired), Bell Helicopter.* (CHAP. 8)

Preface

The purpose of this book is likely to be different from that of other volumes you have read on the subject of environmental management. Its purpose is *not* to summarize current environmental regulations, though you will find such a summary between its covers. Neither does it intend solely to provide step-by-step instructions on environmental tasks, though the information you need to develop effective programs for training, auditing, regulatory affairs, and other requirements is present as well.

What this book *is* about is the challenges you face when you assume responsibility for environmental management in a company small or large. Few roles have greater impact on a company's success and even survival. Few carry with them such personal accountability for decisions made on the job. Yet the person with this responsibility is frequently not the chairman or the chief executive or even head of a division—though you can bet that each of those individuals cares deeply about the decisions the environmental manager makes.

Who is the typical environmental manager? He or she is sometimes an engineer or scientist. In other instances, environmental responsibilities are assigned to a business manager with some technical training. In almost all cases these individuals work with a small or nonexistent staff, and under tremendous pressure to succeed.

And they usually share one more characteristic. Because environmental management is a relatively recent addition to business disciplines, most environmental managers do not have the benefit of either individual guidance in the form of a mentor, or institutional guidance in the form of established corporate policy and practice.

Where many books cover the technical aspects of the environmental field, this volume focuses on management—the day-to-day decisions made by executives and managers in industry today. Because environmental challenges face the chief financial officer as well as the environmental manager, a variety of perspectives are offered. The contributors are experienced executives, managers, consultants, and regulators. They are people who deal with fiscal, ethical, and legal problems every day of their working lives. They include 18 individuals from business, industry, and government with real experience in what works in environmental management—and what doesn't.

Included are environmental managers from The Dial Corp and Textron Inc. who share their ideas about what should go into a company's environmental program mix, and how to manage that program effectively. Managers from TRW and Bell Helicopter remind you that resources outside the company can be as important as those inside: the professional and trade groups that link you with your counterparts around the nation and give you access to the information and technologies you need.

Senior executives from Hill & Knowlton talk about outside input you *don't* need: the negative publicity that can result from an environmental incident. Their chapter details the crisis communcations plan every company must have in today's climate of media frenzy, as well as the daily communication necessary to create and preserve a positive public image.

Training is a fundamental need, and the challenges are different for every company. A training specialist from Northrop Aircraft Division leads you through eight scenarios that have wide application in many industries while identifying the specific training required for everything from environmental awareness to Superfund cleanup. Because cost-effective training is sometimes a case of *should* rather than *must*, in another chapter an experienced training consultant talks about training decisions that focus on reducing risk as well as ensuring compliance. Risk management also merits a chapter of its own, this one written by two leading environmental attorneys who discuss, among other things, the importance of auditing and the common misconceptions surrounding it.

Other contributors let you know what you can expect from regulatory agencies and other enforcement authorities. Senior personnel from both federal and state bodies outline today's regulatory structure and tell you about their agencies' roles as information resources as well as enforcers of the law. An inspector from an air quality authority in Los Angeles brings you into his agency for a view of what developments in the nation's most active environmental region might augur for environmental lawmaking elsewhere, as well as tips on what you *do not* want an inspector to find at your facility.

In addition, a broad spectrum of contributors complete the picture of the state of environmental affairs today. A state legislator describes how the laws that affect you company evolve in the course of the legislative process. Another chapter describes what you can do to get your voice heard on proposed legislation *before* it becomes law. The chief financial officer of a *Fortune* 100 company describes the increasing impact environmental factors have on a company's bottom line, and how it plays out on the balance sheet and in the annual report. The unique challenges at federal facilities are also addressed.

Who should read this book? Members of the board, who share legal responsibility for environmental compliance. The chief executive officer, who has to worry about environmental expense and the headlines that can damage more than public image. The chief financial officer, who must answer to both the board and the CEO for failing to plan for environmental costs. And finally, the environmental director, manager, or coordinator—whatever the title of that poor soul who greets the agency inspector at the front gate and may someday have to face superiors hat in hand with a stunning cleanup bill.

Betty J. Seldner
Joseph P. Cothrel

1

Managing the Environmental Organization

Kenneth M. Ries
Director, Environment and Energy
The Dial Corp

A bucket of snakes: That is, a can of worms, only larger. This frequently describes the routine environmental affairs in any large corporation. The following are real-life examples of what an environmental manager may encounter in a typical day:

- An EPA letter arrives advising that the firm is responsible in a newly named Superfund site for wastes sent by a company the firm sold 20 years ago. It was an asset sale. No one has a copy of the sale agreement and none of the applicable insurance policies can be located.

- A plant manager calls to report a minor spill to the ground. Asking who needs to be notified, he is advised to refer to the SPCC plan he signed 2 years ago. He replies, "What's an SPCC plan? Do I have one?"

- An outside consultant employed by the firm submits an environmental assessment report confirming that no environmental issues exist on a site to be sold. The company attorney wants to close on the sale today. It is almost certain an underground tank was removed from the site years ago, but this fact is not noted by the consultant.

- A subsidiary wants to acquire a manufacturing plant in a foreign country new to the firm. Management has asked to be advised of any environmental risks and also wants a review of the applicable environmental regulations. Subsidiary executives plan to meet in 2 hours and want the environmental input then.

- A plant engineer calls and wants to know where to get rid of a leaking PCB transformer.

- Two highly qualified consulting firms make sales calls, but there are no new projects for which the firm requires their services at this time.

- A consultant submits analytical data on an active remediation project. The data are obviously grossly incorrect, based on prior data. The consultant reviews sampling and chain-of-custody QA/QC and the lab reviews its QA/QC. Both report back the new data are valid.

- The CEO forwards some of his incoming environmental solicitation correspondence for handling. He expects immediate attention to the correspondence he received on global warming and ozone-layer depletion.

- Five brochures in the morning mail announce various environmental seminars, some free, some costing $950. A free one is of considerable interest, but there is no time available to attend.

- Monitoring well data arrive on a piece of scrap paper. The paper gives analytical results, without units, and is signed "Joe." It carries no facility name, location, or date.

- An NPDES discharge permit notice of violation is received. After three lengthy phone conferences, recommendations are issued to the plant manager to bring the facility back into compliance and a suggested response to the state is forwarded.

- A state environmental agency finally issues a "no further action" letter on a site where remediation was completed over a year earlier.

- An investment proposal routed for approval deals with the repair of a leaking roof at a commercial facility. In the justification it mentions, as a footnote, that a white fine-powder residual was left on the floor after the leak 3 months ago. The residual apparently came from friable fireproofing insulation on the roof beams.

- Invoices arrive on four different ongoing remediation projects. One fails to identify which project, and one lacks required supporting documentation. They expect payment in 30 days.

- A memo is issued to all facilities briefing them on the newly passed storm-water discharge permit regulations and the options and deadlines for complying. One major manufacturing facility is found to be exempt; this is confirmed by a call to the EPA hotline number.

- A plant purchasing manager wants to know where to get hazardous-waste labels for drums. Questioning reveals the waste is not hazardous.

- A call is made to a consultant to finalize a contract for a new project. The proposed scope of work requires major revisions and the contract provisions on limitation of liability and indemnifications are unacceptable. Dispute resolution provisions are added.

- A financial subsidiary intends to foreclose on a defaulted loan it made as a lender. The collateral is a shopping center. The environmental assessment reveals soils contaminated by gasoline overfill from a gas station on site and PCE solvent contamination to a depth 80 feet from a dry-cleaning tenant. The groundwater, at 100 feet, has not been impacted yet.

As these examples indicate, the volume and variety of challenges are great. Unfortunately, the staff available to address these challenges is far too small in most organizations. This chapter examines how to maximize the effectiveness of a small staff by managing the internal organization and properly selecting outside consultants.

Managing the Internal Organization

Alphabet Soup

Every field of activity has its own language. One of the greatest difficulties in understanding "environmentalese" is the frequent use of acronyms and abbreviations. While they are admittedly useful in communicating accurate information briefly, their use is effective only when the reader knows their meaning and can decode the message. At a large corporation, rarely do employees not directly involved with environmental work have any understanding of these abbreviations. Therefore, one of the most fundamental lessons to learn is to avoid the use of acronyms or abbreviations except when the recipient already knows them. Even then it is advisable to define the abbreviation when it is first used in written materials.

For example, assume a facility received a letter from the federal government informing it of potential liability in connection with a waste-disposal site it used years ago. The plant manager wants the issue explained. The jargon version might be:

> The EPA has issued you a 104 notice on the XYZ Landfill and you are now a PRP pursuant to CERCLA. EPA has elected to proceed with its RI/FS and intends to issue a ROD soon. As a PRP you should consider joining an SC and explore de minimis settlement.

A translated version, while longer, would be much more effective in communicating (and educating). An example might be:

> The letter you received from the federal Environmental Protection Agency (EPA) is: (1) a request for information you must submit in 30 days, and (2) a notification that our firm is potentially liable for the cleanup costs in connection with a contaminated waste-disposal site called the "XYZ Landfill." EPA has information that your facility may have used that landfill for waste disposal from 1952 to 1972. The EPA plans to investigate soil and groundwater contamination allegedly originating from the landfill. Other similarly named users of the site may form a steering committee to collectively represent the potentially responsible parties (PRPs) and you should consider joining. We have a good chance to be a very minor contributor and if a "de minimis" group is also formed, you will want to consider joining it too.

The Bigger Picture

"Antics with Semantics" was the name of a column written by Sidney Harris for a Chicago newspaper. In the column, Harris would reveal how any single attribute could be perceived in a positive, neutral, or negative way. One example might be:

> I focus on the essential task,
> you are single minded,
> he is a monomaniac.

One trait shared by many competent, technically trained people is the tendency to pursue the technical goal almost to the exclusion of any other concerns. Some of the more humorous examples of too narrow a focus include a consultant neglecting to charge the client for work already performed, a project manager pursuing a project long after the need for its results has ceased to exist, or an employee missing a top-priority meeting because of being engrossed in project work.

It is common for large corporations to assign environmental management positions to technically trained people such as engineers or scientists. When these technical personnel take on management responsibilities, a fundamental change in perception is needed. Environmental management within a corporation is never more than one aspect of any endeavor, and often a minor aspect. Environmental work must be understood within the larger context of company objectives and other interrelated issues.

Another important lesson concerns the different technical disciplines and their respective roles. Persons with academic training in some specialized aspect of environmental work often believe that they are the only ones properly qualified to do work in that area. It is one of the biggest mistakes they can make in their careers. In truth, environmental management today is actually a very young field that encompasses a surprising array of disciplines. That is one reason why such a wide variety of backgrounds is evident in the résumés of people engaged in full-time environmental work. This breadth of backgrounds has enormously enriched, but also complicated, the environmental field.

Some believe the field is too technically complex for a newcomer to understand. Not true. Most people willing to learn and work hard can become reasonably effective if given the opportunity and time to grow. In fact, every effective person in the profession, regardless of academic background, is constantly progressing on his or her own learning curve and the only difference in individuals is their relative position on that curve at any given instant. In this field, not knowing the answer right away is an extremely common and frequent experience.

Money and Time

Businesspeople usually understand money and time. They usually do not understand parts per million or such unfathomable and unpronounceable terms as BTEX (benzene, toluene, ethylbenzene, xylenes), nor do most intend to learn. Managing environmental matters within a company requires that the activities be understandable to others. At a minimum this means explaining them in terms of both money and time, and not just one or the other. These are the two essential inputs businesspeople must have to help them understand its relative priority, to them.

A common problem is that environmental managers are always dealing with inadequate information yet they must communicate the cost and timing aspects to others. When money and timing are not fully known, estimations, based on experience, are essential to make the issue understandable to management. Nicknames for estimating costs and timing in the absence of sufficient information include the "WAG" (wild a ____ guess), the better "SWAG" (sophisticated WAG), and the best, "WAGNER" (WAG not easily refuted).

Surviving with a Small Staff

In today's economic climate, most large corporations have experienced repeated belt-tightening measures. These measures frequently include reductions in force (or RIFs), also referred to as downsizing, right-sizing, and overhead reevaluations. Environmental staff is hardly immune. How can a large corporation cope with the inevitable expansion of environmental activities and exposure while at the same time reducing staff?

Every organization's decision makers have their own ideas of how to address the staffing needs and policies of the firm. Indeed, changes in executives can bring profound and fundamental changes to the firm's environmental philosophies and therefore to the organization as well. It is a very dynamic and frequently changing picture. As someone once cynically remarked, "Organization charts are better done in pencil rather than pen, and with big erasers."

Imagine a multibillion-dollar, multinational conglomerate with 35 operating subsidiaries, a total of 200 industrial and commercial facilities, and an involvement in over 35 Superfund cases. Now imagine a corporate environmental staff of only one person and total subsidiary environmental staffing of less than four equivalent persons. Can such a seeming impossibility work?

This chapter presents a case study of such an organization. The corporate philosophy is based on as small a corporate-level staff as possible, with direct responsibility for environmental compliance driven downward through the line management. Individual facility managers are directly responsible for ensuring the facility's environmental compliance and reducing liability exposure. Even very small units consisting of only a few persons are included. It is further the responsibility of each subsidiary to staff as it sees fit to manage its environmental affairs. Regulatory reporting is by facility, rather than centralized.

Corporate environmental policy in this company is expressed in broad principles rather than detailed procedures. These principles include: (1) timely compliance with all applicable laws and regulations, (2) a respect for the environmental in all aspects of company business, (3) an emphasis on preventing releases to the environment rather than controlling them, and (4) a focus on removing potential environmental liability exposure.

The handful of full-time environmental staff at the corporate level serve primarily as sources of specific information, especially regarding applicable laws, regulations, and codes. They also help in solving specific problems, identify required outside services and products, establish work scopes when requested, review and interpret (translate) technical information, and provide specific recommendations. The corporate staff is usually not directly involved in routine reporting or daily environmental data management, but instead provides an independent oversight of such routine activities, especially when problems arise.

The result is that the "real" environmental staff of this company is actually all the employees. While they do not have "environmental" in their job descriptions, most employees perform a surprising array of environmental duties daily. For example, senior executives set environmental policy and set the tone of how proactive the firm will be toward the environment. Line managers make increasingly frequent decisions affecting compliance matters, and often are directly involved in regulatory reporting. Financial staff coordinate environmental capital project reviews and manage funding. Internal auditors now include environmental compliance in facility audits. Insurance staff handle environmental claims and also provide independent environmental auditing that reduces insurance premiums. Real estate staff consider and often negotiate environmental issues in every real estate transaction, including leases. Attorneys negotiate acquisitions and divestitures to avoid environmental liability and litigate environmental claims. Engineers incorporate environmental considerations in almost every capital project and address procedures to achieve compliance in routing plant operations and preventive maintenance. Supervisors and the rank-and-file hourly workers perform the enormous number of daily tasks needed to keep the company in compliance.

Because there is no centralized environmental staff responsible for environmental affairs, all employees integrate environmental work in their jobs where it is necessary for the company to function properly. The biggest benefit is that responsibility and accountability tend to rest with the individuals most directly involved in performing any act of omission or commission toward compliance.

That is the good news. The bad news is that it requires employees at all levels to educate themselves about environmental matters that they may have to handle. Formal training is simply not practical. An honest lack of knowledge is what most often explains specific noncompliance matters that surface. Another problem is that specific information is highly disaggregated. For example, the total number of underground tanks at any given time and their current compliance status is not readily available information. Centralizing environmental data and keeping it current would require a rather large staff, with many devoted to tedious computer data entry. In this case, having such staff is simply not cost-justifiable. An especially acute problem is in dealing with government agencies who often request difficult-to-get information within an arbitrarily short time span. The disaggregated nature of the information requires the diversion of sometimes considerable overhead resources which often cannot meet the reporting time limits by the agency.

Keeping assigned corporate and subsidiary environmental staff intentionally small is the best possible news to the swelling ranks of consulting firms, law firms, and contractors who provide environmental services to their clients. Large companies necessarily engage many such outside services. This is the other fundamental means by which very small internal company staff proves adequate. Although frequent use of outside skills can be more costly than having the work completed by internal staff, and can also result in some loss of control over ultimate project costs, it nevertheless brings a level of capability and flexibility that cannot be measured solely in monetary terms.

Staying Current with Changing Regulations

People who claim to have a current knowledge of all applicable environmental laws and regulations affecting businesses in the United States have managed to fool at least one person—themselves. The task is not possible, even if that is all one does, full-time. The frequency and number of regulatory changes make such an effort impractical. Unfortunately, the law is clear that ignorance of the law is no defense. In fact, recent case law has held that businesses directly affected by environmental laws and regulations have an affirmative duty to educate themselves as to these applicable laws and regulations. So how might a large corporation with almost no staff time available for such an effort even begin to cope with this task? The answer is that it is a daily task for any full-time environmental staff, no matter what the priority may be of the other daily tasks. Roughly an hour a day is not uncommon in tending to this need for a constant flow of new regulatory information.

People unfamiliar with environmental work cannot appreciate how many different public agencies are actual or de facto environmental regulators. Even 10 years ago, the list was very short in comparison with that of the 1990s. To illustrate the growing number of regulators, consider the following organizations now directly involved in administering and enforcing environmental laws, regulations, or codes:

- U.S. Environmental Protection Agency
- U.S. Department of Justice
- U.S. Army Corps of Engineers
- U.S. Department of Transportation
- U.S. Coast Guard
- State environmental agencies
- State occupational safety and health agencies
- State fire marshals
- State emergency response commissions
- Regional commissions and boards for such media as air or water
- County environmental agencies
- County health agencies
- City health agencies
- Publicly owned treatment works (sewerage commissions)
- Local fire departments
- Local emergency planning committees

In any given environmental matter, identifying which agencies have applicable rules is no longer an easy matter. Indeed, it is increasingly common for two or more agencies to engage in cross-jurisdictional "turf wars." The regulated company has to meet all the expectations anyway, which are sometimes even conflicting. In one instance of a hazardous substance release to the air, for example, no less than five different agencies were immediately notified of the releases. Each expected to be notified, and each expected to be notified first. A sixth agency who was not contacted later complained, saying that the reporting company acted improperly in failing to notify it as well.

Company environmental managers are therefore on a constant quest for current applicable news as to new regulations. Numerous environmental regulatory reporting services exist that offer their subscribers a steady diet of new and revised federal and state laws, regulations, and court cases. Subscription to at least one comprehensive reporting service is indispensable. These services not only issue hard copies of current laws and regulations, as passed, but also provide very timely news of current developments in environmental legislation, regulation, and judicial matters.

For monitoring regulatory developments at the federal level, subscribing to the *Federal Register* is equally advantageous. The *Federal Register* publishes (1) advanced notices of proposed rule makings, (2) proposed rules, and (3) most importantly, final rules, complete with often lengthy discussions of how the final rules were decided. Of course, this reference is of no help in following legislative or judicial matters.

Again at the federal level, the Environmental Protection Agency (EPA) has a growing number of "hot lines" that can be called for current regulatory information. Unique to this free service is that it can provide interpretations as to how a given regulation might apply to a very specific matter of concern to the caller. These hot lines are manned by consultants retained by the EPA, and their sole function is to render accurate regulatory information to callers. There is no charge for the information given and the caller has to identify only the state from which the call originates. The identity of the caller is never requested. Generally, the response to questions is immediate and consistently accurate, with few exceptions. It is one of the greatest values the EPA has made available to the regulated community and one that any environmental manager should consider using whenever such information is required.

The federal EPA also offers numerous written materials. Often there is no charge to be included on the mailing list. Many states also publish environmental regulatory information for the benefit of the regulated community. For example, many states now publish underground storage tank newsletters. Free subscriptions are usually available.

The environmental field is blessed with a large number of trade journals, many of which are free, that are an indispensable source of information on current environmental regulatory, legislative, and judicial issues. In fact, the flow of available regulatory information from just this one source is rather overwhelming.

Some of the larger, well-established environmental consulting firms generate newsletters that are distributed internally and to clients, both current and past. These newsletters are usually very brief and discuss pending legislative or regulatory matters of importance to that consultant and its clients. Many are extremely well written, very timely, and a highly useful source of information. Law firms in the environmental business also publish newsletters, typically focusing on current legislative and judicial issues. These publications are also well written and highly valued for the information they offer. A few of the larger law firms also sponsor annual environmental seminars on new laws and regulations.

Computer reporting services can be used for obtaining regulatory information electronically, and a few are excellent. These services can be costly, and therefore their use should be fully cost-justified beforehand.

The unfortunate truth is that, despite this overwhelming variety and volume of available regulatory information, it is usually not enough in any given specific environmental matter. A time-proven additional strategy for getting the correct information has been to simply contact the relevant regulatory agencies directly. Phone contact works best whenever current regulatory information on a specific matter is needed. The cooperation is usually very high once the right people in the agency are identified and are available. Admittedly, finding them is frequently a frustrating experience. But once the right people are located and respond, the help is usually directly relevant, immediate, and free. It also includes more than just information on current requirements. Required forms, documents, explanation booklets, and filing fee information are often provided as well.

In underground tank work, application for cost recovery from state funds can also be initiated by a call to the state regulator. This is a matter of the highest significance to any tank owner or operator, and is as important as the actual tank project itself. Often the tank regulator will even summarize what specific steps need to be taken and in what order so that the project will conform to the expectations of the regulators. Calls to state environmental agencies sometimes reveal there are other agencies that also need to be contacted, such as a county agency, for example. This is extremely valuable input as the various above-mentioned sources of information about environmental regulation are still relatively ineffective in covering county and local-level regulations. This is unfortunate, as it is increasingly a local or county agency that is actually the lead agency in handling environmental matters in their geographical area. Therefore, these local rules and codes are just as important as the state and federal rules and need to be understood and complied with equally.

In industry there is still a great reluctance by some managers to make direct contact with regulators for applicable regulatory information. It is true agency staff sometimes take an unnecessarily adversarial posture. However, in general there can be no justification for avoiding such an excellent source of timely, accurate information.

Even in a large corporation with a very small environmental staff, the need to keep current on environmental regulation still rests mainly with that small staff. They have an obligation to communicate to facility managers an awareness of current and new regulations likely to impact those facilities and to field specific inquiries from company managers on specific issues. The concept that industrial or commercial facility managers themselves can maintain full knowledge of all applicable environmental regulations impacting them, while laudable, is not a practical reality.

Selecting Outside Consultants

One advantage a large company has over smaller ones is that it is continually contacted by a surprising number of outside firms seeking environmental work. It is equally a disadvantage in that such contacts take up considerable time and are often unproductive for both parties, as the offers always exceed the availability of work.

To illustrate the universe of firms who might actually offer their services, the following is a list of just the *kinds* of firms who would like to be considered for, to take one example, the assessment work associated with an underground tank removal:

- Environmental consulting firm specializing in underground tank removals and associated assessments

- Full-line environmental consultants

- Full-line engineering consultants and contractors who also do environmental work

- Hydrogeology firms, or even geology or geotechnical consultants

- Tank removal contractors who do "turnkey" removals, including the assessment work

- New tank installation contractors who offer tank removals and associated assessments

- Emergency response firms

- Laboratories who also do field sampling work
- Law firms that also do environmental management work
- Asbestos consultants who also offer tank removal consulting

And within each of the above categories, there might exist up to 100 firms who might contact an environmental manager to seek such a contract. It makes the opportunities large indeed, and the selection difficult.

Selection Criteria

Everyone has his or her own methods of selecting outside firms. The process described here is one method that has proved effective for a large manufacturing firm.

Location is the primary consideration. The consultant should have an office close to the project site. The benefits can include (1) less travel time, no airfares, and often no living expenses, all of which help lower the project costs; (2) knowledge of local regulatory practices including specific procedures and standards currently accepted by local regulators; (3) knowledge of local geology and hydrogeology, and possibly even existing contamination near the project site; and (4) knowledge of local contractors who may need to be retained as subcontractors. As every project is ultimately unique and extremely site-specific, local consulting firms have a considerable advantage compared with consultants unfamiliar with the area. Placing location as the primary factor effectively eliminates the strategy of retaining a single large firm for performing all the company's environmental work. Instead, it requires consideration of numerous and often smaller firms. Large national firms, however, have improved their chances of being retained by opening smaller offices in a number of locations.

Second to location in importance is the *ability* to do the work assigned. Consultants are selected based on the client's perception that the consultant is both qualified and capable of completing the work. What really counts is the individuals who are actually assigned and their knowledge, ability, and efforts, almost to the exclusion of who might be their employer. Outstanding work has come from very small, virtually unknown firms, from firms not noted for the kind of work involved in the project, and even from individuals who do not initially seem qualified. By contrast, large firms with high national recognition and reputation, using individuals with outstanding credentials, occasionally produce very poor and even unacceptable work products.

Statements of qualifications, or so-called SOQs, are initially of help in locating firms with individuals having the ability to complete the project. Sought first in the SOQ is a summary listing of all office locations, addresses, phone and fax numbers, and contact names. Next is a summary of the kinds of work the firm does and the kinds of prior work experience the firm has. Third are the individuals the firm might make available for the project, and their backgrounds and work experience.

Direct or even indirect knowledge of proven performance applicable to the project is a major factor leading to a selection. Sometimes references are contacted. Surprisingly, some "satisfied" clients turn out to be not all that satisfied. Regulators are sometimes quite candid about the completeness and timeliness of a prospective consultant's prior work products. Other firms using consultants are another source of relevant and helpful suggestions. In the final analysis, using a new outside firm or a new individual ultimately requires the client to "take a chance." Sometimes the result is unsatisfactory, but more often the result is a delightful discovery of new talent that completes the work extremely well.

Expectations

A client's expectations of its consultants are rarely fully met. A client reviewing hundreds of consulting reports will ultimately see a wide range of quality. Why? It usually has nothing to do with the abilities of the consultants in question.

The most common problem is incomplete or inadequate communication between the consultant and client as to the scope of work. The second most common problem is inadequate communication between consultant and client on administrative matters, including such items as timing, costs, billing, or payments. In solid third place in frequency, after these problems in communication, are problems with the technical work itself. It is gratifying that only rarely do consultants assign project work to individuals who, by lack of training or experience, are simply unable to perform the technical work satisfactorily. But it has happened. When technical issues arise, they are often primarily due to the consultant's having insufficient information to support conclusions, an inadequate understanding of the known facts, or an incorrect interpretation of those facts. Sometimes the problem lies in the consultant's effort to "shoehorn" an experience or strongly held belief where it clearly does not apply.

The following is a list of qualities, in order of priority from highest to lowest, that a client may expect in a consulting report. Consultants that get repeat work are those that come closest to adopting these same priorities.

Timeliness. Environmental work is usually only one, often minor, aspect of some larger project, and project timing is rarely driven by environmental considerations. A property transfer, for example, requires a timely environmental assessment to advise the buyer, seller, and lender of environmental conditions. In an extreme case, a $90 million deal was once held up over a delay in a $1500 environmental assessment wherein the only issue turned out to be $50 worth of corrective asbestos work. By contrast, the interest on that $90 million was over $20,000 per day.

Even where a project is solely an environmental matter, regulatory deadlines, review time for the client, and time needed for approvals will still require very timely submittals by the consultant. Completing the assigned work within the assigned time is frequently, from a client's perspective, the single overriding concern. In fact only rarely is timing not a critically important matter.

Correctness of Scope of Work. Aside from being timely, the consultant's report must also reflect a common understanding between a consultant and client as to exactly what the problem is that is being addressed and exactly what work is to be undertaken. It is best to put this understanding in writing in detail prior to beginning the project, and to have both parties acknowledge it as acceptable. Time spent here will eliminate the most frequently encountered disputes, wherein one party fails to understand or accept what the other thought to be the work scope. A simple example would be agreement on what soil samples shall be composited for analysis versus individually analyzed. Another example might be the choice of specific analytical methods used by a laboratory. Inherent in the notion of a correct scope of work is that the correct problem to be addressed has been identified and that the intended work will be sufficient to produce the desired results. If, after the work commences, it becomes clear that the agreed-upon scope was insufficient, the scope can be adjusted or expanded with little effort if it builds on an initial agreement that was well understood by both parties.

Accuracy. It is essential that the information generated in a consultant's report be factually correct. The problem can be illustrated by an actual case in which a consultant sampled soils for a suspected heavy-oil spill. The testing program included analyses for polynuclear aromatic hydrocarbons (PAHs). The consultant's final report showed no PAHs detected in any of the soil samples except for one, which tested positive for anthracene at 163,000 mg/L. None of the soil showed any visual evidence of free fuel. The value reported was quite obviously in error. The consultant never questioned such an impossible result and so incorrectly reported it as fact.

Opinions and speculation by consultants have little real value in most technical reports. The client sometimes specifically requests opinions or speculation, but even then their value has to be suspect. Of much greater value is correct factual information upon which the subsequent interpretations, conclusions, recommendations, and most importantly, subsequent business decisions can then be based. If the factual information later proves to be incorrect, as it has in some cases, the entire effort may have to be repeated, and usually with a different consultant.

Clarity and Brevity. In the interest of being correct, complete, and comprehensive, and of providing all possible supporting documentation, technical environmental reports are typically too lengthy and too difficult to read. They do not have to be so. Rarely is a report received that is pure joy to read, where the report not only fulfills its function but also is so clear and concise that almost any reader could readily understand it. Once an author of such a report was asked what was the secret. The response was: "My reports are written to be understood by anyone with a sixth-grade education. If I can make it clear to that person, then it is likely the report will be understood by most readers." Too often, technical reports suffer from the inclusion of useless or irrelevant information. It is best left out if it is not helpful. Concise reports are very much preferred by most clients, reports in which factual information is presented clearly and in a form that allows it to be easily found later. Tables, figures, and diagrams are especially helpful in presenting information clearly and concisely. Some reports contain a lengthy but useless legal description of the site and, at the same time, fail to contain either a scaled site plan or even a sketch of the site. A scaled site plan would be clearly superior.

There really are no agreed-upon standards of what constitutes an acceptable technical report, and therefore it is ultimately up to the client to define its own standards. This is especially true in environmental site assessments for property transfers, where so many have made their services available in this exploding new market, and where an inexperienced consultant typically has no idea of what information is really needed. Most comical was a one-page, one-paragraph report from an environmental site assessment wherein the only relevant factual statement was one sentence, which said simply, "I visited the site and it looks okay to me." It was a short, concise, accurate, but completely useless report.

Responsiveness. Consultants who take the time to listen carefully to their clients are much more likely to generate acceptable reports. Where a strong-willed consultant alone decides what is to be done and how it will be done, regardless of the wishes of a client, the results are likely to satisfy only the consultant. Sometimes a client has quite limited funds available, with the result being an abbreviated version of what the consultant would prefer. An ability to listen and fully consider the wishes of the client, whatever their merits might be, is one of the hallmarks of a highly effective consultant. As an appropriate phrase once put it, "Whoever pays the bills can write the rules."

Cost-Effectiveness. If a report has the previous five qualities, it is likely that the work is ultimately cost-effective as well. Cost-effectiveness is not always the same as having the lowest price; instead, it is the ultimate lowest total cost to the client after all aspects of the project have been played out, which could be years in the future. Experienced clients know that a moderately priced effort based on the correct scope of work, completed well and on time, will actually save money compared with a seemingly low-cost effort that later proves incomplete. Therefore, in comparing the proposed costs of competing consultants, common sense teaches that only an "apples to apples" comparison of work of an identical work scope is valid. What is interesting is that there is absolutely no correlation between cost and quality in consulting work—bad work can cost as much as or more than top quality. Thus cost is better placed as the *lowest* priority expectation, not the highest. Instead, look for quality first.

When several quality firms with qualified assigned people are found, only then is it time to do some cost comparisons and, all other things being equal, the lower-priced firm will usually prevail. Consultants themselves have considerable control over costs, in that most of a consultant's charges are for professional time. A high-rate senior person, say over $100 per hour, can often produce a report at a lower cost than a $60-per-hour subordinate. The work is completed in much less time because of the senior person's greater experience.

The best opportunity a client has for cost control, once the work scope is established, is to agree upon a fixed budget amount and fixed time limits. Time is money. Any project that has no cost ceiling and no established time for completion of specific tasks is a project without cost control. Some consultants love such open-ended arrangements and some will even request such "freedom," but it is contrary to the best interests of the client.

2

Converting to Proactive Environmental Management

Paul B. Duff
Director, Environmental Affairs
Textron Inc.

Managing the corporate environmental affairs department of a Fortune 100 company is a daily test of the limits of one's technical and regulatory knowledge, and it can be both rewarding and frustrating. The job has two equal components, both competing for limited resources:

1. Complying with today's laws and regulations
2. Correcting the "sins of the past"

The term "sins of the past" is used despite the fact that, in many cases, companies' disposal activities were consistent with standard industry practice and the laws and regulations in effect at the time.

In the 1990s, a third component has emerged and gained increasing importance: taking the environmental program beyond compliance. Improvements in areas such as waste minimization, toxic chemical usage reduction, product life-cycle design, and selection of off-site disposal facilities go beyond the current regulations to bring real environmental and economic benefits to the company and the community.

In my judgment, the key to successfully managing an environmental organization is the ability to convert the company's program from reactive to proactive. The following discussion provides guidance on successfully making this conversion. I describe the structure of an effective corporate organization and briefly discuss the components necessary to maximize effectiveness without disrupting the autonomy of operating entities. Finally, I outline remedial programs designed to correct problems resulting from historical disposal activities.

Organizing for Effectiveness

Organizational structure is a key element in making any organization effective. This is particularly true for environmental affairs, since the environmental department communicates with every corporate discipline and must have the authority to make things happen. The environmental function is often integrated with the health and safety organization, which is a logical connection since health and safety personnel typically have important responsibilities in the overall environmental program. Some companies establish a separate environmental organization, which gives the function increased independence. Combined or free-standing, the environmental group must report at a sufficiently high level to (1) obtain senior management commitment, (2) be visible to other disciplines in the organization, and (3) have enough clout to get the job done.

The structure that is best for your organization will depend on a number of factors, including the size of your company and the lines of authority in place. Success will also depend on other organization elements such as corporate policy, objectives, and staffing plans.

Corporate Policy

It is imperative that the company's environmental policy be thoughtfully crafted and be incorporated into an official written policy statement. Such an action accomplishes two goals: It ensures that all employees understand the priority placed on environmental compliance, and it tells customers and the community at large that your company is committed to environmental quality. A good start would include advocating full compliance with all federal, state, and local laws and regulations. Specific individuals should then be given the responsibility of ensuring this compliance is achieved. The responsible parties should be those who can directly control activities that impact the environment, such as the managers in charge of company facilities (i.e., general manager or plant manager, whichever is appropriate).

Objectives

The company's environmental objectives should be brief and to the point:

1. Comply with existing laws and regulations
2. Manage present and future risks
3. Remediate existing sites where contamination has occurred as a result of past or present company activities

Keeping objectives brief will allow managers to focus on priorities. Detailed goals can be developed to support the achievement of these objectives.

Staffing

Well-qualified staff should be in place to handle both contaminated sites and compliance at current operating facilities. Qualified staff should exist at both corporate and division levels.

Corporate staff should be organized to perform three major functions:

Assist (the consultant hat)

Assess (the auditor or policeman hat)

Assure (the manager hat)

It is difficult for corporate staff to develop a relationship with division or plant personnel, and at the same time be a consultant, cop, and hard-nosed manager, but that is what it takes. However, corporate staff cannot possibly do the job alone—nor should they be expected to do so. Therefore, additional environmental positions must be designated at the staff and division level.

Each division president should appoint a division environmental coordinator (DEC) who will organize and manage the division's environmental affairs program. The DEC should have a dotted line (some say thin, others thicker) to the corporate Director of Environmental Affairs. These divisional "top guns" should be given special treatment by the corporate office personnel since it is their performance that will ultimately determine the success of the overall company program.

Annual or semiannual get-togethers for DECs should be held to educate and to build esprit de corps. At DEC seminars I have organized, we have held volleyball tournaments and a 5K walk and run complete with souvenir T-shirts. Such extracurricular activities can build a team attitude and replace the happy hour with something that is both healthy for the individual and good for the organization. Each DEC should be assigned to someone who will serve as his or her primary contact with corporate staff. They will get to know each other and, as they begin the process of building trust, will learn to share frustrations and solve problems together in partnership.

Finally, each plant manager should appoint a plant environmental coordinator (PEC) to take charge of the environmental program at the facility level. Again, the focus is on bringing responsibility from the management level to the place where work gets done. This will complete the network of partnerships between the corporate office, division personnel, and plant personnel.

Vehicles to Meet Objectives

To succeed, an environmental program must be quantified, to allow progress to be assessed, and institutionalized, to make compliance part of doing business. A number of vehicles exist to quantify and institutionalize a company's environmental program.

Environmental Policy

A management guide should be prepared that extracts from the overall corporate policies the statements that pertain to environmental affairs.

Environmental Procedures

Listed below are candidates for formal environmental procedures:

1. Responding to governmental requests for information
2. Spill reporting

3. Selling a business or property (environmental assessment requirement)

4. Buying a business or property (environmental assessment requirement)

5. Performing a compliance self-survey

6. Achieving pollution prevention goals

7. Selecting commercial hazardous-waste disposal facilities

Division President's Handbook

This is an executive summary of federal environmental regulations as well as an overview of the corporation's total compliance philosophy, programs, and policy and procedures. This handbook helps senior management to be mindful of resource needs and allows them to ask the right questions.

Environmental Management Guide

This resource document incorporates the President's Handbook, corporate environmental policies and procedures, and other information required by the plant environmental coordinator. It should include, among other items:

1. Calendar with important regulatory deadlines

2. List of books, pamphlets, and videos available on loan from the corporate office

3. Names and telephone numbers of all DECs and PECs—to encourage networking

4. U.S. EPA hotline numbers

Newsletter

Publish and distribute companywide a quarterly newsletter that contains regulatory updates as well as waste minimization success stories. Articles authored by the division and plant environmental coordinators should be encouraged.

Federal Register Tracking Report

This is a monthly summary of environmentally related items (40 CFR) excerpted and highlighted from the daily federal registers. The government even publishes these on Saturdays; in total, Washington publishes about 8000 pages annually applicable to environmental matters. This report can be used by environmental personnel throughout the company as a quick-scan device to determine what regulatory activity is relevant and warrants further investigation.

It is an imperative that each division and plant environmental coordinator have Title 40 of the Code of Federal Regulations (40 CFR), which are the regulations governing environmental matters. It is a modest investment ($600 annually) but is essential to doing the job properly. Title 49, which includes the Department of Transportation's regulations that govern shipments of hazardous materials, would also be useful.

Environmental Alert Bulletins

In addition to the above publications, bulletins should be released on an as-needed basis to summarize late-breaking news regarding significant compliance issues (i.e., new regulations) that will have a significant economic impact on the company.

Programs to Meet Objectives

A number of formal programs are needed to get the corporate environmental affairs group (and the company) focused on making the transition from reactive to proactive.

Compliance Assurance

This program has two elements: a self-survey and a third-party audit. A format should be developed for the self-survey in which the questions that are asked lead the preparer to the conclusion that either a compliance or noncompliance situation exists for each aspect of environmental regulation (air, water, hazardous waste, etc.).

Steps to eliminate noncompliance issues should be outlined in a corrective action plan (CAP). CAPs for all plants should be maintained in a computerized database, maintained by the corporate office, that is set up to track each significant issue.

One word of caution: Once a company identifies environmental noncompliance, it is imperative that these problems be corrected aggressively and in a timely fashion. Failure to do so could result in a charge of willful noncompliance, and that is punishable as a criminal offense.

As a follow-up to the self-survey, an independent auditor should be hired to spot-check the results. For a large, multistate organization, the auditor should check up to 20 percent of the firm's plants in a year. The independent auditor should check compliance for both federal and state regulations; generally, the self-surveys are designed for federal regulations only. The third-party audits should be designed as a check on the company's entire environmental program (i.e., compliance status, quality of staff, effectiveness of the self-survey, quality of training, companywide commitment to environmental policy, etc.).

Training

At a minimum, the following training should occur:

1. Annual basic environmental seminar

2. Biennial regional advanced environmental seminar

3. Special seminars (lawyers, DECs, other focused sessions)

Additionally, each facility should evaluate its training requirements under the environmental laws applicable to that facility.

Pollution Prevention

Specific plans and objectives should be developed to reduce hazardous-waste and nonhazardous-waste generation, toxic-chemical usage, and emissions. Objectives should include specific numerical goals for annual reductions. This program should be a "crown jewel" of the environmental effort. And it should not be just the domain of the environmental personnel. In the past, employees with environmental responsibility were placed at the back of the plant property because their role was perceived as providing treatment at the "end-of-the-pipe." This has changed as environmental personnel work themselves upstream to identify contamination or releases at the source. As environmental engineers gain more credibility because of the contribution they make to the plant operations, they are invited to participate in the overall planning of the manufacturing facility's day-to-day operations.

A successful environmental program must be fully integrated into all disciplines. If environmental compliance is totally the domain of the environmental personnel, the program is doomed to lackluster performance and even failure. Everyone in a facility must be made aware of that entity's environmental impact, and then all employees must collectively take ownership of that responsibility and act accordingly.

More and more Superfund (CERCLA) sites are municipal landfills where industrial waste has created contaminated leachate that migrated into an aquifer. Given this fact, and the rising cost of solid-waste disposal, it seems prudent to also reduce the amount of solid waste generated. Actions can include an aggressive recycling program and finding an appropriate final repository for the remaining material (such as incineration in a trash-to-energy facility).

Hazardous-Waste Disposal Site Selection

A smart decision here can save a tremendous amount of money in future Superfund liability. A few simple rules apply:

1. Do business with large and well-financed companies.

2. Be certain that the other industrial users of those companies are also large and well financed.

3. Inspect the final disposal site to confirm that the facility has all the required permits and is doing things in an environmentally sound manner. Require personnel from the company facility generating the waste to conduct a waste-specific walk-through of the treatment, storage, and disposal facility (TSDF) once per year.

4. Reduce the number of approved sites that are being used by your company.

5. Have the corporate legal department or outside counsel prepare a comprehensive waste-disposal services agreement. If your company is a large multistate operation, this should serve as a basis for negotiating a national contract. This agreement should address key issues such as indemnification from Superfund liability, insurance levels, and notification of TSDF noncompliance.

6. If a plant wants to utilize a TSDF that has not been approved by the corporation, require that prior to such use they conduct an extensive audit and then enter into a formal contract (i.e., use of a purchase order should not be permitted).

Washington Watch

Someone at the corporate level must monitor what U.S. EPA is doing and, if appropriate, submit comments on proposed regulations that may impact the company. In-house efforts can be supplemented by the use of a trade organization, whose research and lobbying resources are typically more extensive than those of an individual company.

State Environmental Coordinator

Since not all wisdom nor all legislative or regulatory activity occurs in Washington, a state environmental coordinator (SEC) should be appointed to monitor state activities in the environmental area. This individual could collect information from any available sources and then pass it along to the other company plants in that state. The networking that occurs is itself a bonus and sufficient reason for such a program.

Summary

In summary, if all of the foregoing hasn't motivated you to "organize for effectiveness" in the environmental area, then you should read the March 5, 1993 draft of the "Recommended Sentencing Guidelines Setting Forth Criminal Penalties for Organizations Convicted of Federal Environmental Crimes." A final draft will be issued by the U.S. Sentencing Commission's Advisory Working Group on Environmental Sanctions in November 1993, and the proposal will be sent to Congress for approval in May 1994.

The guidelines establish a table of basic fines and a formula for increasing the fine amounts by a factor based on the severity of the crime, the past record of the corporation, and the culpability of management. These same guidelines also provide for reducing the base amount to reflect the existence of an effective compliance program to prevent and detect crime, the company's willingness to report any violation promptly to the authorities, and the company's willingness to cooperate fully in the investigation of the offense.

According to the Sentencing Guidelines Commission, an effective compliance program requires at a minimum that you:

- Establish compliance policies, standards, and procedures
- Assign high-level managers to administer these procedures
- Effectively communicate compliance standards to all employees
- Take reasonable steps to assure compliance with these standards (i.e., auditing, monitoring, reporting, and tracking)
- Ensure that regulatory expertise is maintained through regular training and subsequent evaluation of employees with environmental responsibility
- Consistently enforce compliance standards through disciplinary measures
- Take steps to prevent a recurrence after detection of an offense

Effective compliance programs should be viewed as both the first and the best line of defense.

Cost-Effective Remediation

Once you get past the point of being frustrated by the strict and joint and several liability schemes created by the federal government to assure cleanup at contaminated sites, and once you realize that there is no necessary assignment of priorities by the government to clean up the most contaminated sites first, then you can begin the process of planning your company's strategy. For many firms, this is a very expensive undertaking.

The corporate environmental affairs department has an important role in providing direct management of remedial activities that occur at former company manufacturing sites where contamination has occurred, since these sites have usually been sold and there is no other ongoing corporate entity to manage the solution.

For sites that are part of current company operations or sites still owned by a viable entity of the company, the individual entity may assume project management responsibility, but the level of corporate involvement that is necessary is always an issue. Figure 2-1 illustrates one scheme for determining how involved the corporate level must be in a given cleanup effort. In the illustrated scheme, the extreme solutions are typically disregarded. In addition, all sites over $500,000

LEVEL OF CORPORATE INVOLVEMENT				
It's your problem.	Keep us informed. We're available to help.	We'll watch this one. Keep us informed. We're available to help.	This is a big one. We'll be involved.	We'll run the show.
<$200,000	$200,000	$500,000	$1,000,000	>$1,000,000

Figure 2-1 Determining level of corporate involvement for remediation projects on company-owned property.

would be monitored and future cost information, scheduling, and key regulatory dates would be incorporated into a computerized database maintained by the corporate environmental affairs office.

Legislative and Regulatory Remedial Program

There are essentially three ways the government can require a company to clean up a site. Two are very similar in structure: the Superfund Program (CERCLA) and RCRA Corrective Action (40 CFR Subpart S). A step-by-step comparison of the different phases of Superfund and RCRA cleanup programs follows.

Activity	Superfund	RCRA
Preliminary investigation	PA	RFA
Detailed engineering and hydrogeological study	RI	RFI
Review of remedial alternatives	FS	CMS
Installation of a remedy	RD/RA	Corrective action

The reservoir of sites to be evaluated under the Superfund program is known as the CERCLIS list. There are approximately 30,000 sites on this list.

To be a candidate for cleanup under the RCRA corrective action program, the target site must be an industrial site where hazardous-waste (i.e., RCRA-regulated) activity has occurred and where the generator responsible for the hazardous waste activity has filed a Part A RCRA Application (or where a Part A application *should have been* filed).

A third way that the government can order a site cleanup is through the various state property transfer laws (e.g., New Jersey's ECRA, Connecticut's Negative Declaration Process, Massachusetts' MCP/21E), or other state laws analogous to CERCLA. The problem here is avoiding double jeopardy. Double jeopardy occurs when a company cleans up a site under a state order and then the federal government orders an investigation and cleanup. This essentially requires the company to start all over. In my judgment, this is a duplication of effort that wastes resources and impedes the timely execution of what all parties desire—an environmentally sound and cost-effective remedy.

Managing Contractors and Consultants

Now that firms have spent the last half of the 1980s and the first few years of the 1990s studying sites, there is going to be a big push to actually do the cleanups (and therefore spend a lot of money). Much of this work will be performed by contractors and consultants, and you will be in a better position to meet the challenges of remediation if you focus on properly managing these outside firms.

Effective contractor management begins even before the contract is awarded with a well-defined request for proposal (RFP). The RFP should provide as much detail as possible and limit the opportunity for interpretation. If the contractor is interested in doing the job well, before preparing a proposal they will visit the site, talk to the regulators (with your permission), and review historical documents to achieve a sufficiently detailed understanding of the problem and the parameters of a successful solution.

After making your decision, depending on the circumstances, it may be possible to negotiate a fixed-price contract that is very tightly written. In any event, your objective is to define the work sufficiently well at the onset (to prevent poor scope definition) and then agree to a mechanism for implementing change orders (to reduce scope creep).

A word about who you hire to perform the investigation or the remedial activities. Be absolutely certain your project manager is technically well qualified, but also be concerned about his or her administrative skills and his or her commitment to your company and the project. Developing a relationship with the senior management group of the firms you hire is generally a good idea and will pay important dividends in the future.

Once the contractor is on board, a mechanism is required to track progress. It is generally a good idea to require periodic reports. Figure 2-2 presents a format you can use for these reports.

Month _____
Year _____

ENVIRONMENTAL AFFAIRS DEPARTMENT
CONSULTANT/CONTRACTOR
MONTHLY PROGRESS REPORT
(Submit with all Invoices)

The report shall present in narrative form all elements required below other than those noted with an asterisk for which a tabular presentation is required.

1.   Work conducted during month, expressed in general terms.

2.   *Individuals working on the project including their billable hours:

Individual	Title	Billable Hours	Rate

3.   *Tabulation of reimbursable expenses for the month:

Nature of Expense	Paid To	Amount

4.   Summary of analytical data generated during the month in narrative or tabular form.

5.   *Summary of costs: (**NOTE**: Utilize project task descriptions as specifically defined in cost estimate responsive to RFP.)

TIME PERIOD _____

Task No.	Task Description	Cost Estimate (as detailed in original Contract)	Amount Billed This Month	Total Billed To Date	% Complete	Anticipated Future Costs[1]
1						
2						
3						
4						

[1]   If this amount + amount billed to date exceeds original proposal amount, immediately contact Project manager.

6.   Governmental agency interfaces telephone calls/personal visits/written correspondence), by narrative, tabulation, or copies of memorandums/reports, etc.

7.   *Summary of important correspondence issued this month:

Date Sent	Title of Document	Author	Recipient

8.   *Important upcoming activities and/or deadlines:

Date	Nature of Activity and/or Deadline	Person Responsible

9.   Updated Project Schedule (Gantt Chart Format).

Figure 2-2   Format for contractor reports.

The SEC has become increasingly interested lately about the size of remedial efforts under way nationally. Specifically, they want to know whether, in the aggregate, environmental problems for a particular company will be "material" and therefore need to be reported either in the company's annual report or in the 10K. Keep good records to ensure that you can defend your position if it becomes scrutinized.

Lady Versus the Tiger

On a final note, what do you do when confronted with the decision to sign U.S. EPA's model Consent Decree (Lady), or let the agency decide whether to issue a unilateral Section 106 order (Tiger)? And maybe I have the lady/tiger analogy backward.

There are advantages to negotiating a consent decree. A consent decree secures an opportunity to do the work yourself and potentially achieve cost savings. If the EPA hires its own contractor to do the work, you will be obligated to pay whatever the costs are. With a consent decree, you may be able to define the remedial components up front in a scope of work attached to the decree, and thereby limit both costs and future disagreements with EPA. You can avoid the possibility of treble damages provided under CERCLA for failure to comply with a Section 106 order. Entering a consent decree will also provide statutory contribution protection from suits by third parties, if that is a concern.

On the other hand, if EPA issues a 106 order, you may be able to comply with it and achieve the same cost savings as you would under a consent decree by hiring your own contractor. At the same time, you can avoid many of the onerous provisions of the consent decree—stipulated penalties, additional work provisions, and the like. You avoid agreeing up front to do whatever EPA requires and therefore have greater leverage to argue over the reasonableness of EPA's requests. However, if EPA chooses not to issue an order but rather to do the work through its own contractor, you run the risk of increased costs. This risk is mitigated by the fact that you may not be required to pay for the remedy until EPA initiates a cost recovery action—which could take quite some time.

3

Environmental Liability and Reducing Corporate Exposure

Stephen T. Holzer, Esq.
Principal
*Parker, Milliken, Clark, O'Hara &
Samuelian*

Gary A. Meyer, Esq.
Principal
*Parker, Milliken, Clark, O'Hara &
Samuelian*

As public concern continues to focus on environmental safety, the government responds with an ever-expanding web of environmental regulation of business and industry. The federal, state, and local laws enacted to protect the environment impose numerous obligations on managers and directors. Failure to comply with these environmental regulatory schemes may result in harsh civil and criminal penalties.

Liability is also associated with real property transactions. Past and present owners as well as other parties involved in real estate transactions may be liable for contamination and be required to pay tremendous cleanup costs. To protect themselves from such liability, companies must be familiar with the law and adopt a comprehensive and ongoing in-house environmental management program. This chapter will focus on potential liability and the use of environmental audits to meet the ever-increasing legal obligations.

An effective management plan requires becoming familiar with the regulations, keeping current on them, and making certain that they are followed as closely as possible. The principal environmental statutes include the Clean Air Act, the Safe Drinking Water Act, the Clean Water Act, Resource Conservation and Recovery Act (RCRA), Comprehensive Environmental Response, Compensation and Liability Act (CERCLA), and the Toxic Substances Control Act (TSCA). State, city, and county municipal codes must also be monitored and followed.

Criminal Liability

Prior to the 1980s, criminal investigations and prosecutions for environmental crimes were virtually nonexistent. Most matters were pursued as civil or administrative cases. Monetary penalties were relatively small, and the threat of a corporate executive going to jail was unheard of. Commencing in the 1980s, a change of focus toward criminal prosecution began to develop. Multicount felony actions are now regularly filed against corporations and their executives and employees. Prosecutors are no longer satisfied with a "slap on the wrist" fine but seek large monetary payments and often insist on jail time. The shift in focus from civil and administrative enforcement of environmental laws to criminal prosecution for environmental violations has sent shock waves through the regulated community. Both large and small corporations and their individual employees and executives may be subject to prosecution. Moreover, even technical violations of increasingly complex environmental regulations can give rise to criminal liability. The stakes for improper hazardous-waste management have drastically changed in the past decade.

Since the early 1980s, the Environmental Protection Agency (EPA) has employed a staff of criminal investigators. More recently, the FBI has also assigned agents to investigate environmental crimes. These federal agencies, plus others, make referrals to the U.S. Department of Justice. The Department of Justice has a special environmental crimes unit which coordinates case filings and investigations. In addition, state and local enforcement agencies have been given statutory authority to pursue violations criminally.

Virtually every aspect of waste management is subject to regulation, including record keeping, manifesting, labeling, storage, treatment, transportation, and disposal. Each of these activities is regulated by civil as well as criminal penalty provisions. There are certain types of waste management activities which, when combined with other attendant factors, make criminal investigations and prosecutions more likely. While there is no magic formula, and while prosecutorial discretion varies from agency to agency, the following activities and factors are often relevant in a prosecutor's decision on whether to file as a criminal or civil case and on whether to pursue the case as a misdemeanor charge or as a felony.

Suspect Activities

Water Discharge into Public Sewers. Companies which produce waste water through, for instance, their plating operations, are particularly suspect for criminal investigations. Discharged waste water must be checked regularly for pH levels and heavy metal content. Criminal investigators can and often do test a company's waste water flow off-site without a company's knowledge, and the test results can lead to criminal prosecution.

On-Site Spills. In the course of a company's business activities (e.g., manufacturing, storage of chemicals, movement of materials) on-site spills can and do occur. In the case of a business which has been operating a facility for a number of years, these spills may have occurred long before the passage of hazardous waste laws in effect today which make illegal any hazardous-waste discharges onto the ground. Nevertheless, prosecutors have taken the position that spills, even those occurring long ago, constitute an act of illegal disposal. While such cases may be or should be more appropriately handled as a civil cleanup matter, they sometimes lead to criminal charges being filed. Maintaining clean housekeeping practices and the use of proper berming and containment areas can help in this regard.

On-Site Containment and Discharge Pipes. If waste or a chemical flow is being managed (e.g., stored, treated, or transported) on-site through a piping system, it is important to check for inadvertent leaks and to determine the eventual flow or discharge points from these pipes. Prosecutors often theorize about a company's use of a "pirate pipe" or a "bypass" pipe or hose, alleging that the company is trying to manage or dispose of its waste in an improper or covert fashion.

Storage of Drums. The scene of dozens of 55-gallon drums stored on-site often triggers close scrutiny by regulators. This is especially so if the storage occurs near a facility's property line, railroad tracks, or some sort of ditch or drain which leads off-site. Attention should therefore be given to having materials or wastes stored in properly conditioned drums with lids in place and with proper labels and storage records. Proper berming and containment areas are also important. Improperly stored waste can give rise to a host of criminal violations, including exceeding the federal 90-day storage limit (state and local jurisdictions may have even shorter limits), illegal disposals, and the potential for a risk of fire, explosion, and injury.

Asbestos Removal, Demolition, and Disposal. A recent "red flag" for criminal prosecutions involves asbestos. Many buildings and building materials constructed prior to 1979 contain asbestos, a heavily regulated insulation material. Asbestos in a building may be affected during tenant improvements, building restoration, or demolition. EPA has estimated that more than 100,000 demolition and renovation jobs affecting asbestos are done in the United States every year, and that as many as one-half of these projects violate the asbestos regulations under the Clean Air Act. It is important to make sure all asbestos, if removed or tampered with, is handled by licensed companies which follow all regulations.

Transportation and Manifesting. One of the most common charges involves transporting hazardous waste without a proper license and/or without properly filling out a hazardous-waste manifest. Generators of waste can be held liable for the misdeeds of the transporters they engage. Caution in this area is therefore important.

Other Factors Prosecutors Consider

Profit Motive. If an investigation leads to a suspicion that sloppy or otherwise improper waste management was motivated by profit considerations, it is likely that charges will be filed criminally. Prosecutors associate perceived profit motive with "shortcuts" taken by a company with respect to their waste management in order to save money. These money-saving shortcuts, argue prosecutors, are exemplified by the so-called pirate pipe or bypass hose, or the hiring of unskilled or improperly trained workers to handle a company's on-site waste activities. Prosecutors will also look warily on acts which they consider to involve concealment or conspiracy (for example, the mixing of hazardous waste with regular trash to avoid the payment of expensive hazardous-waste-disposal fees).

Egregiousness of the Alleged Act. Prosecutors also consider how egregious or blatant an alleged violation is. The "midnight dumping" of chemicals in an unauthorized location will almost certainly lead to criminal prosecution, as will acts that are perceived to create the potential for serious injury or death.

Financial Condition of Defendants. Criminal charges have been filed against small companies, large corporate conglomerates, individual employees, and corporate presidents. However, the lawsuit against a financially sound company gives the prosecutor possible perceived leverage in requiring expensive cleanups and negotiating for large settlement fines. Cases brought against a company are usually also filed against one or more corporate executives and midlevel management employees.

The EPA and various other federal, state, and local enforcement agencies have broad powers to investigate and prosecute environmental crimes. With the tougher penalties and stricter enforcement of environmental laws, executives at all levels should actively take steps to find and prevent environmental violations.

Liability from Real Estate Transactions

An important but often overlooked area of environmental liability comes in the context of the acquisition, sale, and leasing of real property. The reach of federal, state, and local hazardous-waste statutes is very broad and potentially covers past and present owners of real property containing hazardous substances, as well as lessors, lessees, lenders, corporate officers, and commercial brokers. Very few commercial or industrial properties are immune from the prospect of incurring on-site contamination. Virtually all types of businesses, from manufacturers of all types of products to gasoline stations, hospitals, dry cleaners, printers, office buildings, and developed and undeveloped commercial and industrial real property, are affected. The potential environmental liabilities associated with real property transactions, while often not obvious, can result in tremendous cleanup costs; long delays in the property's development; decreased value or use of the property; and claims from adjacent landowners, lessees, and on-site workers. It is important for companies to be fully aware of potential environmental liability associated with real estate transactions.

The central focus of many recent environmental lawsuits involves the issue of which parties are responsible for cleaning up hazardous waste on real property. The principal federal statute which addresses this question is CERCLA. In the past few years courts throughout the nation have been asked to interpret CERCLA as well as other environmental statutes and have responded by expanding the scope of potentially responsible parties.

Current owners or operators of property containing hazardous waste are liable for cleanup costs. In a recent federal court case the court held that CERCLA imposes "strict liability" on the current owner of a facility from which there is a release of hazardous waste even if the current owner was not responsible for creating the problem. Also under CERCLA, any person who at the time of disposal of a hazardous substance owned or operated the subject property can be held liable. This raises the issue of liability of past owners. Thus, as a current owner of contaminated property a company may be forced to pay for the entire cleanup cost; however, these costs may be recoverable from the prior owner or operator who was responsible for creating the contamination.

Lessees, banks, and even real estate brokers may be subject to liability under the ever-expanding environmental laws. The courts have also recently begun finding company owners and executives individually liable for hazardous-waste cleanup costs. A recent federal case held that the president and vice president of a chemical manufacturing company were individually liable for hazardous-waste cleanup. The president was held liable even though he was not present during the disposal of the hazardous waste in issue. The court found that he was aware of the waste and had actively participated in previous negotiations concerning other similar disposals. The vice president of the company was held liable because he was directly responsible for arranging the disposal and the transportation of the waste. This case demonstrates that new legal theories are developing which hold seemingly remote parties responsible for the hazardous-waste problems of industrial and commercial properties.

In view of the potential environmental liabilities associated with owning or buying real estate, all parties to a transaction should be acutely aware of the risks involved and should seek to protect themselves as much as possible. All parties involved in real estate transactions should take special note of the environmental laws and trends which have already begun to dramatically affect the liabilities associated with the ownership and transfer of commercial and industrial properties. Particular attention should be given and counsel sought regarding the environmental issues relevant to each transaction.

Environmental Auditing: A Solution

To ensure their compliance with environmental regulatory schemes and thus minimize legal exposure, industry and its counsel have from time to time used the concept of the "environmental audit." The federal EPA defines environmental auditing as "a systematic, documented, periodic and objective review by regulated entities of facility operations and practices related to meeting environmental requirements." [EPA "Environmental Auditing Policy Statement," *Federal Register*, vol. 51, no. 131, p. 25006, July 9, 1986 ("EPA Statement").] Businesses should think of environmental audits as they do of any other audits they prudently conduct (e.g., inventory, personnel). The environmental audit is simply a survey to take account of the business' ability to meet its obligations, only in this case we are speaking of the business' legal, as opposed to commercial, obligations. This survey should have as a collateral but important purpose ensuring that the business is meeting its regulatory obligations in the most cost-efficient manner possible.

Why Audit?

There are many reasons why environmental auditing is important to business and industry today:

Auditing helps to evaluate whether a business has all of its necessary environmental permits and licenses. Many times peculiarities of local regulation exist which a comprehensive environmental survey will serve to highlight. As an example, in lieu of simply following state regulations, many cities enforce their own program to prevent hazardous-waste contamination. These local programs many times have their own particular permit and reporting requirements. A business which merely looks at the state's literature on its program would not necessarily focus on such local peculiarities. A thorough audit, however, would provide such focus.

Auditing helps ensure that the business is aware of applicable variances or exemptions from regulation. Because the environmental regulatory scheme is so complex and, in its penalties, so potentially harsh, any variances or exemptions from such regulation are to be treasured. A thorough environmental audit should focus on whether the business in fact qualifies for a variance or exemption. Should a variance or exemption be found applicable to a business' waste stream, it could result in significant cost savings as well as some protection from potential liability.

Auditing helps protect people. This is true in a double sense. First, of course, by helping to ensure that the business is in regulatory compliance, to the extent that the regulations are well grounded, the audit helps to ensure that the environment (e.g., the neighborhood around a plant) is in fact being kept safe; it is a simple truth that a safe environment is good for people. Second, by helping to ensure regulatory compliance, the audit helps to protect company personnel from exposure to personal, civil, and criminal liabilities. It is increasingly the case that prosecutorial authorities will not be satisfied merely with obtaining a fine from a corporate violator and are additionally insisting on civil and criminal accountability from corporate employees responsible for, or who could have prevented, the violations.

Auditing helps lessen government's desire to inspect. The government simply does not have an inspection staff adequate to visit every facility covered by the regulatory scheme. While naturally the government will not promise to refrain from inspecting businesses which adopt a comprehensive environmental auditing policy, as a matter of common sense such businesses can expect the government to focus its inspection priorities elsewhere.

Auditing helps make inspections manageable. Since the audit will make the business' personnel familiar with the business' regulatory obligations, the personnel should in most instances be in a position to discuss those obligations intelligently with the inspector and allay any concern that significant environmental problems are lurking at the inspected facility. Additionally, a thorough audit will detail legal rights as well as obligations and thereby give the business a sense of when to involve its counsel in dealing with inspection requests.

Auditing helps deter prosecutions. This is true for two reasons. First, most prosecutors are in fact motivated by a desire faithfully to protect the public; a technical environmental regulatory violation by a business which has a history of "bad" conduct is more likely to provoke prosecutorial ire than if the violation is seen as an isolated problem encountered by a business with a history of diligent self-policing.

Second, many prosecutorial agencies are geared to statistics; the agency decides to prosecute where it thinks it will win. If the prosecutor is dealing with a business and with business personnel who have shown a history of environmental regulatory awareness through such self-policing measures as audits, the prosecutor may conclude it will be difficult to convince a judge or jury to impose a conviction or, in any event, a harsh sentence. Thus, as the EPA itself implicitly acknowledges, the audit may act as a deterrent to prosecutions: "In fashioning enforcement responses to violations, EPA policy is to take into account, on a case-by-case basis, the honest and genuine efforts of regulated entities to avoid and promptly correct violations and underlying environmental problems. When regulated entities take reasonable precautions to avoid noncompliance, expeditiously correct underlying environmental problems discovered through audits or other means, and implement measures to prevent their recurrence, EPA may exercise its discretion to consider such actions as honest and genuine efforts to assure compliance." (EPA Statement, p. 25007.)

Auditing helps avoid financial problems. The government, of course, is not the only potential litigant threatening the environmental regulatory violator. Private persons who perceive themselves to have been injured by an alleged violation (e.g., neighbors of a plant allegedly polluting the neighborhood ground or air) may institute civil tort suits which may have to be disclosed to a business' lenders and/or to the general public via required filings with the Securities and Exchange Commission. By helping the business avoid noncompliance with the law and thus avoid such suits, the audit helps the business avoid potentially adverse reaction among lenders and investors.

Auditing helps evaluate the risk from the actions of others against third-party lawsuits in the first instance. Under federal CERCLA and similar state statutes, the property owner may be held responsible to clean up a hazardous waste problem even if the owner inherited the problem from others. Similarly, the owner may be held responsible for the activities from other persons using the property (e.g., lessees). Thus, whenever a business is making a property acquisition or granting someone else a leasehold or other interest in presently owned property, the business should make a survey of the potential environmental liability associated with the transaction.

Auditing helps government contractors. The federal government may bar from receiving government contracts or subcontracts businesses which have had a history of environmental regulatory noncompliance.

For instance, for any business convicted of violating the Clean Air Act or Clean Water Act such bar is mandatory. The EPA, which has little employed this "blacklisting" device in the past, has indicated that the device will be used more frequently in the future. By helping to ferret out environmental problems in order that they may be promptly corrected, the audit serves as a tool for such contractors and subcontractors to avoid such disastrous consequences.

Auditing may help save money. Businesses generating hazardous waste cannot ship, generally, their waste off-site except for costly disposal at a properly licensed facility and via a properly licensed hauler. As a result of, among other things, adverse public opinion, licensed sites for any types of waste are becoming either increasingly rare or at least increasingly remote, with consequent increase in the cost of disposal. A thorough environmental audit should explore the possibilities of alternative legitimate methods of dealing with waste generated at a facility, such as whether the waste can be treated on-site and/or recycled as opposed to being simply discarded. Such alternative methods may produce significant savings to the business when compared with the ever-escalating costs associated with landfill disposal. Indeed, some state governments have made provisions for financial assistance in certain situations to encourage such alternative technological approaches to the management of hazardous waste.

Concerns About Auditing

Businesses understandably have a few legitimate concerns about the wisdom of conducting an environmental audit. However, on balance, these concerns do not dictate abandonment of the auditing concept.

One concern about auditing is that a thorough audit may reveal problems which are simply too expensive or too time consuming to cure or may serve as a violation "road map" for government investigators and prosecutors. (For a discussion supporting the view that auditing runs the "road map" risk, see Edmund B. Frost, "Voluntary Environmental Compliance Audits: A DOJ Policy Failure," *BNA Toxics Law Reporter,* Sept. 18, 1991, p. 499.) However, at least for businesses in communities with aggressive prosecutors and for businesses whose livelihood depends on government contracts and subcontracts, it may in the long run prove too expensive not to cure environmental problems. Indeed, given the substantial risk of criminal and civil prosecution of corporate officers and other responsible employees, it would seem that, for any business dealing with hazardous or potentially hazardous waste, the auditing effort on balance should enjoy at least a favorable rebuttal presumption.

A second concern about auditing is that it may disclose environmental regulatory violations which, upon discovery, may have to be reported to the government. However, in many instances environmental liability cannot be avoided simply by deliberate failure to investigate. A business may have a duty to find out and report on certain issues anyway, and therefore it seems sensible to encompass the business' complete environmental situation in one survey.

A third concern about auditing is the expense of the audit itself. Depending on the size of the facility being audited, this expense can easily run into thousands of dollars. However, there are methods to keep the expense as low as possible—for example, an outside auditor can identify various issues (e.g., that the business must have a procedure to ensure that its waste haulers are licensed), and where appropriate, the business can then utilize in-house personnel to follow up on those issues. If the audit is viewed properly as an investment the business is making in ensuring a future free from regulatory difficulties, then expense should seldom prove a controlling factor in deciding whether or not to audit.

Conducting the Audit

The auditing task must be a cooperative effort involving both lawyers and scientific experts because it invariably involves both legal and scientific judgments. In auditing a business, for instance, the experienced environmental lawyer will know it is essential to review the business' material safety data sheets for information as to whether a given product contains materials falling within certain legally defined "hazardous waste" criteria. The lawyer may need the assistance of scientific expertise to interpret whether or not various technical data on the safety sheets in fact fall within or without such criteria, however. While more than legal expertise is needed for the audit, it is advisable to have it conducted under the supervision of counsel. There are several reasons for this:

First, the environmental regulatory area is statutorily and administratively complex and often without judicial precedent. The regulatory scheme offers both legal pitfalls and potential exemptions to which environmental counsel will be attuned.

Second, in many instances whether a particular material is "hazardous" is in the strictest sense a legal judgment call. For example, the government in a given jurisdiction may have promulgated a list of several hundred chemicals which are deemed "potentially" hazardous; however, it would still possibly be an open legal question as to whether a business must treat a chemical as actually hazardous just because the chemical appears on this list. The decision a business makes in this regard will obviously be highly dependent on the advice of counsel about the courts' ultimate resolution of this question.

Third, conducting the audit under the auspices of counsel will give the audit some measure of legal confidentiality. It is quite simple: Audit reports and recommendations to management from counsel are privileged. The attorney-client privilege applies, and in certain jurisdictions the attorney work-product privilege may apply as well. It is important to stress, however, that these privileges cannot be used to shield from the government information which the business has a legal obligation to reveal. While some courts have also recognized a distinct privilege for "self-evaluation," the statute of this privilege is shaky and cannot be viewed as a substitute for the privilege available through the involvement of counsel.

Fourth, regarding information given to the government, any claim of trade secret or propriety data protection must be made in compliance with the specific requirements of the regulatory scheme. Obviously, a business will need to look to counsel for an opinion that such requirements have been fulfilled and that the secrets and data are, in fact, protected from disclosure.

Fifth, it should be also noted that the businesses engaging an environmental scientific consultant for auditing and/or more general purposes often find a contract for services presented which places all potential liabilities on the business and completely indemnifies the consultant. Such a situation is purely a matter of contractual agreement and not a matter of law; and counsel can assist the business in evaluating its exposure under the consulting contract and in negotiating a better deal.

In making the commitment to audit, a business must grapple not only with the issue of the respective roles of lawyers and scientists but also with the issue of whether the auditor should be in-house and/or outside personnel. Obviously, the utilization of in-house counsel or scientists minimizes expense. On the other hand, in-house personnel may lack the expertise or simply the time to devote to a thorough audit. Moreover, although by no means universally the case, in-house personnel may not feel completely independent and comfortable reporting to management adverse conclusions and potentially expensive recommendations. The EPA has stressed the auditor's independence as a key to successful auditing: "The status or organizational locus of environmental auditors should be sufficient to ensure objective and unobstructed inquiry, observation, and testing. Auditor objectivity should not be impaired by personal relationships, financial or other conflicts of interest, interference with free inquiry or judgment, or fear of potential retribution." (EPA Statement, p. 25009.)

The principle of auditor independence, then, should be respected. How each business ensures such independence (i.e., through the use of outside or in-house personnel or of both) may vary within the discretion of sound business judgment.

Where to Audit

Any business engaged in manufacturing or recycling activities would benefit from an environmental audit. However, even service-oriented businesses which handle chemicals (e.g., the printer or beautician) may benefit.

For example, while a jurisdiction may have an exemption from regulation for households which discard products containing hazardous materials, this exemption would not necessarily apply to commercial activities. Thus, while a household may be free to throw into the regular garbage a can of hairspray containing a hazardous material, the beauty supply shop may not be free to do so. How many beauticians know this? An audit would tell them.

Additionally, a business with more than one facility should consider auditing all of its facilities. The business should not assume that a problem solved in one state can safely be left for another day in its plant in another state. For example, Arizona received a grant from the EPA to set up a nine-state computerized information bank concerning licensing problems, civil suits, indictments, and administrative proceedings. Thus a corporate environmental problem in any one of the participating states will become known to authorities in all of these states, potentially triggering investigations in any of these states where the business' property is located. Accordingly, a business environmental audit should be companywide.

When to Audit

One safe rule to observe is that auditing should be associated with change. When a business undergoes significant change, an audit should be conducted to ensure that new processes are environmentally safe and to ensure that new management and/or other key employees are confident they may safely continue past practices. From this commonsense principle one can conclude a business should consider an environmental audit whenever (1) there has been a significant amendment to applicable laws and/or regulations, (2) there has been a change in the manufacturing process of the business, (3) there has been a transfer of an interest in real property, or (4) a stock offering is contemplated.

Additionally, an audit should be conducted whenever a business learns it is being investigated by the government. If the investigation ultimately leads to litigation, the prelawsuit audit should enable the business' litigation defense counsel to "hit the ground running." Moreover, the audit will serve to arm such counsel with information so as to enable counsel in appropriate circumstances to approach the government intelligently before litigation is even instituted. If counsel can, in the prelitigation phase of the investigation, make an informed argument to the government that the business is generally in compliance with the environmental regulatory scheme, the government may be convinced to regard the matter under investigation as an isolated incident rather than as part of a pattern of business practice. In such event, the prosecution, doubting it has a "bad actor" on its hands, may be somewhat less zealous in the pursuit of penalties.

Information Included in an Audit

Advising a business about the status of its environmental regulatory compliance involves both legal and scientific judgments. A sound environmental audit should include the following information:

- Prior to any audit pertinent personnel should be given a "preaudit questionnaire" to answer. Based on the auditor's experience and preliminary review of the facility, the questionnaire should focus on the regulatory areas most likely to be involved in the functioning of the plant. The information submitted in response to the questionnaire should enable the auditor immediately to focus attention upon potential problem areas.

- The audit should ensure that the business is adequately providing both training and warnings to employees about potential dangerous products they may encounter in the workplace.

- The audit should focus attention on the business' storage, if any, of chemicals in tanks and drums. State and local agencies extensively regulate underground storage tanks regarding leakage. Additionally, some localities regulate chemical storage in above-ground tanks.

- The audit should review any chemical discharges by the facility into the air, the ground, waterways, or the sewerage system. The discharge of hazardous waste into waterways, for instance, can be violative of not only federal laws such as the Clean Water Act but also of various state and local laws.

- If the facility sends any waste off-site, the audit should review whether or not the facility has adequate procedures to ensure the waste is being transported by properly licensed hazardous-waste haulers to properly licensed disposal facilities.

- The audit should review whether or not there are any electrical transformers at the facility, and if so, whether or not the transformers contain PCB oil. If so, there are special federal regulations which may apply.

- The audit should review whether or not facility buildings have any asbestos problems. Many older buildings have asbestos. While this fact alone may not present any environmental risk requiring immediate remedial action, in many jurisdictions there are very strict regulations governing disclosure of the presence of asbestos and governing the handling of such asbestos in the event the material is disturbed by activities such as repairs or reconstruction. The audit, therefore, should alert businesses to this fact so that management can properly plan ahead of time for such repair or reconstruction to be done in compliance with the regulatory scheme.

- It is important for the audit not only to consider what is presently being done at the facility but also to ascertain what may have been done on the same property by others in the past. A business can bear cleanup responsibility even for things done by its predecessors. The audit should focus on the prior history, if any, of government inspections in an effort to infer what activities of the facility have interested the government in the past.

- The audit should, of course, review any and all government permits and licenses, or applications for the same, pertaining to the facility; and the audit should consider the facility's eligibility for any appropriate variances or exemptions.

Just as business commonly accepts that it must undergo financial auditing, so, too, is business coming to understand the concept of environmental auditing. While auditing does involve the commitment of precious financial resources, the commitment may well be worthwhile considering that environmental violations left unremedied can and have ruined employees' careers and businesses' reputations. The environmental audit should be viewed by business as an important tool which, appropriately utilized, can help provide invaluable personal and corporate protection from unwanted, and needless, confrontations with government and private litigants.

4

Inspections and the Enforcement Process

Steven J. Jones

Supervising Air Quality Inspector
South Coast Air Quality
Management District

The Role of the Inspector

The cries echo through the industrial community: "oh no, they're here!" To most people involved in the business world, they are the ogres, the fire-breathing dragons, the bad guys with a badge in one hand and their other hand in your pocket. These demons of the deep are regulatory agency inspectors. They come in many sizes and shapes, and there are always too many of them.

And I'm sure you are tired of hearing they are a necessary evil. But, despite rumors, inspectors are human. They are born of human parents (well at least most of them are), live and raise their families in the same locales, eat at the same restaurants, and aspire to the same standards of life as you do: the ability to breathe clean air, drink uncontaminated water, eat foods free of carcinogens and pesticides, raise a family in a crime-free, clean neighborhood instead of a landfill, and not to have others transgress upon their rights.

Today, the regulations appear to be never-ending versus the "good old days." Many regulations are brought on by a new awareness of exposures to various chemicals from everyday products. Some are warranted; others overkill. Unfortunately, we are trying to reverse or solve the problems "dumped" on us by our ancestors. Not so long ago, regulations didn't exist for the disposal of chemicals, especially solvents. Today, we have the legacy of countless years of dumping wastes "out back," and need to correct these problems so our future generations won't have to. Regulatory agencies are sensitive to industrial needs. However, I would like to see my grandchildren breathe clean Los Angeles air, and not have to suffer as I did growing up in the San Gabriel Valley. So a happy median will have to exist.

Like me, most inspectors are believers in their agency's cause and are not just out to get a paycheck. I've been employed with the South Coast Air Quality Management District (SCAQMD) for more than 10 years. Most of these years were spent as an inspector or supervisor in the enforcement division. The SCAQMD is one of the largest air-pollution agencies in the world and has the difficult task of cleaning up the air in the Los Angeles area. The district is chartered by the state of California primarily to enforce federal, state, and local air-pollution regulations for stationary (non-motor-vehicle) sources. Except for a few rare cases, the motor vehicle sources are handled by the state Air Resources Board. The district is the forerunner in air-pollution control measures and regulations. Other air-pollution agencies may duplicate our regulations once their feasibility is determined and the bugs are worked out of the system.

Unlike most other areas in the United States, Los Angeles has the ideal conditions for the production of photochemical smog. The city lies in a natural basin surrounded by mountains, is subject to inversion layers (which work like a lid on a pot), and has an abundance of sunshine. Mix these all together and you get photochemical smog. The "smog" associated with other areas of the United States, such as New York City, is a combination of combustion by-products from coal and fuel oils mixed with the fog that occurs during the winter months. Photochemical smog is a reaction involving nitrous oxides (NOx, by-products from fuel combustion) and hydrocarbons (HC or solvents) in the presence of sunlight. The main component of photochemical smog is ozone. Ozone is good in the stratosphere, but not so good at ground level, where it is an irritant and causes property and plant damage. Someone once suggested that we pump the ozone from Los Angeles to the hole in the ozone layer. This probably came from the same person who recommended installing giant fans to "blow" the smog out of Los Angeles.

The Los Angeles air basin is a nonattainment area—that is, does not meet minimum standards—for carbon monoxide (CO), particulate matter less than 10 micrometers (PM 10), ozone (O3), and nitrous oxides (NOx) according to the federal and California Clean Air Acts. When the Los Angeles Air Pollution Control District was created in 1947, the formation of "smog" was little understood. The first enforcement programs went after visible sources of emissions such as smokestacks, motor vehicles, and backyard incinerators. Once the complex reactions forming smog were known, enforcement turned to the most cost-effective strategies of controlling the reactants. Controlling NOx emissions was too costly and the technology was not available; therefore, regulations were developed limiting solvent emissions from industrial sources such as vapor degreasers and solvent cleaning operations. Regulations were also developed to reduce emissions from gasoline dispensing, refineries, chemical plants, power utilities, bulk loading racks, paints, and landfills. When the technologies were available, NOx regulations were developed to control emissions from water heaters, boilers, and internal combustion engines. Today the district is developing regulations to control emissions from smaller sources and consumer products such as charcoal lighter fluid, propellants in aerosol spray cans, and chlorofluorocarbons from automobile and air-conditioning units. The district is also developing regulations which will affect the lifestyles of Los Angeles residents, such as trip-reduction requirements (carpooling) for employers with 100 or more employees.

As you can see, the district has numerous regulations affecting companies that range from dry cleaners to auto body repair shops, office buildings, large aerospace firms, and oil refineries. There are relatively few companies that are not affected by our regulations in one form or another. Most homeowners are not aware that the water heater they just bought is equipped with a low NOx burner required by the district, or that water-based paint needs to comply with our architectural coating regulation.

The last subject I'd like to mention about the district concerns our funding. Everyone wants to know if their tax dollar is being spent wisely. The SCAQMD is not funded through our tax dollars. Rather we have a permit system and annual fees that comprise the majority of our budget. We are a large agency with 1100 employees and an annual operating budget of $111 million. I've heard it said that companies are paying us so we allow them to pollute. The way I see it, companies are paying us to enforce the regulations.

The Enforcement Process

As previously mentioned, I've been in enforcement for more than 10 years and have gained a great deal of knowledge about air-pollution regulations and equipment. I've been involved in some of the largest penalty cases the district has ever handled. For these reasons, I am commonly requested to speak before various groups on the subject "What does an inspector look for?" The groups range from college environmental classes to professional organizations to companies just wanting to know what is expected of them. I mostly discuss rules, regulations, permit requirements, record keeping, and interactions with district staff. It gives me an opportunity to tell some "war stories," and discuss enforcement actions, penalties, and creative settlements, while interjecting some humor to smooth over the harsh reality of noncompliance.

The largest settlement in district history and probably the largest settlement for a local air-pollution agency involved a large aerospace firm who had previously hidden behind the guise of national security. I was the first inspector allowed in these areas, and at the conclusion of the inspection a Notice of Violation was issued for over 7000 violation counts, and the potential existed to triple that number. The majority of the violations were for improper or no record keeping of their solvent and coating usage. Other violations were for not having Permits to Operate on several pieces of equipment and exceeding coating and solvent limits of prohibitory rules.

The company reached an agreement with the district and settled for $1 million. Although the fine is a nice round number, it's the compliance plan that we're the most pleased with. The plan outlined several steps to ensure future compliance and originally was estimated to cost the company $2.5 million to set up and implement. The compliance plan required condensing all coatings and solvents into centralized chemical cribs, computerization of coating and solvent usage, purchasing high transfer efficiency spraying equipment long before the rule required its use, and purchasing enclosed automatic spray gun cleaners.

Condensing coatings and solvents into centralized chemical cribs is a necessity for any large usage facility, especially if they have numerous types of coatings and various applicable regulations. There are several reasons for centralized chemical cribs; however, the main benefit is *control*! The cribs can maintain records of all coating and solvent use, e.g., amounts purchased, amounts used on each project, and the amounts disposed of (great for SARA and other reporting requirements). In addition, there is control over who uses the material and if it is used properly, e.g., proper substrate, regulation, etc.

Once you add a computer to this system, your whole nightmare of endless hours of report preparation is reduced to a punch of a button. The above company would have spent up to 3 months preparing annual reports. Today, the reports are ready in a few hours. Imagine the ideal situation where an employee needs a coating to paint a part. All coatings and solvents are bar coded once they enter the crib. Employees go to the crib and pass their ID badge through a scanning reader which accesses their personnel file to see if they have had a recent physical or proper training to use that material. The project paperwork is scanned and the attendant then scans the coating and places it on the automatic scale which records the weight and cross-checks if the material is permissible in this application. The returned material is reweighed and records the amounts of material disposed of and which drum the waste is placed in. All the information is now in the database, and reports can be generated for any material, employee exposure, daily usage, project expenditure, or waste generated. This technology is almost a reality. I predict further reliance on automated record keeping in the near future, and it possibly could show up as a rule requirement.

I got off the course a little, but aren't all inspectors a little off base? Anyway, the other compliance plan items are for the benefit of reducing air pollution by utilizing more efficient and less polluting equipment.

Another large settlement that I was involved with also had a comprehensive compliance plan which included installing centralized chemical cribs, conducting mandatory record keeping classes, the auditing of chemical usage areas (including audits of the auditors), and purchasing enclosed automatic spray gun cleaners. An interesting twist to this settlement is that the company placed a significant sum of money into a separate bank account with the district. If the company meets or beats the deadlines (or milestones) for implementation of each section of the compliance plan, they get a portion of this money back. If they fail to meet the deadline, the district keeps that portion of the money. It's like placing the carrot in front of the horse. It's an interesting concept that should motivate the company to comply because few people would want to explain to their bosses why they didn't meet the deadline and had to forfeit the monies to the district.

And, by the way, no bonuses or awards are given to the staff who worked on these settlements. The fines that are collected from large settlements normally go into one of our research funds from which we issue contracts (or grants) for companies to develop new air-pollution technologies, such as alternate fuels or low volatile organic compound (VOC) coatings or solvents. The $1 million fine went into our clean fuel fund to research fuel alternatives to gasoline or diesel, such as flex fuels, methanol, LPG, electric, and solar; therefore, it is possible for a company to receive a portion of their fine back if they are willing to develop air-pollution technology. In the long run it can be a win-win situation for air pollution.

I am also involved in our Regulation XV (Trip Reduction/Indirect Source) Section, also known as carpooling. In an effort to minimize the number of vehicles on the roadways, companies with 100 or more employees are required to submit trip-reduction plans outlining the incentives offered to employees so they can meet a targeted average vehicle ridership (AVR). Depending on your work location, you have a targeted goal of 1.3, 1.5, or 1.75 persons per vehicle. The 1.75 target is for heavy traffic areas such as downtown Los Angeles. The district is very serious about compliance with this regulation, and large fines and innovative compliance plans have resulted from noncompliant companies. For example, some companies were required to convert some or all of their fleet vehicles to clean fuels such as LPG, provide advertising for clean air, or develop vehicle maintenance classes.

The district is actively pursuing a "kinder and gentler" approach to fines and penalties. Some fines are greatly reduced if the district obtains a compliance plan that ensures company compliance and will help to reduce air pollution.

So after this lengthy discussion on fines and penalties, what's my point? The purpose, of course, is to demonstrate what could happen to you if you are not in compliance with not only SCAQMD regulations but other regulatory agencies as well. Some agencies have "cease and desist" authority, and others, like the district, have an Order for Abatement, which limits or ceases the violating operation. With these heavies, it's no wonder people don't like regulatory agencies. They can put you out of business in a hurry.

Working with the Agency

However complicated the regulations are, it is in your company's best interest to make sure they are in compliance with every agency's regulations, and to maintain a good working relationship with them.

Some agencies have a "consultant" service that works side by side with enforcement. If you have any problems or questions, you call the "consultant" service and they give you assistance and possibly more time to come into compliance. Normally, they involve enforcement only if you fail to comply within the allotted time frame. You should ask each regulatory agency if they have this service and keep the telephone number handy. The district is developing a "consultant" service for small businesses since many of our current and future regulations impact smaller and smaller sources.

One of the main points from my speeches is that you should be calling me and asking questions and not have me at your door asking the same questions. If you have a question concerning permits or a rule interpretation, call your inspector. Be up front and don't beat around the bush. Also, take specific notes on your conversation with time, date, and whom you spoke with. We're not perfect and sometimes we can be forgetful. If the interpretation is critical, write a letter and ask for a written response. These letters and notes could save you and your company undue grief, especially when a "new" inspector shows up at your door and isn't familiar with your operation or specific regulations.

Within Enforcement we have several inspectors who are designated as "rule coordinators." These inspectors are well versed on their specific rule and can answer most of your questions concerning rule applicability or interpretation. Get to know the inspector who is the rule coordinator for your specific operation. For example, I'm the rule coordinator for aerospace, wood, paper, rubber, and glass coating regulations. If you have a question about a coating and if it's subject to the wood coating rule, you give me a call and document my response (remember; I may not).

Interactions can be extended to other regulatory agency divisions and not just Enforcement. You should get to know your customer service representative. At the district, our reps are assigned alphabetical company listings such as A through D. Your rep is your best friend when it comes to straightening out billings, permits, address and name changes, fees, or where to refer you for answers to specific questions.

Another division you need to be familiar with is Engineering. Usually, you will have one engineer who will process all of your applications for permits and plans. This person is your best contact on permit processing before problems can occur. Learn to start asking questions before beginning that "big" project. Additional equipment or processes may be required to bring the project into compliance, and these may be cost prohibitive. Once again, ask first so you don't have to pay later. For example, your company may want to install two additional paint booths and increase their paint usage by 10 gallons a day.

You wouldn't think this would be a big deal, and it may not be for some agencies. However, the district has several regulations covering new equipment. For example, do you have emission reduction credits or other mitigating emissions to offset these increases? Even then, you would be subject to Best Available Control Technology (BACT) review. For coating and solvent control, BACT is an afterburner. Afterburners for paint booths may cost in excess of $500,000, have high operating costs, and require a large space for installation. This is probably more than you budgeted for. Now suppose you already installed the booths without a permit and exceeded your facility usage limit for 100 days before an inspector happened to stop by your shop on a routine inspection. The inspector would issue you a Notice of Violation for installing two pieces of equipment without a permit and 100 days of excess emissions (one count per day). The district fines have limits of $1000, $10,000, or $25,000 per day per count. The higher fines are emissions-related and can be filed civil or criminal, depending on whether negligence or intent is demonstrated. Let's say you were negligent in this case since you have permits on other paint booths and are familiar with district regulations. You could therefore be subject to the following maximum fines:

Installing equipment without permit: 2 counts $\times$ $10,000 = $20,000

Operating equipment without permit: 2 booths $\times$ 100 counts
$\times$ $10,000 = $2,000,000

Excess emissions: 100 counts $\times$ $10,000 = $1,000,000

For this violation, you could be subject to $3,020,000 in fines, plus you may not be able to operate this equipment until you install BACT (possibly an afterburner), which in itself is costly. As you guessed, this was a large capital investment that just went down the tubes, and your job is probably on the line. If you had conducted some research first, this scenario probably would never have occurred. This case sounds rather severe, and in most cases the district would negotiate for a reduced fine if we can ensure compliance and mitigate the excess emissions. For example, install an afterburner equipped with a continuous monitor for hydrocarbons and NOx, plus install a urea injection system to abate NOx emissions, and the fines could be greatly reduced.

This scenario would also bring you into contact with another one of our divisions, Legal. On the positive side, the district has a "desk duty" attorney who is available to answer, or get the answer, to various legal or rule interpretation questions. Sometimes the rule coordinator isn't available and, for example, you need an interpretation on what constitutes a "facility." The desk duty person should be able to help you.

If you are involved in a specific industry such as aerospace, another person you should get to know is the Air Quality Specialist (or engineer) from the Rules Division. The Rules Division is responsible for adopting and amending the district's regulations. Let's use an example to demonstrate how a rule is adopted (or amended), and show possible areas for your company's input. The district proposes a new rule on VOC emissions from bovines. The strategy is outlined in the district's Air Quality Management Plan (AQMP), which is our "map" to ensure compliance with federal clean air standards by the year 2010. The proposed rule is assigned to a staff person. The staff person researches EPA, Air Resources Board, and other documents on bovine emissions. Through a series of internal workshops with bovine experts from Enforcement, Engineering, and Technical Services, a draft of the rule is released for public comments, either written or through public workshops. If your company is gravely concerned about this regulation and its impacts on milk production, you can express your views or research to the Rule Specialist. Comments are evaluated, and if reasonable, changes are incorporated into the proposed rule. Sometimes several public workshops are held if major changes are made. You should always participate in these workshops, because it is tougher to change the rule once it has been adopted. The final draft goes before our governing board for adoption. The board reviews the rule, makes comments, and opens the floor for public comments. Here's another opportunity for you to express your concerns about milk production. The rule is either adopted or sent back for a rework. Thus a rule is born and is ready for implementation with input from both sides.

In order to keep abreast of information about new or proposed regulations, rules, new technologies, or fee changes, I highly recommend that you sign up for our subscription service. For a service fee, you will receive notifications of pending regulations, board meetings, and other district news. You can leaf through the documents and attend any meetings that potentially have an impact on your industry. Also, the district's Public Information Center has a plethora of air quality information, manuals, and other publications.

As you can see, the district is a full service information agency. We try to provide good customer and information services. So take advantage of it! I'm sure other regulatory agencies have similar setups, involving similar divisions, and available information. Research what information and services are available from each agency and take advantage of them. With information, knowledge, and ability to have someone answer your questions, you've taken the first major step in keeping your company in compliance. It's a full-time job, and all medium-to-large companies should have trained staff dedicated to ensure compliance with the regulations.

If the project is complex, or if you don't have environmental staff, a company may hire the services of a consultant. There are many reputable consultant firms, and some that are not. Before you commit to a consultant, check with your friends, neighbor companies, your professional association, or companies within your association. I've worked with several outstanding consultant firms and others that usually result in a violation notice being issued. So be very careful and deal only with respectable firms (or individuals).

Not all enforcement actions are negative. The earlier case reduced months of paperwork to a push of a button. Some actions will save the company money in the long run, although it may not be apparent in the beginning. When I first started as a fledgling inspector, I inspected a heavy-use perchloroethylene (perc) dry cleaner. In those days, BACT wasn't required and a dry cleaner would need to install control equipment only if they exceeded 320 gallons of perc in a year. I was amazed when the total perc usage for the previous year exceeded 3500 gallons! I issued a Notice of Violation for not having control equipment, and needless to say the owner was not very pleased with me. After 20 minutes of verbal abuse, I made my escape. I remembered the tirade the following year when the inspection was due. Instead of the anticipated verbal attack, I was verbally praised! The owner installed the control equipment (in this case a refrigeration unit), and reduced perc usage to under 500 gallons in a year. At $6 a gallon (at that time), they not only saved about $18,000 during this time, but also paid off the fine, the cost of the unit, and the first year's operating costs. I wish all stories ended this way, a benefit to the company and a big benefit for air pollution.

A word of advice: don't try to falsify records or reporting requirements. You will eventually be caught; take it from an expert who knows. You can fool some of the inspectors some of the time, but it's bad news if you're caught. Intentionally falsifying records is a criminal misdemeanor, punishable with fines of up to $25,000 per day per count and possible jail time. Recently, I went out to a company with one of my inspectors. During the course of the inspection I noticed something unusual about their paint usage records. Upon closer examination of their record-keeping logs, I noted the entries were almost identical. It soon became apparent that the company made a few minor changes and photocopied the previous month's log. The entries, coatings, handwriting, and amounts used were almost identical. Since this company is a specialty shop, it is almost impossible for them to use the same coatings day in and day out, let alone for the last 3 months. The owner admitted in so many words that he faked the records, and his case was recommended for criminal prosecution.

So don't try it. I'm sure your company president doesn't want to sit in the same jail cell with you.

In summary, here's a list of "keepers" to use and keep your company in compliance with the regulatory agencies, and not have to roll over.

- Get to know each of your regulatory inspectors.

- Ask the inspectors questions to avoid having them ask you the same questions during an inspection.

- Get to know all of the available services and staff members from each agency.

- *Use* these services!

- Get and maintain copies of all applicable regulations.

- Sign up for all subscription services and mailing lists.

- Be actively involved in the rule-making process.

- Research permit requirements prior to beginning new projects.

- Use only reputable consultants.

- Do not cheat or manipulate records; it will catch up with you.

- And above all, be cooperative with your inspectors. You can catch more flies with honey than...well, you know.

References

California Air Resources Board (CARB), California Air Pollution Control Laws, 1991.
South Coast Air Quality Management District (SCAQMD), Rules and Regulations.
SCAQMD, Air Quality Management Plan, Draft, December 1990.
SCAQMD, Policies and Procedures, Enforcement Division.

5

The Role and Function of the United States Environmental Protection Agency

Glenn Heyman
Environmental Scientist
U.S. Environmental Protection
Agency, Region IX

The U.S. Environmental Protection Agency (EPA) was established by the U.S. Congress on Dec. 2, 1970, as an independent agency in the executive branch of the federal government. EPA was given the mandate by Congress to protect human health and the environment. Prior to this time, the responsibility for environmental regulation was dispersed among 15 components of 5 executive departments and independent agencies. The environmental responsibilities of these diverse groups were consolidated within the EPA.

Some of the major statutory authorities consolidated in the EPA include:

1. Air-pollution control, solid-waste management, radiation control, and drinking-water programs, inherited from the Department of Health, Education, and Welfare

2. The federal program for controlling water pollution and part of a pesticide research program from the Department of the Interior

3. The authority to register pesticides and to regulate their use from the Department of Agriculture

4. The responsibility to set tolerances, or legal residue limits, for pesticides in food from the Food and Drug Administration

5. The duties of the Federal Radiation Council and some responsibility for setting standards for environmental radiation from the former Atomic Energy Commission

EPA currently implements 16 major federal laws dealing with the environment:

- The Clean Air Act
- The Clean Water Act
- The Safe Drinking Water Act
- The Comprehensive Environmental Response, Compensation, and Liability Act (CERCLA, or more commonly "Superfund")
- The Emergency Planning and Community Right-to-Know Act
- The Resource Conservation and Recovery Act (RCRA)
- The Federal Insecticide, Fungicide, and Rodenticide Act (FIFRA)
- The Toxic Substances Control Act (TSCA)
- The Marine Protection, Research, and Sanctuaries Act
- The Uranium Mill Tailings Radiation Control Act
- The Indoor Radon Abatement Act
- The Ocean Dumping Ban Act
- The Coastal Zone Management Act
- The Pollution Prevention Act
- The National Environmental Policy Act
- The Federal Facilities Act of 1992

The Role of the EPA

The role EPA plays in protecting human health and the environment is defined by federal legislation, which specifies the regulatory framework within which EPA works. EPA reviews the scientific literature and supports research within the agency and in academia to determine the specific actions necessary to carry out these laws.

EPA works with governmental organizations and private groups on all levels that focus on public health and the environment. These groups include local and state agencies, Native American tribes, environmental organizations, and industry groups.

EPA Policy Evolution—From "Command and Control" to Incentives for Compliance

EPA historically adopted a "command and control" approach to implementing the statutes provided by Congress. Under this approach, EPA set standards and developed procedures for the regulated community to meet and follow. The incentive to meet the standards has been limited to the threat of fines, closure, or court action.

During the early 1970s, EPA resources were directed toward developing the statutes passed by Congress and the regulations and guidance necessary to implement these statutes. This was followed by a period of aggressive enforcement of the regulations, which was accompanied by a large increase in the Office of Regional Council staff. In the late 1970s and throughout the 1980s, EPA implemented the regulations while attempting to refine the legislation by working with Congress to develop amendments and reauthorize the statutes. Finally, in the late 1980s and into the 1990s, EPA has applied total quality management (TQM) principles to all phases of environmental management and has developed a strategic approach for implementing the statutes.

The strategic approach developed by EPA is an attempt to define environmental problems, place them in the proper context, prioritize each relevant issue, and apply the appropriate tool (including cross-program coordination) to solving the problems. This includes working with the public, industry, and environmental groups to develop new approaches to developing regulations, maintain and improve the environment, and clean up problems caused by inadequate chemical and waste management practices of the past. In this context, EPA is developing market-based regulations with economic incentives, encouraging industries and communities to take voluntary actions to reduce existing levels of pollution, and promoting pollution-prevention activities to eliminate or reduce pollution at the source.

Measuring the Benefits of Environmental Programs

EPA is developing measuring criteria, known as environmental indicators, to measure the effectiveness of its programs in removing human and ecological risks from the environment. These measuring criteria are designed to allow EPA to determine the real environmental benefit of its programs and to more clearly report these results to Congress and the public. Using environmental indicators will result in focusing EPA's resources in areas with both the greatest risk and the most benefit.

Encouraging Voluntary Solutions

EPA is urging industry to participate in voluntary programs to reduce production of hazardous waste and conserve energy. The Industrial Toxics Project, also known as the 33/50 Project, requested companies involved to reduce total emissions of 17 toxic chemicals by one-third by the end of 1992 and by one-half by the end of 1995. When a company joins EPA's Green Lights program, it agrees to survey all its facilities and install new lighting systems that save energy, to the extent that the new systems do not increase costs or compromise lighting quality.

The Enterprise-for-the-Americas initiative, begun in 1990, uses economic incentives to help Latin American countries protect their endangered rainforests and other natural resources. The United States has told Latin American governments that their public debt owed to the U.S. government can now be renegotiated, at a discount rate, and converted into local currency earmarked for environmental and conservation projects.

Program Delegation

In most statutes, there are clear provisions for states to assume responsibility for the programs. Programs such as RCRA and programs in the Clean Air Act and the Clean Water Act are good examples of delegable legislation. On the other hand, CERCLA, or Superfund, as it is popularly known, is the largest program which is not designed to be delegable. Once a state is authorized for a given program, EPA and the state agencies involved enforce the state regulations. EPA can also modify the base program which has been delegated. EPA supports the activities of the state in many ways, including:

- Providing grant money to fund the program
- Providing technical support
- Enforcing those state regulations that meet the delegable EPA regulations
- Monitoring the ongoing operation of the state program to assure that it continues to meet or exceed the federally legislated mandate.

As an example, the RCRA program can be delegated to a state when that state puts into place and demonstrates the ability to enforce a program that meets or exceeds the requirements of the federal legislation. When a state demonstrates this capacity, a program application is submitted to EPA and a determination is made on the state's ability to carry out their program.

EPA's Organization: Headquarters, the Regions, and ORD

To carry out its mission, EPA is subdivided into three general branches: (1) headquarters, located in Washington, D.C.; (2) 10 regional offices located across the country (known as the regions) which implement the programs; and (3) research groups organized under the Office of Research and Development (ORD). There is also a Science Advisory Board, which operates under the Federal Advisory Committee Act (FACA) to provide advice to the EPA administrator on scientific and engineering issues. This section discusses the roles and responsibilities of each of these entities.

Headquarters—Regulation Development and Coordination

Once environmental legislation is passed by Congress and signed into law by the President, EPA is mandated to develop a comprehensive set of regulations. Regulations are legal mechanisms that define how a statute's broad policy directives are to be implemented. Headquarters develops a set of proposed regulations or guidance procedures in a similar way using the general process outlined below. Initially, headquarters prepares a set of proposed regulations with input from the public, interest groups, and state and local governments. Headquarters submits these for formal review and public comment, then submits the revised regulations to the Office of Management and Budget for review and approval. Once a new regulation has been approved through this rigorous formal review and comment process, the regulations are published in the *Federal Register*.

During daily operations of EPA, headquarters acts as an interface between the regions, the Congress, and the executive branch. In their oversight role, members of Congress or Congressional committees routinely request information which only the regions can supply. Headquarters may organize the effort to respond to these inquiries, especially when the requests require accumulation and collation of data from multiple regions. As part of these interface duties, headquarters routinely analyzes the impacts of the various EPA programs on industry and the environment and reports to both Congress and the President. Headquarters is also responsible for preparation of EPA's annual budget and presentation to the executive branch.

Headquarters is responsible for coordinating and responding to input from interest groups and the public during the development of all official regulations and guidance documents. An effort is made to include the interest groups in the early stages, where appropriate, especially when developing industry-specific regulations. Finally, when a lawsuit is brought against EPA, it is headquarters' responsibility to defend against the suit.

Additional major functions of headquarters include:

- Advising on international environmental policy and providing technical assistance to foreign governments

- Ensuring national program progress and consistency through mandatory reporting requirements

- Providing regulatory interpretations to all the regions in response to specific problems or questions

- Setting priorities for both the Office of Research and Development (ORD) and the regions and in some instances coordinating activities between them

- Controlling the ORD and regional budgets

- Coordinating development of training courses for regional and state staff to assist in implementing the programs

- Interacting with the National Governors Association, the Association of State and Territorial Solid Waste Management Organizations (ASTSWMO), and other state organizations to offer them direct input on major national environmental issues

The Regions—Program Implementation

The primary role of the regional offices is to implement the environmental programs, assist the states in becoming authorized for all delegable programs, report on program progress to headquarters, and assist in program development. There are currently 10 EPA regions, as shown in Fig. 5-1, with an eleventh proposed for Anchorage, Alaska. Relative to other federal agencies, EPA is decentralized and the regions have been informally delegated to many authorities. In addition to the primary program implementation role described above, the regions:

- Serve as a source for public information and education.

- Negotiate with the states the disbursement of grants to fund federally mandated programs.

- Provide information to Congress and headquarters as requested.

- Assist in technology transfer to states.

- Advocate for their states with headquarters and serve as a conduit for state's concerns.

- Assist Native American tribes and the U.S. Island Territories in program implementation and development.

- Assist with program development both with direct input to headquarters and through the Lead Region program. Each region serves as the lead in developing and coordinating regional input to continually improve the environmental programs. The Lead Region for each program rotates annually.

Office of Research and Development—Technical Support

The Office of Research and Development conducts an agencywide integrated program of research and development relevant to pollution sources and control, contaminant transport and fate processes, health and ecological effects, measurement and monitoring, and risk assessment. ORD disseminates its scientific and technical knowledge. Upon request, it provides technical reviews, expert consultations, technical assistance, and advice to EPA managers and regional staff, as well as state, local, and foreign governments.

While not officially a part of ORD, the Science Advisory Board

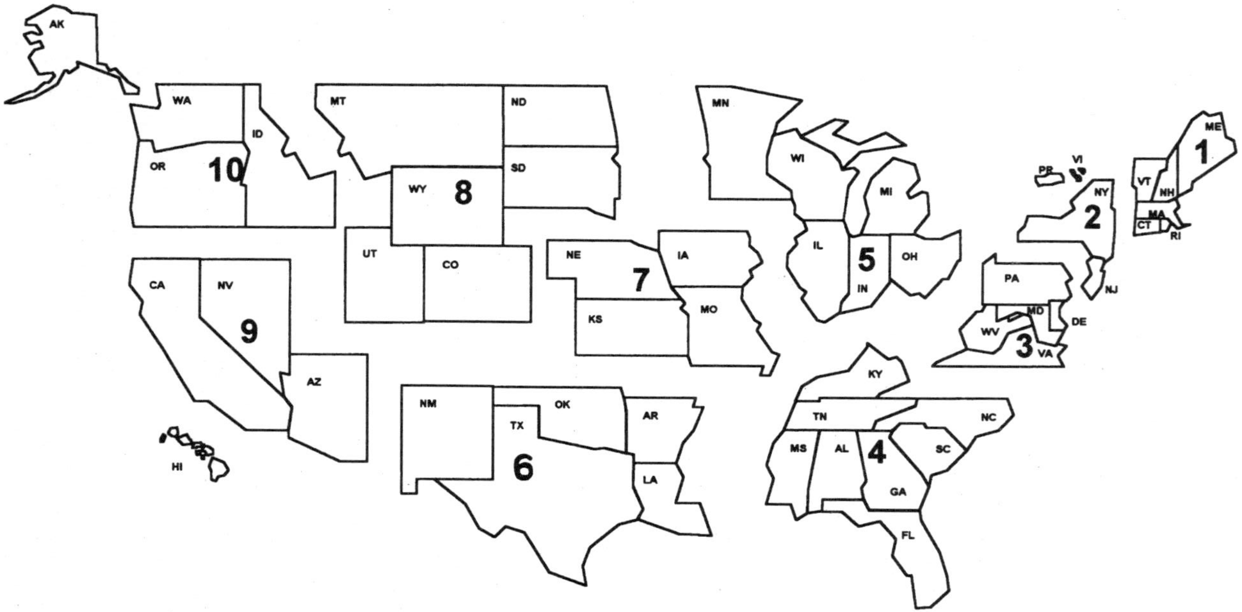

Figure 5-1. EPA regional offices. (*Source: U.S. EPA.*)

U.S. EPA Region 1
JFK Federal Building
Boston, MA 02203
(617) 565-3424

U.S. EPA Region 2
26 Federal Plaza
New York, NY 10278
(212) 264-2515

U.S. EPA Region 3
841 Chestnut Street
Philadelphia, PA 19107
(215) 597-9370

U.S. EPA Region 4
345 Courtland Street NE
Atlanta, GA 30365
(404) 347-3004

U.S. EPA Region 5
230 S. Dearborn Street
Chicago, IL 60604
(312) 353-2072

U.S. EPA Region 6
1445 Ross Avenue
Dallas, TX 76202
(214) 655-2200

U.S. EPA Region 7
726 Minnesota Avenue
Kansas City, KS 66101
(913) 551-7003

U.S. EPA Region 8
999 18th Street
Denver, CO 80202
(303) 293-1692

U.S. EPA Region 9
75 Hawthorne Street
San Francisco, CA 94105
(415) 744-1020

U.S. EPA Region 10
1200 Sixth Avenue
Seattle, WA 98101
(415) 744-1020
(800) 424-4EPA

68

(SAB) was set up to ensure that EPA's programs and actions are based on fundamentally sound science. This group consists of independent experts who provide advice to the administrator on scientific and engineering issues. The SAB was established by Congress and consists of 80 members and over 200 consultants who advise the agency on technical matters. The members come from academia, industry, and independent labs specializing in physics, chemistry, biology, mathematics, engineering, ecology, economics, medicine, and other fields. The SAB's agenda is set by specific requests from EPA and by the members themselves.

Implementing the Programs: How It Works

Headquarters is subdivided into four main environmental program divisions, each supported by ORD and the Office of Enforcement. In addition to the specific statutes for each program, each division also has responsibility for implementing parts of the Pollution Prevention Act. The divisions and specific statutes each is responsible for implementing are listed below.

Solid Waste and Emergency Response Division

- Comprehensive Environmental Response, Compensation and Liability Act of 1980 (CERCLA), as amended by the Superfund Amendments and Reauthorization Act of 1986
- Emergency Planning and Community Right-to-Know Act (EPCRA), SARA Title III
- Resource Conservation and Recovery Act (RCRA), as amended by the Hazardous and Solid Waste Amendments of 1984 (HSWA)
- Oil Pollution Act of 1990
- Clean Air Act of 1990 (CAA), as it relates to accidental chemical releases
- Hazardous Materials Transportation Uniform Safety Act (HMTUSA)

Water Division

- Safe Drinking Water Act of 1974 (SDWA), as amended in 1986 and by the Lead Contamination Control Act of 1988
- Clean Water Act of 1972 (CWA), as amended by the Water Quality Act of 1987

- Marine Protection, Research and Sanctuaries Act of 1972, as amended by the Ocean Dumping Ban Act of 1988
- Shore Protection Act
- Coastal Zone Management Act

Pesticides and Toxic Substances Division

- Toxic Substances Control Act (TSCA)
- Federal Insecticide, Fungicide, and Rodenticide Act (FIFRA) as amended in 1988
- EPCRA
- Asbestos Hazard Emergency Response Act (AHERA)
- Asbestos School Hazard Abatement Act (ASHAA)
- Asbestos Information Act (AIA)
- Federal Food, Drug, and Cosmetic Act (FFDCA)

Air and Radiation Division

- Clean Air Act Amendments of 1990

The environmental programs are generally divided into three divisions in most regions:

- Solid and hazardous waste
- Water
- Toxics and pesticides (which typically includes the air and radiation programs)

Each region has the authority to organize the programs to best suit the conditions in their states. Therefore, the rest of this chapter discusses the programs under Solid and Hazardous Waste, Water, Air, Toxic Chemicals, and Pesticides.

Solid and Hazardous Waste

The two main programs which deal with the management and cleanup of hazardous waste are the Resources Conservation and Recovery Act (RCRA) and the Comprehensive Environmental Response, Compensation, and Liability Act (CERCLA). These two statutes are discussed in the following section. The other programs dealing with waste material (i.e., TSCA) are discussed later.

The Resource Conservation and Recovery Act

The Resource Conservation and Recovery Act was enacted in 1976 to address how to safely manage the huge volumes of municipal and industrial solid waste generated nationwide. The RCRA regulations have been described as the most complex federal regulations other than the Internal Revenue Service codes. The goals set by RCRA are:

- To protect human health and the environment

- To reduce waste and conserve energy and natural resources

- To reduce or eliminate the generation of hazardous waste as expeditiously as possible

The Solid Waste Disposal Act of 1965 was the first federal attempt to improve solid-waste-disposal methods in this country. It established grant programs for the development of solid-waste management plans by states and/or interstate agencies. This was amended in 1970 by the Resource Recovery Act, and again in 1976 by RCRA. RCRA reorganized this country's solid-waste management system and added provisions pertaining to hazardous-waste management. The scope and requirements of RCRA were significantly expanded by the Hazardous and Solid Waste Amendments of 1984.

The RCRA legislation is currently divided into 10 subtitles. However, just four of these subtitles lay out an integrated framework for solid-waste management:

- Subtitle D—States develop comprehensive plans to manage primarily nonhazardous solid wastes such as household garbage.

- Subtitle C—A system for controlling hazardous waste from the time it is generated until its ultimate disposal or destruction.

- Subtitle I—Regulates certain underground storage tanks.

- Subtitle J—Regulates medical waste management.

Subtitle D—Management of Solid Waste. Subtitle D of RCRA establishes a framework for federal, state, and local government cooperation in controlling the management of nonhazardous solid waste. The framework established to manage solid waste has two main components:

1. Criteria for classification of solid-waste disposal facilities and practices (40 CFR 257 and 258)

2. Guidelines for the development and implementation of state plans
   (40 CFR 256)

The federal regulations provide minimum national standards for siting and operating municipal solid-waste landfills, and provide for technical assistance to states for planning and developing their own programs. The actual planning and direct implementation of solid-waste programs remain state and local functions. EPA retains the authority to enforce the appropriate standards in a given state.
RCRA defines the term "solid waste" as:

- Household garbage or industrial refuse such as metal scrap, wallboard, and empty containers

- Sludge from a waste-treatment plant, water-supply treatment plant, or pollution-control facility, such as scrubber sludges

- Other discarded material, including solid, semisolid, liquid, or contained gaseous material resulting from industrial, commercial, mining, agricultural, and community activities, such as boiler slag and fly ash

Waste materials not included under the RCRA definition are:

- Domestic sewage (defined as untreated sanitary wastes that pass through a sewer system)

- Industrial wastewater discharges regulated under the Clean Water Act

- Irrigation return flows

- Nuclear materials, or by-products, as defined by the Atomic Energy Act of 1954

The Subtitle D criteria are used to determine which solid-waste-disposal facilities and practices pose a reasonable probability of adverse effects on health and the environment. The criteria include general environmental performance standards addressing eight major topics:

- Floodplains
- Endangered species
- Surface water
- Groundwater
- Land application

- Disease

- Air

- Safety

These criteria serve as minimum technical standards for solid-waste-disposal facilities. Those facilities that meet the criteria are classified as sanitary landfills. Facilities failing to satisfy any of the criteria are considered open dumps. State plans developed pursuant to the Guidelines for Development and Implementation of State Solid Waste Management Plans must provide for closing or upgrading all existing open dumps within the state. Each facility must comply with the criteria; otherwise it is classified as an open dump and must upgrade operations or close.

The revised criteria for MSWLFs are presented in 40 CFR 258, along with new information requirements for owners and operators of industrial solid-waste-disposal facilities and demolition debris landfills. These are landfills that may receive household hazardous waste or hazardous waste from small-quantity generators, as defined under Subtitle C. These requirements outline conditions for MSWLF location, design and operation, groundwater monitoring, corrective action, closure and postclosure care, and financial responsibility.

The Guidelines for State Solid Waste Management Plans outline the minimum requirements for state plans and detail how these plans are approved by EPA. While all state plans must follow the same guidelines, each plan is tailored to the needs of the state. These plans are intended to promote recycling of solid wastes and require closing or upgrading of all environmentally unsound dumps. The state plans ensure that adequate facility capacity exists to dispose of solid waste in an environmentally sound manner, coordinate the activities of all state environmental programs dealing with solid waste, and ensure public participation in the waste-management process.

Subtitle D presents an integrated waste-management hierarchy to be used consistently across the country. The goal is to encourage complementary use of source reduction, recycling, combustion, and landfills to continually reduce the amount of waste generated and disposed of. Finally, all current and future landfills must be operated in a manner ensuring protection of public health and natural resources.

Subtitle C—Management of Hazardous Waste. The Subtitle C program developed under RCRA created a federal system to manage hazardous waste (including provisions for cleaning up releases to the environment) from its generation to the disposal or destruction of the waste. Hazardous waste is a subset of solid waste. A solid waste is hazardous if it is not excluded from regulation as a hazardous waste under 40 CFR 261.4(a) and (b), is not excluded as a recycled hazardous waste (under 40 CFR 261.6 or 266), and meets any of the following conditions:

- Exhibits any of the characteristics of a hazardous waste including ignitability, corrosivity, reactivity or Toxic Characteristic Leaching Procedure (TCLP) toxicity

- Has been named as a hazardous waste and listed as such in the regulations (a "listed" waste)

- Is a mixture containing a listed hazardous waste and a nonhazardous waste (the "mixture" rule)

- Is a waste derived from the treatment, storage, or disposal of a listed hazardous waste (the "derived-from" rule)

The mixture and derived-from rules have been successfully challenged in court; therefore, EPA is working to develop a new definition of hazardous waste. However, until a new definition is published in the *Federal Register,* the above general definition of hazardous waste remains in effect. The full regulatory definition of hazardous waste is given in 40 CFR Part 261.

A difficult issue is the regulation of mixtures of radioactive and hazardous waste, or mixed waste. Since mixed waste is considered hazardous under RCRA and radioactive under the Atomic Energy Act, the Nuclear Regulatory Commission (NRC) and EPA comanage these wastes.

The regulatory framework for hazardous waste recognizes that there are generators; transporters; and treatment, storage, and disposal facilities (TSDFs). Subtitle C focuses responsibility on these generators, transporters, and TSDFs for ensuring sound management of hazardous wastes. Subtitle C also includes regulations to clean up past or present releases of hazardous waste at permitted or closing facilities.

Generators are subdivided under RCRA based on the volume of waste they generate into large-quantity generators (LQGs), small-quantity generators (SQGs), and conditionally exempt SQGs. The following definitions apply:

- LQGs: Over 1000 kg per month of hazardous waste or over 1 kg of acutely hazardous waste per month

- SQGs: Greater than 100 but less than 1000 kg of hazardous waste at a site per month (and accumulates less than 6000 kg at any one time) or less than 1 kg of acutely hazardous waste per month (or accumulates less than 1 kg at any one time)

- Conditionally exempt SQGs: Less than 100 kg per month of hazardous waste and less than 1 kg per month of acutely hazardous waste

While some Subtitle C requirements are less restrictive for SQGs and conditionally exempt SQGs, these generators are still responsible for the safe management of hazardous waste. The basic requirements for safe management include obtaining EPA identification numbers; properly handling and storing wastes while on-site; proper manifesting to track the movement of hazardous waste from the point of generation to the point of ultimate treatment, storage, or disposal; and specific record keeping and reporting. Finally, the generator is responsible for determining if the hazardous waste is subject to land-disposal restrictions (LDRs) and, if so, certain notification requirements.

A transporter is any person engaged in the off-site transportation of manifested hazardous waste by any means. Transporters are regulated both by EPA and by the Department of Transportation (DOT). Once a manifested hazardous waste is taken off-site, the transporter is responsible for complying with the manifest system and for handling any waste discharges. The transporter may store the hazardous waste for up to 10 days. However, if the storage time exceeds 10 days, the transporter is considered a storage facility and must comply with the regulations for such a facility. Also, transporters who bring hazardous waste into the United States or mix hazardous wastes of different DOT shipping descriptions in the same container are classified as generators and must comply with the regulations for generators.

The most extensive and complex regulations under Subtitle C apply to TSDFs. All TSDFs that handle hazardous waste must obtain an operating permit and abide by TSD regulations. The TSD regulations establish design and operating criteria as well as performance standards that owners and operators (O/Os) must meet.

Two categories of TSDFs were originally established under the original RCRA legislation. The first category was made up of interim status facilities, which do not have permits. The second category is made of facilities that have permits. The interim status category allows O/Os of facilities in existence on Nov. 19, 1980 (or brought under Subtitle C regulation due to an amendment), who meet certain conditions, to continue operating as if they had a permit until their permit application is issued or denied. However, incinerators that did not submit a final permit application by November 1986 lost interim status in November 1989, and land disposal facilities that did not apply by November 1985 lost interim status in November 1985. All other facilities lost interim status in November 1992 unless they submitted an application by November 1988. These facilities are now either permitted, their permits are under review, they are in the process of closing, or they have postclosure permits.

The regulations for interim status facilities are in 40 CFR 265, and for permitted facilities in 40 CFR 264. The administrative and nontechnical standards for both types of facilities are nearly identical and cover:

- Who is subject to regulation
- General facility standards
- Preparedness and prevention with respect to releases and other emergencies
- Contingency plans and emergency procedures
- Manifest system, record keeping, and reporting

The technical standards ensure that O/Os operate TSDFs in a way that minimizes the potential for releases of any sort during the treatment, storage, or disposal of hazardous waste. General technical standards include groundwater monitoring requirements, closure and postclosure requirements, and financial requirements. Specific technical standards apply to the waste-management methods employed at each facility.

The Subtitle C regulations cover the requirements for corrective action of past or current releases. The term "corrective action" refers to the process of investigating and remediating releases of hazardous waste from solid-waste-management units (SWMUs) or regulated units at TSDFs. Corrective action regulations were included in HSWA to strengthen EPA's authorities for addressing releases of hazardous waste. All RCRA regulated and Superfund sites receive a ranking of their environmental priority, based on the threat each site poses to human health and the environment. Under RCRA, each site is scored under the National Corrective Action Priority System (NCAPS). This is similar to the Hazard Ranking System (HRS) in Superfund. For interim status facilities, corrective action normally occurs under an enforcement order. For permitted facilities, corrective action normally occurs under a permit schedule of compliance.

SWMUs are discernible units at which solid wastes have been placed at any time, irrespective of whether the unit was intended for the management of solid or hazardous waste. Such units include any area at a facility at which solid wastes have been routinely and systematically released. Regulated units are a subset of all SWMUs and consist of surface impoundments, waste piles, land treatment units, or landfills that received waste after July 26, 1982. Corrective action for SWMUs is included in proposed 40 CFR 264 Subpart S and for regulated units in 40 CFR 265 Subpart F.

The corrective action process is initiated by one of several events:

- Possible or actual release of hazardous waste at a high-priority site as a result of the preliminary assessment and site inspection (PA/SI)

- Detection of groundwater contamination during routine detection monitoring required at all regulated facilities

- Discovery of a previously unreported SWMU at a permitted facility

The steps involved in RCRA corrective action essentially parallel the investigation and remediation steps developed under CERCLA. The formal steps of the corrective action process include:

- RCRA Facility Assessment (RFA)
- RCRA Facility Investigation (RFI)
- Corrective Measures Study (CMS)
- Corrective Measures Implementation (CMI)

These steps are summarized in Fig. 5-2 and are discussed below.

- *RFA.* An RFA is conducted at every facility seeking an RCRA permit and at interim status facilities with evidence of a release as determined during the PA/SI. The RFA typically consists of a review of the existing information at a site and a visual site inspection. Soil or groundwater sampling may be conducted if warranted by the site conditions. The objective is to identify all SWMUs and confirmed or suspected releases needing further investigation. The RFA results in a recommendation of either (1) no further action, (2) an RFI, or (3) interim corrective measures where necessary to prevent imminent exposure to a release.

- *RFI.* If an RFI is recommended, it will be required of the O/O either under a permit schedule of compliance or under an enforcement order. The RFI is intended to confirm a suspected release and characterize all documented releases in each environmental medium. The responsible regulatory agency compares release characteriza-

Figure 5-2. RCRA corrective action process. (*Source: U.S. EPA.*)

RCRA Facility Assessment (RFA)	RCRA Facility Investigation (RFI)	Risk Assessment (RA)	Corrective Measure Study (CMS)	Corrective Measure Implementation (CMI)

INTERIM CLEANUP MEASURES OCCUR WHEN NECESSARY

RFA

EPA
Reviews files and inspects site to identify hazardous waste releases

Prepares RFA report summarizing results

Issues corrective action order or permit based on findings

PUBLIC
Reviews and comments on draft permit (public hearing)

RFI

OWNER
Develops RFI workplan

Conducts facility investigation

Develops RFI report summarizing results

Proposes and implements interim measures as appropriate

Establishes information repository

Develops summary report or fact sheet for public

EPA
Reviews RFI workplan

Provides field oversight of facility investigation

Reviews RFI report

Approves and oversees implementation of interim measures

RA

OWNER
Develops risk assessment workplan

Conducts risk assessment

EPA
Reviews risk assessment workplan

Reviews risk assessment

Establishes cleanup requirements based on RFI and RA results

CMS

OWNER
Develops CMS workplan

Identifies and evaluates cleanup alternatives

Prepares CMS report

Recommends corrective measures

EPA
Reviews CMS workplan and report

Evaluates recommended corrective measures

Solicits public comment

Selects corrective measures

Modifies permit or order to include corrective measures

PUBLIC
Reviews and comments on RFI, draft CMS report, proposed cleanup levels, and recommended corrective measures

Reviews and comments on draft permit modification

CMI

OWNER
Develops corrective measure design and construction plans

Constructs corrective measure

Conducts operations and maintenance activities

Reports monitoring results to agency

Keeps public informed of progress

EPA
Reviews and approves corrective measure designs and construction plans

Provides field oversight of construction

Reviews operations and maintenance activities

Reviews monitoring reports

PUBLIC INVOLVEMENT ACTIVITIES OCCUR THROUGHOUT THE PROCESS

YEAR 1	YEARS 2-3	YEARS 4-5		YEAR 6

Note: Steps may occur simultaneously.

tion data against established health and environmental criteria to determine whether a CMS is necessary. EPA also places a high priority on identifying and implementing during the RFI any interim measures needed to prevent the spread of a contaminant release.

- *CMS.* The data acquired during the RFI must be sufficient to determine the need for a CMS and to aid in the selection and implementation of these measures. In most cases it is possible to begin the identification of potential corrective measures as the RFI progresses and to conduct treatability studies where warranted. This step may begin midway through the RFI and continue through the CMS. This is also true for conducting a risk assessment to identify risk-based cleanup levels where appropriate. While public involvement is encouraged throughout this process, it is required prior to finalizing selection of corrective measures.

- *CMI.* The CMI includes designing, constructing, operating, and monitoring the selected corrective measures. Facilities are required to demonstrate financial assurance for corrective action prior to implementation. The RCRA corrective action program, as well as the Superfund remedial program, is heavily dependent on support from outside contractors and ORD for review of all technical documents and development of all technical solutions to hazardous-waste remediation.

There are two essential elements to RCRA's enforcement program: compliance monitoring and enforcement actions. Compliance monitoring is used to determine a handler's level of compliance with RCRA's regulatory requirements. Compliance monitoring data are collected by either inspections by state or federal officials, or reviews of reports required of each handler.

A primary goal of enforcement actions is to bring facilities into compliance and keep them there. Enforcement actions are taken when a facility is found to be out of compliance with applicable Subtitle C regulations, or when releasing nonhazardous or hazardous solid waste or hazardous constituents. At federal facilities, EPA has been limited to negotiating compliance agreements. However, authorized states may issue administrative orders or take other enforcement actions.

Delisting of hazardous wastes to remove them from the RCRA regulatory requirements can happen in a number of ways, including:

- EPA will consider petitions based on facility-specific variations in raw materials, processes, or other factors.

- Facilities that treat listed wastes can successfully demonstrate that a treated listed waste is no longer hazardous. The wastes may then be disposed of outside the regulations of Subtitle C.

- When a hazardous waste ceases to exhibit any hazardous characteristic, it is automatically dropped.

Subtitle I—Control and Prevention of Underground Storage Tank Leaks. Subtitle I was enacted to control and prevent leaks from underground storage tanks (USTs). This is the only program under RCRA that regulates both products and wastes. Subtitle I applies to underground tanks storing regulated substances, petroleum products, and Superfund-defined hazardous substances. Tanks storing RCRA hazardous wastes are regulated under Subtitle C. However, there is a large list of primarily noncommercial underground storage tanks which are not regulated under RCRA.

EPA has developed performance standards for new tanks and established requirements that a state UST program must meet in order for EPA to approve the program. Existing USTs must comply with all requirements for new tanks by Dec. 22, 1998, or they must be closed.

The Superfund Amendment and Reauthorization Act of 1986 (SARA) added authority for EPA to clean up releases from UST systems or require O/Os to do so. It also establishes a trust fund to finance some of these activities.

The approximately 1.4 million tanks regulated by Subtitle I are subject to notification requirements, performance standards, leak detection, corrective action, financial assurance, and closure. Inspection authorities are included to ensure compliance with the regulations. To use the Leaking Underground Storage Tank Trust Fund established under Subtitle I, states must enter into a cooperative agreement with EPA that details how the money will be used.

Subtitle J—Management of Medical Waste. During the summer of 1988, widespread mismanagement of medical waste led to washups of syringes and other medical material on the Atlantic seaboard. In response to this problem, Subtitle J was added to RCRA in November 1988. A 2-year demonstration project ensued to track medical waste from generation to disposal in selected states. While this project has been completed and the report submitted to Congress, the Subtitle J regulations have not yet been finalized.

CERCLA, or Superfund

The Comprehensive Environmental Response, Compensation, and Liability Act (CERCLA), or Superfund, was enacted in 1980 as a 5-year program to address the 400 worst abandoned and uncontrolled hazardous-waste sites in the nation, and gradually be phased out of existence. The Superfund legislation provided $1.6 billion to accomplish this goal; funding was made available from taxes on crude oil and commercial chemicals. However, it quickly became clear that the total number and distribution of hazardous-waste sites far exceeded any of the original estimates.

SARA—Expanding the Scope of Superfund. The Superfund Amendments and Reauthorization Act (SARA) was passed in 1986 to expand the scope of the Superfund program. Among the major changes and additions SARA made to the Superfund program are the following:

- Increased the trust fund to $8.5 billion and provided an additional $500 million for cleanup of leaks from underground storage tanks. The additional monies come from excise taxes on petroleum and feedstock chemicals, a tax on certain imported chemical derivatives, an environmental tax on corporations, appropriations made by Congress from general tax revenues, and money recovered or collected from responsible parties.

- The focus was placed on permanent cleanups at Superfund sites.

- Superfund actions are required to consider the standards and requirements found in other federal and state environmental laws and regulations (also known as conforming to applicable or relevant and appropriate requirements, or ARARs).

- Involve the public in decision processes at sites, and encourage states and tribes to actively participate with EPA.

- EPA's research, development, and training responsibilities were expanded and enforcement authority was strengthened to get responsible parties to clean up hazardous-waste problems they have created.

Title III—Emergency Planning and Community Right-to-Know. Along with SARA, Congress passed the Emergency Planning and Community Right-to-Know Act, known as Title III. Title III mandates that each community be prepared to respond to emergencies resulting from release or explosion of chemicals and establishes reporting requirements for industrial and commercial facilities on the quantities of substances present in their facilities and released to the environment on a routine basis. These reports then become a part of the Toxic Release Inventory (TRI).

Title III authorizes the federal government to respond directly to releases, or threatened releases, of hazardous substances that may endanger public health, welfare, or the environment. Legal actions can be taken to force those responsible to clean up those sites or reimburse the Superfund for the costs of cleanup. If those responsible for site contamination cannot be found or are unwilling or unable to clean up a site, the EPA can use money from the Superfund to complete the cleanup.

NCP—National Contingency Plan. The Superfund response effort is guided by the National Oil and Hazardous Substances Pollution Contingency Plan, commonly known as the National Contingency Plan (NCP). The plan outlines the steps that EPA, the U.S. Coast Guard, and other federal agencies must follow in responding to situations in which hazardous substances or oil are released into the environment. The NCP predated Superfund and has been revised three times: first to incorporate the 1980 Superfund program, then in 1985 to streamline the Superfund process, and again in 1990 to address the changes resulting from the passage of SARA.

The Superfund Remedial Process—How It Works. The Superfund remedial process is summarized in Fig. 5-3. This remedial process begins with site discovery. After discovering a site, EPA or the state conducts a Preliminary Assessment to determine whether there is an imminent threat which would require immediate attention or whether additional investigation is needed. Discovery of an imminent threat usually results in a short-term action by EPA to stabilize or clean up the immediate hazard.

If contamination remains at the site, or if a site investigation is required, a decision is made to rank the relative national priority of that particular site. The Hazard Ranking System (HRS) was developed to score each site. If the HRS score is high enough, the site is added to the National Priorities List (NPL), which is the official list of hazardous-waste sites warranting attention under Superfund. In addition, each state may propose to list a top-priority site.

For sites included on the NPL, the Remedial Investigation/Feasibility Study (RI/FS) process is initiated. The RI is designed

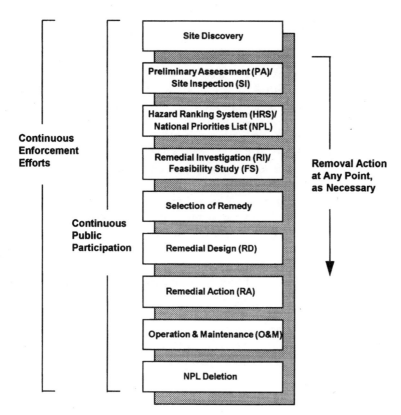

Figure 5-3. Superfund remedial action process. (*Source: U.S. EPA.*)

to define the nature and extent of the problem and to provide information needed to develop and evaluate cleanup alternatives. The possible alternatives for cleaning up a site are evaluated during the FS. Each alternative is compared with nine criteria to determine the suitability of each method. After the public has had a chance to comment on the RI/FS, the most effective remedy is selected and published in the Record of Decision (ROD). This process was used as a model for the RCRA RFI/CMS process.

To implement the ROD, the Remedial Design (RD) is conducted to prepare the engineering plans and specifications. This is followed by the Remedial Action (RA), which consists of the construction phase to implement the RD. This is accompanied with an Operation and Maintenance (O&M) plan to ensure that the cleanup methods are working properly and that the site remedy continues to be effective long into the future. This process was used as the model for the RCRA CMI process.

Superfund's Enforcement Program—Requiring Responsible Parties to Pay. One of Superfund's major goals is to have responsible parties pay for and conduct cleanups at NPL sites. The foundation of the enforcement program is CERCLA's strict, joint, and several liability standard. Under this standard, each potentially responsible party (PRP) may be fully liable for all site cleanup costs, regardless of waste share or fault. PRPs include owners, operators, generators, and transporters of hazardous waste at a site.

SARA provided enforcement tools to facilitate settlement negotiations, and enhanced the enforcement measures available to EPA if PRPs do not settle. At the beginning of the NPL listing process, EPA conducts an investigation to determine and locate those who may be liable for contamination at the site. Once they are identified, the PRPs are each sent a general notice letter notifying them of their potential liability. Information is exchanged between EPA and the PRPs concerning site conditions, their connections to the site, and other PRPs.

Based on the information gathered during the search and information exchange process, EPA may issue special notice letters to PRPs, which begins a formal negotiation period and establishes a moratorium on certain response and enforcement activities. If within 60 days PRPs make a "good-faith offer" to conduct the response action, the moratorium may be extended to provide additional time for reaching a final settlement.

EPA and the PRPs may reach settlement agreements to conduct an RI/FS or an RD/RA. Settlement agreements are usually formalized in an administrative order on consent (AOC). If PRPs do not settle, EPA can either issue orders to force liable, financially viable PRPs to conduct the response action, or spend Trust Fund money and recover the costs from the PRPs later. For RD/RAs, EPA routinely issues unilateral administrative orders (UAOs) to force nonsettling PRPs to implement the remedy themselves. Noncompliance with a UAO can result in civil penalties of $25,000 per day, and if Trust Fund money is spent, EPA may seek triple the cost of the response action in cost-recovery litigation.

Water Divisions

The Water Management Divisions are responsible for protecting the quality of both surface and groundwater from pollution. The principal law which gives EPA, the states, and Native American tribal governments the authority to deal with water pollution is the Clean Water Act of 1972 (CWA). The CWA's goal is to "restore and maintain the chemical, physical, and biological integrity of the nation's waters." To carry out the provisions of the CWA, EPA has developed regulations and programs to reduce pollutants entering all surface waters, including lakes, rivers, estuaries, oceans, and wetlands. In 1987, Congress passed the Water Quality Act of 1987 that reauthorized and strengthened the CWA. The amendments ensured continued support for municipal sewage-treatment plants, initiated a new state-federal program to control nonpoint source pollution, and accelerated the imposition of tighter controls on toxic pollution.

The Safe Drinking Water Act (SDWA) of 1974 created major legislative authority for protecting drinking-water resources. This act, amended in 1986, requires the establishment of additional drinking-water standards as well as protection of underground sources of drinking water from underground disposal of fluids. The 1986 amendments also established two new major groundwater protection programs: (1) the wellhead protection program to protect areas around public drinking-water wells and (2) the sole-source aquifer demonstration program to protect unique underground water supplies.

To protect the marine environment from the harmful effects of ocean dumping, Congress enacted the Marine Protection, Research, and Sanctuaries Act (MPRSA) in 1972. This act established a permit program to ensure that dumping of wastes in the ocean does not cause degradation of the marine environment.

Surface Water

The four major surface-water pollutant sources are municipal, industrial, nonpoint, and dredge and fill activities. Each source is discussed below.

Municipal Pollutant Sources. Municipal sources primarily consist of household and industrial facility wastewater, and storm sewer discharges. Pollution is controlled by proper construction of household septic systems, municipal sewage systems, and industrial pretreatment prior to discharge to the sanitary sewer. Until passage of the 1987 amendments, the Clean Water Act mandated grants to share the cost of sewage-treatment plant construction with states and local governments. Prior to CERCLA, this program constituted a major part of EPA's budget and activities. The 1987 amendments provided for phasing out this program and replacing it with state revolving funds, with initial seed money provided to the states by EPA.

The CWA also requires EPA and the states to use a water-classification and permitting system to control water pollution from every facility that discharges waste into water. When acting as the permitting authority, the states must designate each of their surface-water resources as suitable for specific uses. All states must then adopt water-quality standards for each water body that protect its designated use. The CWA created the National Pollutant Discharge Elimination System (NPDES) permits which are issued by the states in most cases. NPDES permits establish the amount of each pollutant that the plant may discharge based on national maximum contaminant levels or the quality of the water as determined by state water-quality standards.

Industrial Pollutant Sources. Industrial sources of surface-water pollution include discharges to sewers under permit from the local sewer district, to surface waters under a NPDES permit, into injection wells (regulated by the SDWA), or unauthorized releases from leaks or spills. In many cases, facilities must pretreat their wastewater prior to discharge according to limits specified in their permits. Spills or leaks, whether past or present, are addressed under the RCRA, CERCLA, or TSCA waste programs.

Nonpoint Pollutant Sources. Nonpoint sources constitute the largest class of water pollutants. Nonpoint sources are multiple, diffuse sources of pollution such as runoff from roads and cultivated fields as opposed to point sources such as underground storage tanks or a discharge pipe from a factory. The major nonpoint source pollutant is sediment, but oil and gasoline, agricultural chemicals, nutrients, heavy metals, bacteria, and viruses are also major nonpoint pollutants.

Dredge and Fill Activities. Dredge and fill activities are governed by Section 404 of the CWA and the Marine Protection, Research, and Sanctuaries Act (Title I). The problem with dredging waterways comes both from the churning of bottom sediments and the pollutants which may be buried there (PCBs and heavy metals), and the filling of sensitive ecosystems. The regulatory programs are overseen by the Army Corps of Engineers and EPA.

The Watershed Initiative—Encouraging States to Adopt an Integrated Approach to Surface-Water Protection. To coordinate EPA's surface-water protection efforts, the Watershed Initiative has been adopted to encourage states to focus actual protection and restoration activities in specific watersheds. Programs in these targeted areas will emphasize integrating traditional control technologies such as water-quality standards, permits, and enforcement actions with a broader use of nonpoint source control and prevention programs, the technology information network, education, and public outreach.

Drinking Water

EPA's drinking water focuses on two areas: (1) protecting groundwater and (2) assuring that water being consumed meets health-based standards. EPA has adopted a comprehensive approach for protecting groundwater involving development of Comprehensive State Ground Water Protection Plans, Wellhead Protection Programs, and Sole Source Aquifer Demonstration Program, and Underground Injection Control. Under the SDWA, EPA has established Maximum Contaminant Levels (MCLs) for a continuously increasing number of important pollutants in drinking water.

Protecting Groundwater Resources

Comprehensive State Groundwater Protection. EPA provides guidance to each state to develop a Comprehensive State Ground Water Protection Program (CSGWPP), which is intended as a groundwater basin approach to comprehensively protecting groundwater resources. This represents a resource-based approach which reaches beyond controlling a few federally regulated sources to the safeguarding of all groundwater resources from the full range of potential threats. The eventual goal of the CSGWPPs is to provide a state-level framework that integrates the various federal, state, and local government groundwater activities. Through these plans, states can address nontraditional sources of groundwater contamination, many of which are so localized that they would be overlooked in a larger-scale watershed approach.

A fully integrated CSGWPP means that the groundwater protection efforts will be coordinated and focused across all federal, state, and local programs. It is based on a state's understanding and decisions regarding the relative use, value, and vulnerability of its groundwater resources, including the relative threat of all actual or potential contamination sources. The first step is for each state to develop a "core" CSGWPP, which includes completion of the following steps:

1. Establishing a groundwater protection goal to guide all relevant programs in the state

2. Establishing priorities to direct all relevant programs and activities in the state toward the most efficient and effective means of achieving the state's protection goal

3. Defining authorities, roles, responsibilities, resources, and coordinating mechanisms across relevant federal, state, tribal, and local programs for addressing identified groundwater protection priorities

4. Implementing all necessary efforts to accomplish the state's groundwater protection goal consistent with the state's priorities and schedules

5. Coordinating information collection and management to measure progress, reevaluate priorities, and support all groundwater-related programs

6. Improving public education and participation in all aspects of groundwater protection to achieve support of the state's protection goal, priorities, and programs

Wellhead Protection. The Wellhead Protection Program encourages states and municipalities to develop local wellhead protection efforts, including using zoning changes, public education, and other management techniques to protect groundwater.

Underground Injection Control. The underground injection control (UIC) program has broad authority to regulate and enforce against threats to underground sources of drinking water. Subsurface emplacement of fluids is a practice of many industries including petroleum, chemical, food manufacturing, product manufacturing, solution mining, and many small specialty plants and retail establishments. Recoginition of the extreme vulnerability and adverse impact on groundwater resources posed by underground injection prompted passage of the SDWA.

UIC program requirements are designed to prevent contamination of underground sources of drinking water (USDWs) as a result of injection-well operations. Injection-well constuction standards and operational constraints applicable to deep, high-technology wells help to ensure that injected fluids remain isolated from USDWs. This federal program also establishes minimum requirements for effective state UIC programs. The SDWA provides for delegation of the UIC program to the states and for funding to states that have been delegated the program.

Sole Source Aquifer Demonstration. The SDWA authorizes the EPA administrator to designate an aquifer as a sole source if the aquifer provides 50% or more of the drinking water for an area and if the contamination of that aquifer would result in a significant public health hazard to the people relying on that aquifer as their only source of drinking water. That authority has since been delegated to regional administrators. Projects receiving federal financial assistance undergo a review by EPA to ensure that these projects would have no adverse effects on the water quality in the aquifer.

Petitions for sole source aquifer (SSA) designations are reviewed and approved by each regional administrator, after input by the WMD, UIC, PWSS, and other interested regional programs. Once granted, projects within the SSA areas are reviewed to ensure the aquifer is not adversely impacted. Interagency MOUs are also developed with other federal agencies to ensure that SSA reviews are conducted on proposed projects.

Oceans, Estuaries, and Wetlands

Regulation of oceans and coastal programs is covered under the CWA, which regulates coastal and ocean discharges, and the MPRSA, which regulates ocean dumping and monitoring. EPA's Office of Marine and Estuarine Protection was established in 1984 to administer EPA's ocean and coastal programs. Strategic initiatives enacted in response to major specific pollution problems include the Great Lakes Program and the Chesapeake Bay Program. The National Estuary Program and the Near Coastal Water Initiative are examples of geographically targeted approaches to the protection and restoration of an area. Significant improvements in eliminating discharges of conventional contaminants have been made in these areas. However, the remaining problems require a multimedia and multiprogram approach that stresses geographically focused efforts.

Section 404—Regulating Discharge into U.S. Waters. Wetlands are sensitive ecosystems protected under Section 404 of the CWA and, in part, by other federal and state regulatory authorities. Section 404 regulates the discharge of dredged or fill material into waters of the United States. Since most wetlands are waters of the United States, wetlands automatically are accorded the protection of all sections of the CWA.

This has resulted in a strategy for protecting wetlands which integrates various Office of Water programs.

Section 404 is jointly administered by EPA and the U.S. Corps of Engineers. EPA and the Corps jointly developed the environmental standards that the Corps uses to evaluate permit applications for the discharge of dredged or fill materials. The Corps has the daily administrative responsibilities for the program. EPA has responsibility for: (1) reviewing discharge permit applications for adverse environmental impacts resulting from the discharge, (2) defining areas that constitute wetlands, (3) approving state assumptions of the 404 program, and (4) enforcing against unpermitted discharges.

Other state and federal agencies with resource management responsibilities have authority over certain wetland and coastal protection issues. These agencies, collectively known as the Natural Resources Trustees (NRTs), include such federal agencies as the U.S. Fish & Wildlife Service, Bureau of Land Management, the Department of Interior, and the National Oceanographic and Atmospheric Agency (NOAA).

Air Pollution Control

The first federal legislation to control air pollution was enacted in 1955, and strengthened in 1963, 1965, and 1967. However, it was the Clean Air Act (CAA) of 1970 which created the framework for all subsequent air-related regulatory efforts. The CAA has been reviewed and amended in 1974, 1977, and 1990, but the basic principles of the 1970 CAA have remained intact.

The Clean Air Act of 1970 and Its Amendments

The fundamental objective of the CAA is the protection of the public health and welfare from harmful effects of air pollution. While the lead role for preventing and controlling air pollution was given to the states, EPA is required to set National Air Ambient Quality Standards (NAAQS), toxic emission standards, and visibility standards. In 1974, the Energy Supply and Environmental Coordination Act modified some air quality requirements following the oil shortages of the early 1970s. In 1977, additional revisions were enacted, including nonattainment requirements applicable to new sources. The Clean Air Act

Amendments of 1990 represents the most sweeping changes since the passage of the Act in 1970.

NAAQS and NESHAPS—Setting Air Quality Standards. EPA has set both primary and secondary NAAQS for distinctly different purposes. Primary NAAQS define the air quality standards required to prevent any adverse impact on human health. Secondary NAAQS set standards to protect visibility, vegetation, property, or other environmental components. NAAQS have been set for only six pollutants to date: ozone, particulate matter, carbon monoxide, sulfur dioxide, lead, and nitrogen dioxide.

EPA was also required to set toxic emission standards. The National Emissions Standards for Hazardous Pollutants (NESHAPS) set limits on hazardous pollutants that contribute to an increase in mortality or serious illness. However, there was disagreement about regulations of cancer-causing pollutants, and only eight NESHAPS were set prior to the 1990 amendments.

State Implementation Plans—Complying with CAA Requirements. The CAA was designed to be implemented by states through State Implementation Plans (SIPs), which document how a state will comply with the CAA requirements. The original SIPs from 1972 were designed to attain CAA air quality standards by 1977, but the standards were not achieved in many areas. The 1977 amendments required a second round of SIPs to attain air standards by 1982, with certain exceptions delayed until 1987. Again, there were numerous nonattainment areas, particularly with respect to ozone, carbon monoxide, sulfur dioxide, and particulate matter in major urban areas. The regulations also provide for the development of Federal Implementaiton Plans (FIPs) if states do not meet the deadlines for SIP approval.

The 1977 amendments set different guidelines for mobile sources versus stationary sources. The mobile source guidelines focused on reducing emissions from cars and other vehicles. Stationary sources are subdivided into new versus existing sources. For new stationary sources, the regulations sought to establish the "best" technology-based standards. For existing stationary sources, the regulations required facilities to install reasonably available control technology (RACT).

The 1977 amendments also provided new features for industrial projects with new plants or construction leading to increased emissions. For projects in attainment areas, the regulations required that the projects "prevent significant deterioration" (PSD). In nonattainment areas, the regulations required installation of the most stringent control technology and to offset any new emissions with decreases from other emission sources.

The 1990 Clear Air Act Amendments

The 1990 amendments require newly revised SIPs for all nonattainment areas. These SIPs must provide for additional control requirements to ensure that the standards will be achieved by specified deadlines. Deadlines are to be set based on a sliding scale that is linked to the severity of the nonattainment. Application of the RACT guidelines was also greatly increased.

For mobile sources, the 1990 amendments increase auto emission standards. This includes the requirement for petroleum refiners to produce alternative cleaner fuels and for the auto industry to produce fleet vehicles capable of using the alternative fuels. These cleaner fuels include methanol, ethanol, mixtures of these fuels with gasoline, reformulated gasoline, natural gas, liquefied petroleum gas, and electricity. While the new emission standards apply nationally, the clean fuel requirements apply specifically to the nine most polluted urban areas.

Difficulty in developing NAAQS and NESHAP standards for toxic air pollutants led Congress to require that new control standards be set for a list of 189 hazardous air pollutants and promulgation of new control technologies for most sources of these emissions. The rules require companies to install the Maximum Achievable Control Technology (MACT) for these pollutants. After the MACT standards have been met, certain facilities may be subject to further reductions in emissions based on the residual risk to exposed individuals. The amendments also provide for the phase-out of the productions and use of chlorofluorocarbons and several other chemicals believed to cause destruction of the stratospheric ozone layer.

To address the problem of acid rain, the amendments require power plants to reduce emissions of sulfur dioxide and nitrogen oxides. The new standards are dual-phased in by 1995 and 2000. A market-based system has been developed to provide power plants with "emissions allowances" that allow them either to reduce their emissions or acquire allowances from other facilities to achieve compliance.

A new permit program was also established to define the requirements applicable to each air-pollution source. Whereas the SIPs reflect the air control need for each "air basin" and impose specific requirements on sources in the region, the permits will detail the specific requirements applicable to individual sources. This will allow for better compliance monitoring and enforcement of the regulations.

Indoor Air Problems

Indoor air pollution has rapidly become a major health issue in the United States since most people spend most of their time indoors. EPA regulates the indoor air-pollution problem under a variety of environmental laws, including the Toxic Substances Control Act (TSCA), the Federal Insecticide, Fungicide, and Rodenticide Act (FIFRA), RCRA, the Asbestos in Schools Hazard Abatement Act of 1986, the Uranium Mill Tailings Radiation Control Act, and SARA. These authorities require regulations to control such indoor pollutants as radon, environmental tobacco smoke, asbestos, volatile organic compounds, biological pollutants, and pesticides.

Toxic Chemicals

The Toxic Substances Control Act (TSCA) of 1976 authorizes EPA to control the risks that may be posed by the thousands of commercial chemical substances and mixtures that are not regulated as either drugs, food additives, cosmetics, or pesticides. Under TSCA, EPA can, among other things, regulate the manufacture and use of a chemical substance and require testing for cancer and other effects.

One of the first tasks EPA completed under TSCA was compiling an inventory of all chemicals commercially produced or processed in the United States between Jan. 1, 1975, and July 1979. In 1986, manufacturers and importers were required to report current data on a subset of the substances on the inventory and to update the information every 4 years. EPA can also collect information on use and exposure for selected chemicals which may pose unreasonable risks.

Since enactment of TSCA, EPA has focused on problems associated with a shorter list of specific chemicals including polychlorinated biphenyls (PCBs), asbestos, dioxin, and chlorofluorocarbons (CFCs). These are discussed briefly below.

PCBs

Congress specifically directed EPA to ban the manufacture, processing, distribution, and use of PCBs except in totally enclosed electrical equipment. PCBs were originally used widely because of their desirable physical properties, but they have been found to bioaccumulate with serious health and environmental effects. EPA's regulations strictly limit the use of PCB-containing electrical transformers and establish requirements for disposal and cleanup of PCBs and PCB-contaminated media.

Asbestos

Two statutes have been passed by Congress to address asbestos-related problems in schools. The Asbestos School Hazard Abatement Act of 1984 provided interest-free loans or grants to schools for asbestos control projects. Under the Asbestos Hazard Emergency Response Act (AHERA) of 1986, which amends TSCA, schools are required to identify and respond to their asbestos problems. EPA has also studied asbestos in public and commercial buildings and provided recommendations to Congress on how to address the problem.

Dioxin

Dioxin refers to a family of chemicals with similar structure, the most common of which is 2,3,7,8-tetrachlorodibenzo-p-dioxin, or TCDD. Dioxin is an inadvertent contaminant of the chlorinated herbicides 2,4,5-T and silvex, which were used until recently in agriculture, forest management, and lawn care. It is also a contaminant of certain wood preservatives, the defoliant Agent Orange, and is formed along with furans during the combustion of PCBs. The use of dioxin-containing products has been banned in the United States, and cleanup and disposal of dioxins has been strictly regulated.

CFCs

To control the use of CFCs, EPA banned their use as a propellant in aerosol cans and other nonessential uses in 1978. EPA also joined with 30 other nations in agreeing to the Montreal Protocol in 1987, which places restrictions on the production and use of CFCs by developed nations.

Pesticides

The Federal Insecticide, Fungicide, and Rodenticide Act (FIFRA) was first enacted in 1947 to be administered by the U.S. Department of

Agriculture and was intended to protect consumers against fraudulent pesticide products. The responsibility for enforcement of FIFRA was assumed by EPA in 1970. In 1972, the act was amended to shift the emphasis to health and environmental protection. Regulation of pesticides residues in food is shared between EPA and the U.S. Food and Drug Administration (FDA), which set "tolerance levels" in food under the authority of the Federal Food, Drug, and Cosmetic Act.

FIFRA requires all pesticides used in the United States to be registered with EPA. A pesticide manufacturer must submit all test data and information related to health and environmental risks. The options open to EPA after reviewing the data are to refuse registration of that pesticide, to restrict its use to certain applications, or to require that only certified applicators apply the pesticide. Those pesticides existing in 1972 were required to be reregistered with submittal of the most current risk data. EPA also has an aggressive enforcement policy which includes issuing civil or criminal penalties for violations of FIFRA.

The states and Native American tribes have primary responsibility for enforcing laws and regulations regarding pesticide use through cooperative agreements with EPA. Each state is encouraged to develop a Pesticides State Management Plan (SMP). If specific pesticides are shown to have leaching potential, those pesticides cannot be registered in selected vulnerable states (or counties) unless the state develops and EPA approves a SMP tailored to the localized groundwater vulnerability. Each generic SMP includes (1) a listing of the state authorities for regulating pesticides, (2) provisions for monitoring groundwater for pesticide contamination, (3) prevention plans, (4) response plans in the event of groundwater contamination, (5) enforcement mechanisms, (6) public participation requirements, and (7) administrative requirements. The states are also encouraged to have a management plan for each pesticide used within the state.

Summary—Working Toward a Safe and Healthy Environment

Future EPA activities will complement its traditional implementation approaches by encouraging program integration to efficiently solve environmental problems, and prevent further problems through pollution prevention, outreach to industry, and education of the public. Pollution prevention started with the idea that traditional methods are not sufficient to attain greater levels of environmental cleanup. The gains that can be made by "end-of-the-pipe" controls have been or soon will be attained. More initiatives like the 33/50 program, the Green Lights program, and other EPA-industry partnerships will be developed to reach goals which cannot be attained by traditional methods. However, EPA's primary responsibility is to enforce the regulations to maintain public confidence in the agency.

EPA is initiating a strategic approach for priority setting and program implementation based on environmental needs, public concerns, and comparative risk concepts. EPA will continue to support state program development, attempt to use the appropriate level of government to solve problems, and conduct outreach activities to compel communities to help solve current problems and prevent new problems from developing. As EPA, state and local agencies, the public, industry, and environmental groups come to terms on reasonable environmental goals and work cooperatively to reach these goals, we will find that it is possible to have both a healthy economy and a safe environment in which to live and work.

References

EPA, Environmental Progress and Challenges: EPA's Update, EPA-230-07-88-033, August 1988.

EPA, RCRA Orientation Manual—1990 Edition, EPA/530-SW-90-036, 1990.

EPA, The Superfund Program: Ten Years of Progress, EPA/540/8-91/003, June 1991.

EPA, Preserving Our Future Today, Your Guide to the United States Environmental Protection Agency, 21K-1012, October 1991.

EPA, "The New Clean Air Act: What It Means to You," *EPA Journal*, vol. 17, no. 1, 21K-1004, January 1991.

6

Understanding Federal, State, and Local Environmental Regulation

Norman L. Weiss

Compliance Manager
EMCON Associates

For almost any business, complying with regulations intended to protect our environment, public health, and quality of life is a complex and costly endeavor. The costs take many forms; they derive from what we are required to do, what we choose to do, and in many instances, what we choose not to do. Understanding these costs—and justifying them to upper management—can be the most difficult task of all, since the structure and logic of today's regulatory environment are not always apparent to those who must live by its dictates.

The Regulatory Process

Government bureaucracy and its by-product, regulation, have sometimes been thought of as the major threats to the functional sanity, economic well-being, and future development of mankind. Many believe that government bureaucracy and regulation have been specifically designed to create a nightmare for business and industry. Obviously, only a sinister plot in the dark halls of government could explain the endless reams of paperwork and thousands of pages of environmental regulations that control our every action.

However, for better or worse, there is no grand scheme or ethic that guides the development of environmental laws and rules in the United States. It is essentially a process of consensus building and compromise, and the results are determined more by local and immediate concerns than by overarching principle.

The give and take is usually most pronounced in Congress or the state legislature, where environmental laws are passed. In these forums, elected officials have an opportunity to participate in drafting a legislative bill through various committees and subcommittees. If the bill is fortunate enough to survive this process it is sent to the floor, where all the members have the opportunity to vote on it. If the bill is passed, it is then sent to the president or governor for signature, at which point it may or may not be signed into law in accordance with our system of checks and balances.

The adoption of a rule, however, follows a quite different process. A rule can be based upon the discretion of a single person, such as an agency director, or the wishes of several people, such as a board or commission. Negotiation can also play a major role. While special-interest groups participate in both the regulatory development and legislative process, the number of decision makers actually involved in the process of rule making is substantially fewer.

Something that is usually not considered in the rule-making process is whether the rule is written in a clear and understandable manner. If the rules cannot be understood by the average person, how can the bureaucrats be expected to enforce them? More importantly, how can companies and individuals be expected to comply? Some say another plot is at work here, this one hatched by environmental lawyers and consultants to promote their livelihood—except that the dimensions of the problem suggest a level of organization and cooperation far beyond what they have shown themselves capable of to date.

The complicated nature of environmental systems and processes and the diversity of environmental conditions have contributed to the complexity of environmental regulations. Since our rules are usually command-and-control–oriented, they must provide precise direction on a multitude of specific conditions and actions. Where precision has been achieved, it is usually in the service of enforcement rather than general understandability. Court interpretations of the law are another factor in the increasing complexity of our environmental regulations.

Most environmental rules are adopted through a formal process prescribed by law. Generally, an agency or board operates by statute. It should be important to note that there is a fundamental difference between rules and statutes. Statutes usually define the general or specific authorities that establish a foundation for public policy making. By contrast, rules are adopted to implement the law or policy, usually at the administrative level of government. Most administrative rules have the force and effect of law; subsequently, the violation of a rule may include administrative, civil, or criminal sanctions. This can vary considerably from state to state and between jurisdictions.

The command-and-control nature of environmental protection means that most regulations state that you "shall do this" or you "shall do that." The sanctions for noncompliance are usually economic penalties; however, many environmental regulatory programs now have criminal sanctions associated with "intentional" or "knowing" acts of noncompliance.

While we can spend much time and effort discussing the arguments for or against specific environmental regulations, it is important to acknowledge that, for most citizens of our country, and therefore also for their elected representatives, environmental protection has become a priority. The underlying concept in environmental regulation is that there is a direct correlation between environmental protection and the protection of public health. There is also a secondary correlation between environmental protection and "quality of life," the definition of which varies widely.

Economic development and environmental protection do not need to be considered conflicting goals. When our programs are well thought out and our community, state, and national environmental actions are guided by the same objectives, they can in fact be mutually supportive. Today, legislators show an increasing awareness of the burdens that regulation places on business, and an increasing tendency to scrutinize environmental action from a cost-benefit perspective. By communicating our needs to elected officials and the public, we can all work to achieve the balance that is needed.

Environmental Roles and Responsibilities

The roles and responsibilities of the government in environmental protection vary based upon the level of government and the services provided. Each level of government has its unique perspective and capability to provide environmental protection programs and services. It is important to recognize that some environmental protection programs can be implemented more effectively at the national level, such as those which have national and interstate implications. Likewise, programs that have statewide implications are best handled within a state, provided there is adequate authority, funding, and commitment to implement the program.

Ideally, the lower the level of government, the more effective and responsive are the services provided to the public. For this reason, programs that have local environmental implications are best handled at the city or county level. In some cases, however, local agencies may not be able or desire to implement environmental programs owing to the lack of authority or funding, or a perception that other jurisdictions should assume responsibility.

Environmental protection programs developed early roots within public health programs. Historically, many of the environmentally related functions of government—such as wastewater treatment, emergency response, and solid-waste disposal—have been provided by local agencies. It is important to realize that local environmental problems and needs are not necessarily the same as regional, state, or national needs. It is equally true that national priorities are not necessarily the same as state and local priorities. This situation can create conflicts and fragmentation in government agencies and environmental programs. The differences in perception of priority or ability to respond negatively impact the effectiveness of the agency in serving the public.

Role of Congress and the U.S. Environmental Protection Agency

Over the last 25 years in the United States, countless environmental laws have been enacted that affect our daily lives. The earliest environmental mandates fundamentally dealt with water quality, air quality, drinking water, and the environmental impacts associated with federal government actions. The later mandates have dealt with hazardous waste, solid waste, control of toxic substances, and cleanup of the environment.

Many of the early federal laws were very broad-based, establishing national goals and policies, yet leaving much discretion to the U.S.

Environmental Protection Agency (EPA) with regard to implementation of environmental programs. Some argue that the large degree of discretion given to the EPA left the door open for vast differences in interpretation of the law. The result has been numerous lawsuits in which the courts have been required to rule on widely divergent interpretations of the laws.

In some of the more recent national laws, such as the Resource Conservation and Recovery Act (RCRA) Amendments of 1984, and others, Congress appears to have written rules into the statutes. An example of these are the "hammer" provisions in RCRA, which relate to land disposal restrictions and other requirements. If EPA fails to adopt certain rules or take certain actions based upon a specific deadline as defined in the law, the requirements automatically become effective.

The provisions of the act concerning land disposal required the EPA to evaluate all hazardous waste to determine which wastes should be banned or restricted. The RCRA Amendments of 1984 required EPA to establish certain methods or levels of treatment for certain categories of waste. The purpose of establishing treatment levels or methods of treatment was to reduce the toxicity of the waste and thus minimize potential impacts to public health or the environment. The amendments established statutory deadlines. Dioxins and solvent wastes were one of the first priorities for establishing land ban restrictions. Wastes that were identified as restricted were required to meet certain treatment standards; otherwise they could not be disposed of on the land. If EPA failed to set the required standards by certain statutory deadlines, the waste was automatically banned from being disposed of on land.

Some would argue that this type of approach to regulation does not offer sufficient flexibility to the EPA, which should have the expertise and discretion to implement the federal law. Perhaps owing to legal challenges to EPA's interpretations or past inaction by environmental administrators, Congress has felt it has needed to intervene.

Many of the federal environmental mandates, such as the Clean Air Act, the Clean Water Act, the Safe Drinking Water Act, and RCRA, have provisions and incentives for the adoption of state programs. This is inherently a recognition by Congress that states are in a better position to adopt a particular program and provide for effective service, provided they have the expertise, authority, funding, and commitment. Typically, the state may be provided with federal funding as seed money to develop state programs. The state programs must meet specific national criteria before they can be authorized or delegated by the EPA.

The federal criteria may include minimum standards for enforcement authority, penalties, inspections, permitting, state rules, and funding. Federal funding usually diminishes once the state assumes delegation or primacy. In most cases, state laws or rules can be no less stringent than the federal requirements; however, they may be more stringent if specifically authorized.

State Environmental Protection Programs

Many state environmental protection programs are influenced by federal laws and requirements. Many states have taken the opportunity to participate under the "umbrella" or auspices of the federal program. Other states have elected to leave certain environmental programs to the federal government. This may be due to the lack of financial resources, the absence of legislative authority, or the desire to avoid the inevitable conflicts with the EPA over what constitutes an adequate state program.

EPA clearly does not have the resources, personnel, or expertise to administer environmental protection programs in all the states. Consequently, one may ask what incentive is there for a state to assume primacy or delegation of a federally mandated program?

The answer may be found in the structure and workings of the EPA. The EPA does not have an office in most states. Operationally, most EPA programs are administered through 10 EPA regional offices. In most areas of the country, the nearest EPA office may be hundreds of miles away. In most cases, the EPA office is located in another state. EPA officials may not be very close to the local environmental problem or needs in a state because of physical distance and limited resources. The EPA may not have a sensitivity to competing interests or priorities which may impact local economic or environmental conditions. EPA regional office accountability, for the most part, is directed to EPA headquarters and Congress.

States may choose to participate in a federally mandated program to assume primacy to provide for more effective service delivery, to minimize duplication in state or federal programs, or in some cases, just to keep the EPA out of the state. There are also some disincentives for states that do not choose to participate or maintain adequate federal standards. For example, under the Federal Superfund Amendments and Reauthorization Act (SARA) of 1986, states that do not develop a

Hazardous Waste Capacity Assurance Plan to demonstrate that the state has adequate treatment and disposal capacity for hazardous waste may have federal Superfund moneys withheld. This may slow down toxic waste cleanup. Other examples include sanctions for failing to maintain air-quality standards or to implement air-pollution-control strategies. The primary sanction in these cases is the withholding of federal highway funds.

The above are examples of what is called the "carrot-and-stick" approach to encourage state participation in federal programs. Another approach to leverage states is to provide for the opportunity of citizen suits, a provision currently found in many environmental protection programs. One example of using the citizen suit provision to leverage a state is found in the Wellhead Protection Program authorized under the Safe Drinking Water Act Amendments of 1986. Under this program, if states do not adopt a program to protect groundwater wells that are used to provide drinking water by a certain date, a citizen can sue the state for noncompliance. In this and other applications, the citizen suit provisions of federal environmental laws are powerful tools that may be brought against a state or industry for noncompliance with standards, permits, or federal rules. The citizen suit concept has also found its way into many state environmental laws, to pressure companies or localities to comply with state law.

Because state priorities are often not the same as federal priorities, many states have found it necessary to adopt environmental protection programs to meet their unique needs. Some of these overlap with federal programs, some are more strict than federal programs, and others have nothing to do with federal programs. Examples of these may include environmental programs related to the protection of groundwater resources, delivery of solid-waste services, management of special wastes, and protection of riparian habitats or groundwater recharge areas.

States that take the prerogative to adopt their own programs are frequently frustrated when, at a later time, the federal government authorizes a new program to protect the environmental concern that the state already effectively regulates. Examples include state solid-waste management programs and groundwater protection programs with which the federal government has only recently become interested or involved. When this occurs, states may actively lobby to request the federal government to provide maximum flexibility so that the state program can fit into the federally mandated "program mold" with minimal disruption to the existing state program.

Paradigm for the Future

The processes and priorities used to establish environmental protection programs undoubtedly will change over time. Areas of future regulatory development may include the integration of programs to manage and control toxics as well as the reauthorization of many of our existing environmental laws at both the state and federal levels.

There may also be continued specificity in newly enacted or reauthorized federal laws. This will continue to minimize the flexibility and discretion of the EPA and, in turn, may minimize the flexibility and discretion of the states in the adoption of rules and programs.

There may continue to be experimentation in the rule-making process through a concept which is known as negotiated rule making. This is an approach which has been used by both the federal EPA and some states. The concept is to utilize the expertise and interest of diverse interest groups through a process of negotiation and consensus building in the rule development process. Under this approach, the regulatory agency may be a participant and usually maintains final decision-making authority.

As the federal fiscal and budget constraints grow more acute, it is likely that additional funding measures will emerge at the state and local level to provide revenues for the development of new programs or the maintenance of existing programs. These measures may include increased permit and inspection fees, waste-related surcharges, or taxes.

Perhaps the greatest changes will occur in the role of the public in environmental regulation. The management of the environment is a complex task that requires the balancing of interests, priorities, and costs. Ultimately, it is a process of negotiation, compromise, and consensus building. Active participation by all parties—industry and individuals alike—will be required. The general public is the most powerful voice in the process. Unfortunately, the voice of the majority is not frequently heard. When the public does speak, it is usually a loud reaction to a problem or situation as opposed to constructive input to solve the problem. Effective citizen participation in the process is a challenge that remains to be fully considered in our regulatory process.

7

Industry Associations— How They Work

Kraig H. Scheyer
*Manager, Safety, Health,
and Environmental
Affairs, TRW*

Industry associations have become an important part of successful compliance programs for many companies. However, achieving the benefits of membership in these organization—and avoiding the pitfalls—requires an understanding of the many types of associations and the various levels of involvement that are possible. The benefits can include a substantial and cost-effective source of up-to-date information, and the ability to have an impact on environment-related laws and regulations beyond that which is possible for a company working independently. Conversely, association involvement can be a drain on a company's resources with little return value if the choice of association and level of involvement are not carefully managed.

Types of Associations

The Encyclopedia of Industry and Trade Associations lists some 30,000 associations registered and operating in the United States. Many of these associations can provide some level of support with respect to environmental programs. Although a great variety exists in the structure and activities of these groups, they can generally be divided into two types: formal and informal. The formal type are usually tax-exempt nonprofit organizations with memberships ranging from several hundred to a thousand or more. These formal associations usually have dues of $500 to $30,000, hold regular member meetings, and generally have been in existence for many years. In addition to paying dues, members may be asked to contribute additional funds to pay for specific studies or other activities.

Formal associations have well-defined bylaws, organizational structures, and member services. Clearly defined charters provide the direction that the association will take as various issues are presented for action or consideration. The organizational structure is normally defined by the association's bylaws, which set forth the rights and responsibilities of members and officers, the methods by which officers are elected, criteria for membership, and other rules governing the activities of the association. The services provided by formal associations to members can include consulting, lobbying, information gathering, and publications such as newsletters.

The structure of formal associations typically includes a chairman, a steering committee, and officers. The chairman and steering committee are normally elected based on their contribution to, and support of, association activities. They are key to the direction, philosophy, and success of the association. The larger associations have paid staff members to support the association's administrative and technical activities.

Informal associations differ from formal groups in having fewer members and less well defined structures. Frequently, they are temporary groups formed to address a specific issue and disband when the issue is resolved. These informal associations have minimal or no dues, but they may require funding of a specific study or other paid-for service (e.g., consultant, lobbyist) in order to be a member. They are usually created by a few interested individuals (e.g., representatives of companies) with a common need or issue to be resolved.

The structure of informal associations generally includes a leadership role. All members then share in the work or activities performed. Consequently, informal associations generally require a much higher level of involvement and input from individual members. In many cases, members not capable of a commitment may not be accepted.

While the demands are greater in informal organizations, the benefits gained by each member can be correspondingly high. Where larger more formal associations tend to be driven by the input of the steering committee and other major members, small organizations give individual members more influence.

	Formal Associations	Informal Associations
Charter	Well Defined	Initially Defined, but May Change or Drift Over Time
Structure	By-Laws Exist, Officers Elected	Generally No By-Laws or Officers; Leaders Appointed or Develop
Duration	Long-Term	Generally Short-Term, May Dissolve After Issue Is Resolved
Level of Involvement by Members	High to Low Depending on Role in Association	High, in Most Cases
Cost	Annual Dues Ranging from $500 to $30,000	Little or No Dues

Figure 7-1. Formal and informal organizations compared.

A summary of the key differences between informal and formal associations is presented in Fig. 7-1. The type of association that is right for a company depends on the results the company seeks. For a company with a wide range of goals, membership in several organizations should be considered. Common to both formal and informal associations is the belief that working through such groups, rather than independently, adds value to a company's efforts in many areas.

In addition to the formal-informal characterization, associations can be further categorized as follows:

- *General industry associations,* which cover all types of issues (e.g., taxes, human relations, transportation, technologies, health and safety, environmental) for a wide range of industries. An example is the National Association of Manufacturers, which includes all types of manufacturing.

- *Industry-specific associations,* which cover all types of issues for a single industry. The Chemical Manufacturers Association is one example.

- *Environmental associations,* which focus only on environmental issues. Examples include the Sierra Club and the Environmental Defense Fund.

- *Industry- and environment-specific associations,* whose sole charter is to focus on environmental issues specific to a particular industry. For example, the California Aerospace Environmental Association addresses the environmental issues unique to aerospace firms.

As the importance of environmental compliance has grown over the last few years, the general industry associations and industry-specific associations have begun to focus specifically on the environment through standing committees. In addition, the last decade has seen a substantial growth in environment-specific associations and emerging industry- and environment-specific associations. Although they are not industry associations, environmental associations should not be overlooked as a potential source of information and as a potential public relations avenue for environmentally conscious companies.

Following is a summary of the key characteristics of each of these types of associations. These key characteristics of each type of association are also summarized in Fig. 7-2.

General Industry Associations

These groups normally focus on state- or national-level issues and cover a wide range of environmental topics. Their activities include informing members about changing laws and regulations and general trends in environmental compliance. Lobbying or regulatory activity is generally focused on issues that affect members in general. Industry-specific issues are avoided to minimize conflict between members and to maximize membership. The larger general industry associations have a staff that performs one or more of the following activities: meeting planning and coordination, lobbying, preparation of newsletters, and developing and maintaining membership. As mentioned above, although these groups are not focused on environmental issues, their members are affected by environmental laws and regulations, and therefore they typically have environment-specific standing committees or at a minimum hold meetings or conferences with environmental themes.

Industry-Specific Associations

Similar to the general industry associations, these associations have standing environmental committees or focused meetings or conferences on the environment. The advantage here is that their concerns are limited to a specific industry, and thus they are more likely to address the issues facing an individual member. The size of these organizations, which is dictated by the size and number of companies in the industry, is directly related to the impact the association has on regulations. Associations with limited membership are not likely to have a substantial impact unless the potential problem is severe.

	General Industry Associations	Industry-Specific Associations	Environmental Associations	Industry and Environment-Specific Associations
Methods of Addressing Issues	Standing Committees, Ad Hoc Committees	Standing Committees, Ad Hoc Committees	All Meetings, 100% Focus	All Meetings, 100% Focus
Relative Size	Large	Medium to Large	A Few Large, Many Small	Generally Small
Membership Mix	Broad Representation Across Industries	Representatives from One Major Industry	Mostly Interested Individuals; Low Industry Involvement	Environmental Professionals from One Major Industry
Organizational Structure	Formal	Formal	Semiformal	Range from Formal to Informal
Geographical Focus	National	National	A Few Focus on National, Many Focus on Local	National, Regional and Local
Dues and Fees	High	High to Medium	Low	Low to Medium

Figure 7-2. Organization characteristics compared.

Environmental Associations

Environmental organizations provide information and a potential public relations avenue for environmentally conscious companies. The dues are small for individuals ($25 to $100) and relatively small for companies (e.g., the National Resource Defense Council provides company membership for $5000). These associations are not a forum for working on industry-specific issues; rather, they are a forum for finding out about public and community issues and are a potential vehicle for participation in community environmental activities.

Industry- and Environment-Specific Associations

In these groups, the focus is 100 percent on environmental issues affecting a specific industry. In general, these associations are smaller in size, operate in an informal manner, and rely heavily upon member action to sustain them. Responsibility for specific actions is typically distributed evenly among members. Involvement at a level comparable with that of other members is expected. If active involvement is not sustained, the inactive member will most likely be shunned by the active members.

The Value of Associations

A wide variety of benefits are available from associations, depending on their charter and focus. Within an association, members will get different benefits from different levels of involvement. The following discussion presents some of the specific benefits from membership in associations.

Current Information

Probably the most common and consistent benefit provided by associations is information. In many associations, the real value added is purely that of learning about developments in progress. Associations offer an abundance of information on current developments in law, regulation, and technology. In most cases, the agendas of standing committees address current developments in the environmental arena. In addition, environmental conferences and workshops are a great source of information, with speakers covering the state of the art in environmental management. Most associations invite regulators, lawmakers, and other experts to provide guidance and give overviews of current topics. Last but not least is the information available from other members. They are one of the best sources of information on current developments.

Lobbying and Regulatory Interface

Because of the number of members they represent, associations have a greater ability to influence legislators and regulators than independent companies. This influence can be a positive or a negative, depending on how it is exercised. The key is developing a relationship with the legislative and regulatory community based on integrity and credibility. This relationship must be maintained with ongoing, positive contact with individuals in that community. In California, the California Manufacturers Association has successfully represented California manufacturers before the state's legislative body. In many cases, proposed bills have been revised, and laws promulgated, to the greater benefit of the industries affected.

Industry-Specific Studies

Associations perform a wide range of studies that would be impractical or impossible for companies to perform independently. These include evaluations of the effect of proposed regulation and legislation, the results of which are used by the association's lobbyists. Industrywide studies collect performance data that can be used by individual members in appraising their own operations, as discussed below. In many cases, the companies would not be able to afford the cost of such studies individually.

Benchmarking

Benchmarking is the process of comparing the performance and organization of a given company against that of other companies in the same industry. In an association, benchmarking can be performed formally through studies, as an ongoing agenda item in association meetings, or independently between members. The information gained is useful for evaluating resource levels committed to compliance activities and for evaluating the success of specific compliance activities.

Professional Networking

Networking is one of the benefits of attendance at association meetings and conferences. Association members develop professional liaisons that can be tapped as questions arise while developing new programs and evaluating different courses of action. The ability to poll other companies is often critical to ensuring that a company's program is on the right track; a professional network is critical to this task.

Levels of Involvement

The level of involvement should be commensurate with the benefit expected from the association. For example, if regulatory lobbying is of prime importance to the company, a very active role is required to ensure that the company's position is appropriately considered by the association. By contrast, if information is the only goal, a low level of participation, such as attending a few meetings and conferences or even just reviewing a newsletter, may be acceptable. The following describes the various roles and potential benefits which can be expected. Figure 7-3 provides an overview of the benefits of various levels of involvement.

Steering the Association

Steering an organization requires a substantial commitment to time and effort by the individual member. In many cases a formal position such as chairman, committee leader, or other office will be necessary. At a minimum, active regular and ongoing involvement is required.

Committee Participation

Another way to ensure that the individual member's issues are addressed is through active participation in committees. This level of involvement is more focused and can be limited to the duration of a committee's activities on a specific issue.

Levels of Involvement	Benefits
Steering the Association (i.e., Officer or Leader)	Direct activities and focus resources on issues of interest
	Ensure that issues of interest are addressed
Committee Participation	Provide input to focus resources on a particular issue
	Ensure that issues of interest are considered
	Obtain detailed information on issues and regulations
Periodic Meetings	Obtain current information on issues and regulations
	Identify developing trends
	Develop professional network
	Obtain benchmarking information
Information Mailings	Obtain limited information on issues and regulations

Higher levels of participation produce stated benefits plus those of lower levels.

Figure 7-3. Participation levels and benefits.

Meeting Attendance

By attending meetings on a monthly, quarterly, or even semiannual basis, a member can gather useful information on potential impacts of new regulations, developing trends in the profession, and upcoming agenda items in the government and private sector that may be of interest to the company.

Mailings

This is probably the lowest level of involvement with an association, but it does have benefits. Routine mailings such as newsletters, regulatory updates, and meeting agendas can provide useful information. Upcoming legislation and regulations are routinely covered in newsletters. In many cases, key issues of interest to members are highlighted. Separate discussion and action correspondence may also be sent out to members on the association mailing list. The only disadvantage to this low level of involvement is the cost; most likely you will pay the same dues whether you are a fully involved member or just receiving the mail.

Summary

In summary, some of the key questions to answer when considering participation in an association include:

- What benefits do you want from your involvement with the association (i.e., lobbying your interests, current information, professional networking, etc.)?
- What method of involvement will result in the desired benefits (ranging from active participation in leading the association down to reading a newsletter)?
- How much are you willing to pay for what you want to get out of the association? (Consider dues, miscellaneous fees, and the time and effort required.)

Answering these questions before you join an association will ensure cost-effective participation and results consistent with your expectations.

8

Profiles of Four Trade and Professional Associations

Robert Young

Manager (Retired)
Environmental Services
Bell Helicopter

The environmental manager in today's manufacturing industry has an enormous task. Compliance with federal environmental regulations alone requires knowledge of a stack of written materials 18 inches high. Correcting 30 years of environmental sins while avoiding citations along the way is no small task. It is even more challenging—and in fact may be impossible—for the manager who remains isolated from the regulatory community and his or her industrial peer group.

Annual inspections and the permit application review process offer neither the opportunity nor the proper setting in which to effectively communicate with agency personnel. The busy schedules of enforcement and permitting personnel generally prevent meaningful discussions of topics outside of those directly related to the visit. Additionally, these agency personnel may or may not be knowledgeable in all aspects of the agency's functions, policy decisions, and long-range planning.

The effective manager of today must have recognition within the regulating body which governs the firm's environmental actions, an active and comfortable rapport with peer groups, and a vehicle by which to influence regulatory language. One small voice from an isolated manufacturing facility is easily lost among the millions of public comments on a proposed environmental regulation. Trade and professional organizations offer the manager an opportunity to be heard, communicate with regulatory agencies, converse with peer groups, and be recognized within the regulatory community without extensive "political training." The manager must, however, exercise care to ensure that he or she chooses those affiliations which best fulfill the company's needs and which are respected within the industry and regulatory community. In the following sections, I discuss the background and purpose of several associations that have played a prominent role on behalf of specific industries or professions in the United States. Where describing local activities, I have used the state of Texas, where my involvement has focused, and which I believe to be fairly representative of local activities nationwide. Please be aware that these are merely a sample of the many organizations that can assist you and your company in addressing environmental and other challenges in industry today.

Aerospace Industries Association

Trade associations such as the Aerospace Industries Association (AIA), Chemical Manufacturers Associations (CMA), and Machinery Allied Products Institute (MAPI) are structured to represent a specific industry in all aspects of its business before the Congress, the public, and regulatory bodies. In today's business environment, federal regulatory bodies include the Environmental Protection Agency and the Occupational Safety and Health Administration (OSHA). Trade organizations are renowned for their ability to effect change, moderating and even eliminating proposed or existing regulations that impose undue burden upon their member companies. The political clout of such organizations is derived from the number of companies they represent and the financial impact their industry has upon the U.S. economy. Their effectiveness within the regulatory community is a product of competent leadership and prudent use of the given powers. Trade associations have the ear of both the Congress and the Environmental Protection Agency but generally refrain from becoming directly involved with state or local issues, which are usually addressed by professional organizations.

The history and structure of the AIA is typical of a large, well-organized trade organization. Like many such organizations, the AIA has a history that reaches back to the origins of the industry. The association was founded in 1919 with a charter membership of 100. The purpose of the group was "to foster, advance, promulgate and promote aeronautics." Early members included such notables as Orville Wright and Glenn Curtiss. Today, AIA represents 68 member companies including Boeing, Bell Helicopter–Textron, Chrysler Technologies, Northrop, General Dynamics, IBM, and Westinghouse Electric. Member companies produce aircraft and associated aerospace products.

It is important to note that trade associations represent their members from a technological as well as a trade standpoint. A group such as AIA is a uniquely powerful source of knowledge of expertise related to the science and technology of its particular industry. When providing input to federal agencies seeking to rule on complex technological and scientific matters, trade groups frequently lend a level of expertise that does not exist anywhere else in the world, even within the regulatory community itself. Congress in particular does not (and cannot be expected to) master the intricacies of every industry. Thus, in participating in the regulatory and legislative processes, AIA provides both tangible and intangible benefits to the private and public sectors of the United States.

In addition to the role it plays in the regulatory and legislative process, the AIA undertakes a variety of projects of interest to its members. The AIA has established national standards for aerospace manufacturing. It has participated in a long-range program with the National Aviation Education Council to produce instructional materials for higher education. Its work also includes the development of programmed tool systems in a joint effort with the United States Air Force Material Command and the Massachusetts Institute of Technology.

The association currently publishes the AIA newsletter with an audience of 15,000 in industry, government, academia, the financial world, and the media. Environmental initiatives are annually among the association's top 10 issues. The association and its member companies are committed to protecting the health and safety of aerospace workers and surrounding communities and to being conscientious stewards of the environment while ensuring that there is no sacrifice to product quality or damage to the competitive position of American aerospace products in the international market.

The general meeting of the Environmental Health and Safety Committee of AIA convenes twice annually for 2 to 3 days. Meetings are formal, but all member companies are allowed an opportunity to express views or concerns upon an agenda item or topic. The Executive Committee and AIA Committee Representative meet prior to the general meeting in order to plan future meetings, collect subcommittee reports, and conduct other committee business. The Executive Committee is elected by the member companies and the AIA Committee Representative is employed by AIA with committee approval.

Activities outside of the annual meetings offer an opportunity for member company representatives to discuss topics of interest or concern with peers in an informal setting. These discussions often provide the environmental manager with invaluable technical information or program ideas. Meetings removed from the normal work setting also encourage the manager to concentrate on focused issues or program needs rather than on day-to-day problems.

Environmental managers with membership in the AIA have an opportunity to speak directly with EPA officials involved in policy decisions, have a voice in Congress through AIA's legislative initiatives, and can converse with the premier environmental engineers and managers in the nation. For the manager who is not involved with the aerospace industry, the Chemical Manufacturers Association (CMA) and Machinery Allied Products Association (MAPA) boast similar histories, accomplishments, and member benefits.

American Water Works Association

Unlike the trade associations like the AIA, professional associations such as the American Water Works Association (AWWA), Water Environment Federation (WEF), and Air & Waste Management Association (AWMA) are not industry-specific but rather attract pollution-control experts (consultants, chemists, and engineers) for many industries as well as government and academia. Also in contrast to trade organizations, which are active in all areas of regulatory control, professional associations generally channel their efforts in a specific field such as air, water, or hazardous-waste management.

The AWWA was formed in 1881 to "promote public health through the improvement of the quality and quantity of public water supplies." Its early efforts included the development of standards for filtration, disinfection, and distribution of municipal water supplies. In recognition of the importance of operations training, the AWWA developed a system of regional water utility associations that provide water plant operators with hands-on training, technical literature, and other resources not available from other sources. It has also promulgated the standards by which the design engineers prepare plans and specifications for new facilities. Today, the AWWA's training programs are the standard for utility operator training.

In keeping with the organization's goal to disseminate scientific and technical information, a major activity of the AWWA is the publication of books, journals, and other materials. Its regular publications include the *Journal of the American Water Works Association* (JAWWA), read by water utility personnel around the world; *WaterWeek*, a biweekly newsletter for breaking news; *Mainstream*, a newsletter on covering water-supply issues and the AWWA activities; and *OpFlow*, a newsletter for operators. Information is also exchanged at regional and national conferences sponsored by the AWWA.

The regional water utility associations give operators a local source for education, training, and technical information. In the state of Texas, for example, water utility operators can benefit from association with the Texas Water Utilities Association, the Professional Water Operations Division of the Water Environment Federation.

The regional organizations also organize and conduct the training and education programs required for licensure of plant operators. Through the local water utilities associations, operators can earn the continuing education credits required for maintaining licensure.

Water Environment Federation

Formerly known as the Water Pollution Control Federation, the Water Environment Federation (WEF) is a 40,000-member group dedicated to preserving and enhancing water quality worldwide. Dating back to 1928, the WEF was originally formed to address the problems of sewage treatment. Like the AWWA, it rapidly developed as a standards-making body for water treatment, facility design, and operations.

The WEF formed the Professional Water Operations Division (PWOD) specifically to address the needs of water utility operators. This organization, in conjunction with the AWWA organizations, supplies the treatment plant operators with hands-on literature, training, and technical information.

The WEF publishes more than 80 technical publications that present members with the most recent information on water utility design and operation. Its periodicals include *Water Environment & Technology*, covering industry trends; *Water Environment Research*, a peer-reviewed journal presenting recent research findings; *Operations Forum*, for operators; and *Industrial Wastewater*, a magazine for environmental specialists in industry. The WEF's five newsletters cover member activities, water analysis, professional opportunities, safety, and regulation.

Among the association's major activities is the WEF Annual Conference and Exposition, which brings together more than 13,000 water-quality professionals from around the world. In addition to seminars and guest speakers, the conference includes exhibits from more than 500 companies.

In addition to the national-level organization, WEF has a strong organization on the state level. The Texas Water Pollution Control Association, a member of the WEF, has over 1750 members in all areas of the state, as well as an annual meeting which has been attended by over 500 for the past 3 years. On the local level, sections exist in Houston, Dallas–Fort Worth, and Austin. These sections meet every other month for dinner and a professional program directed at the environmental engineer or manager.

Air & Waste Management Association

The Air & Waste Management Association (AWMA) was formed in 1907 as the Air Pollution Control Association to address the problems of air pollution related to power generation and metal production. Like AWWA and WEF, it is responsible for the development of standards of sampling, modeling, and implementation of air-pollution-control technologies. Unlike AWWA and WEF, it has not strongly addressed the operations-level staff, instead focusing on the engineers, chemists, and management-level personnel.

An international organization with an annual convention, the AWMA publishes the *Journal of the Air and Waste Management Association* (JAWMA) and a bimonthly newsletter, *News & Views*. In addition to the international organization, AWMA has a strong organization on the state level. The Texas Section of the Air & Waste Management Association has members in all areas of the state, as well as an annual meeting. On the local level, chapters exist in several major cities, including Dallas–Fort Worth. This chapter meets every month for lunch with a professional program directed at the environmental engineer, chemist, or manager.

The 14,000 members of the AWMA can participate in specialty conferences, broadcast seminars, 1- and 2-day workshops, and a wide variety of training courses. Events are located throughout the United States.

9
Employee Training: Eight Scenarios

Mark G. Busch
Senior Environmental Control Engineer
Northrop Aircraft Division

This chapter addresses training issues in a comprehensive environmental management program. Obviously the needs of each company may vary to some degree; but the requirements, in terms of both legal mandate and good business sense, are often applicable across the board. The intent of this chapter is to discuss the levels of training that may be required by an industrial organization. Wherever possible, information is provided concerning the "how to's" of an environmental training program (how to set up a training support program, how to implement training to meet specific training needs, etc.). The scenarios and case studies used in this chapter are hypothetical but are based on real incidents experienced by this author.

Introduction

In setting up an environmental training plan, a large manufacturing company considered three sources for information to determine training needs:

- *Federal and state requirements for training.* Employees with expertise in environmental regulations reviewed federal and state law to identify the training required by law. (For smaller companies without environmental experts, a consultant or lawyer could provide the same service.)

- *Federal and state requirements for employees to adequately perform certain tasks.* Some federal and state regulations do not mandate training specifically but rather require that employees perform certain tasks with a specific level of accuracy. An example of such a task would be reviewing Uniform Hazardous Waste Manifests for correctness and completeness prior to signing. A company may need to train employees for such tasks.

- *Notices of Violation and company environmental inspection reports.* Notices of Violation and internal inspection reports are sources of information about deficiencies that exist in a company's environmental program. These sources were reviewed to identify any patterns of deficiencies that could also be addressed through awareness training. The inspection reports also provided a baseline to determine success of the environmental training. In the first year in which training was provided, inspection reports indicated an 80 percent drop in the number of environmental deficiencies. While other factors contributed to this dramatic decrease as well, these reports served as one indicator of the success of the training program.

From this information, the training plan illustrated in Figs. 9-1 and 9-2 was developed. Where possible, courses were taught by company environmental staff. In cases where the trainer must be certified to teach the course, as with HAZWOPER training addressed below, vendors were contacted to provide the training. Each employee was evaluated by job title, classification, or specific tasks to be performed to determine whether the company would require that he or she attend the training courses.

The legal obligation to provide for training in the hazardous-materials (hazmat) field has been in existence for several years. This obligation was originally directed toward employees whose job involved Hazardous Waste Operations and Emergency Response (commonly referred to by the acronym HAZWOPER). As the understanding of the need for effective employee training in the area of hazardous materials and hazardous waste grew, training was extended to a greater number of employees.

Many of the training modules discussed in this chapter reflect current requirements for a company operating in the state of California, whose environmental laws are among the most stringent in the nation.

Directions:

Please use this form as a guide to determine requirements for employees in your department and to complete the Hazardous Waste Materials Training Plan.

	Hazardous Waste Training for Generators	Hazardous Waste Mgmt for Focal Points/Monitors	Overview of Hazardous Waste for Non-Generators	Hazardous Waste Manifest/Land Ban Overview	Hazardous Waste Ops & Emergency Response	Hazardous Waste Ops/Emerg Response	Pretreatment Plant Operations	Rule 109 Recordkeeping Annual Review	Rule 109 Recordkeeping/Computer Input	Agency Inspection Guidelines	Spray Booth Permit Requirements	Hazardous Material Shipping Regulations	Transportation of Hazardous Matls (Carriers)	Transportation of Hazardous Matls (Shippers)	Forklift Operation	Industrial Tow Motor Operation	Liquid Propane Refueling	Confined Space Entry	Hazard Communication	Handling Asbestos-Containing Matls	Health & Safety Trng for Emerg Resp Personnel	Health & Safety Trng for Emerg Resp (Refresher)	Respirator Training
	ENVIRONMENTAL																TRANS		EQ OP LIC		SAFETY		
Generators	X																		X				
Environmental Focal Points & Monitors	X	X																	X				
CMS Operators & Transporters	X	X		X	X					X		X						X	X			X	
Environmental Professionals, Management, etc.		X				X													X				
Functions Requiring Additional Training																							
- Asbestos Handlers	X																	X	X				
- Designated Confined Space Entry Personnel	X															X	X					X	
- Equipment Operators (Licensing)	X												X	X	X	X							
- Fire Protection	X																	X	X	X			
- Hazardous Waste Manifest Signers	X		X															X					
- Health Industrial Hygiene Personnel	X																	X	X	X			
- Oil Discharging Equipment Maintainers	X																	X					
- Pretreatment Plant Operators	X				X													X					
- Respirators Required in Work	X																	X					X
- Rule 109 Recordkeepers	X					X	X											X					
- Spray Booth Operators	X								X									X					
- Transportation (Carriers)	X										X							X					
- Transportation (Shippers)	X											X						X					

NOTE: 1st Line Supervisors receive same courses as generators and other courses as appropriate.

Figure 9-1. Hazardous materials training matrix.

Directions:

Please indicate the training required for each employee in your department who handles, stores, or transports hazardous virgin material or hazardous waste by checking off (√) one or more of the courses listed. Keep original in department files and send one copy to your Environmental Focal Point.

Manager: _____ Focal Point: _____
Dept/Zone: _____ Date: _____
Extension: _____ Page: _____ of _____

NAME	EMPL #	JOB TITLE		

Column headers (rotated):

ENVIRONMENTAL
- Hazardous Waste Training for Generators
- Overview of Hazardous Waste Mgmt for Focal Points/Monitors
- Hazardous Waste Manifest/Land Ban Overview
- Hazardous Waste Ops & Emergency Response
- Pretreatment Plant Operations
- Rule 109 Recordkeeping/Computer Input
- Agency Inspection Guidelines
- Spray Booth Permit Requirements
- Hazardous Material Shipping Regulations
- Transportation of Hazardous Matls (Shippers)
- Transportation of Hazardous Matls (Carriers)

TRANS
- Forklift Operation
- Industrial Tow Motor Operation
- Liquid Propane Refueling
- Confined Space Entry

EQ OP LIC
- Hazard Communication
- Handling Asbestos-Containing Matls
- Health & Safety Trng for Emerg Resp Personnel

SAFETY
- Health & Safety Trng for Emerg Resp Personnel (Refresher)
- Respirator Training

NOTE: 1st Line Supervisors receive same courses as generators and other courses as appropriate.

Figure 9-2. Hazardous materials training plan.

Requirements can vary from state to state and between state and federal agencies. A look at current legal and political trends suggests that the requirements in place in California will eventually be adopted by other states. A proactive manager should consider the California requirements as a basis for future legislation in his or her state and look to establishing a training package to meet anticipated as well as current guidelines.

Because HAZWOPER training was among the earliest to be specified by law, it is discussed first in this chapter. Other types of environmental training are discussed later, as are guidelines for establishing an environmental training and record-keeping plan. This chapter will also suggest an environmental management program that can be implemented within the framework of a company's existing employee base.

Essentially, the HAZWOPER requirement (29 CFR 1910.120) is a health- and safety-related form of training. Its original intent was primarily to protect employees performing spill response and site remediation operations. Its guidelines also serve as a foundation for the concept of employee environmental training, and it therefore is the logical place to start any examination of environmental training.

Scenario 1

A tool and die maker is returning from break and walks near a process tank line. As he passes by the line, he notices a large pool of an unidentified liquid underneath. He goes to a nearby company telephone, dials the phone extension for the company's security department, and reports the incident.

Shortly after the employee hangs up, a security officer arrives. The officer blocks off a nearby drain hole to prevent the liquid from flowing in, and keeps a small crowd of curious employees at a safe distance.

Meanwhile, a crew from the company's hazardous-waste team arrives. The company's industrial hygienist is also on-scene to identify the material and coordinate with the waste-team members. The industrial hygienist is also available to act as company liaison with outside agencies inquiring about the release.

Upon investigation, waste-crew members discover a small rupture in the line and are able to plug it. The line is closed and purged. Later that day, employees from the company facilities department are able to repair the line and return it to operation. No injuries or property damage resulted from this incident.

This scenario depicts the intended result of the training mandated by 29 CFR 1910.120, "Hazardous Waste Operations and Emergency Response." Specific training allowed each employee to perform his or her role in a hazmat incident safely and effectively.

The tool and die maker functioned at the *First Responder* level. As the term implies, this individual is the first person to notice the incident. The only action required of the First Responder is to immediately notify the appropriate company representative, in this case the company security department. No other action from this individual is needed, expected, or authorized. Training at this level is limited to that which is adequate to provide the employee with the ability to recognize a hazard and report it. No minimum or maximum time limit for the length of training is imposed.

The security officer arriving on the scene performed *First Responder Operations* level activities. The officer kept employees at a safe distance and tried to stop the spread of the spill. Further action could then be taken by members of the company hazardous-waste team and the industrial hygienist. Training at the First Responder Operations level must be 8 hours long and must include such items as hazmat terminology, use of personal protective equipment (PPE), and knowledge of company emergency procedures.

The hazardous-waste team members functioned as *Hazardous Material Technicians*. Training at the Technician Level is 24 hours long. It must contain training equal to that included in the First Responder Operations level course, and must also impart specialized knowledge related to the company emergency response plan, field survey equipment, hazard and risk assessment techniques, advanced control and containment procedures, etc. This training would also be necessary for these employees in their normal duties as hazardous waste and materials handlers in the company's controlled material storage facility.

The industrial hygienist served as the incident *Hazardous Materials Specialist*. Training at this level must also be at least 24 hours long and equal to that at the Hazardous Material Technician level, although a more in-depth evaluation of some of the topics (e.g., hazard and risk assessment, decontamination procedures, site safety) is included.

Twenty-four hours of training is also required for employees working in a company's *Treatment, Storage, and Disposal Facility (TSDF)*. The content of this training is not specified, but it must provide employees with sufficient knowledge regarding hazardous waste and material handling to perform their assigned duties. Initial 24-hour training may be waived if the employer can show that an employee's prior experience and/or education gives the employee a level of understanding that meets or exceeds the training. However, whether or not an employee receives the initial 24 hours of training, he or she must attend an 8-hour annual refresher each year. Recent additions to the California Code of Regulation imposed by the California Occupational Safety and Health Administration (Cal-OSHA) currently mirror federal requirements. Should the state requirements exceed federal regulations, they would supersede these federal standards.

Scenario 2

A factory is demolished and the land where it sat is put up for sale. Soil samples taken at the site indicate high concentrations of polychlorinated biphenyls. U.S. EPA officials designate the land as a Superfund Amendments and Reauthorization Act (SARA) cleanup site, and an authorized cleanup crew is called in.

The individuals cleaning the site would need 40 hours of training before they could begin this assignment. The training would include 3 days of field experience under the supervision of an instructor experienced in these operations. Few companies have employees who would be called upon to perform a major site cleanup or respond to a major hazardous materials incident (an oil spill or a train derailment involving hazardous waste, for example). These duties are usually handled by municipal or county fire departments or other appropriate agencies.

The greater likelihood is that employees may be involved in incidents described in Scenario 1. Ironically, many employers provide their employees with a level of training required for incidents that they are not likely to encounter. In many cases, a 40-hour course is provided to employees who respond to non-SARA spills like the one described in the first scenario. The rationale is that, if training is good, more training is better.

Providing the right training, and the right amount of training, serves the best interests of both the employer and the employee. Neither party benefits if the training the employee receives is inappropriate. The regulations mandating training were put into effect to ensure that an employee's health and safety are protected. Employers are expected to meet these legal requirements. The issue therefore is "what training is needed to protect employees and meet legal standards?"

At one company, *Awareness* level training has been provided to all employees whose job assignments put them in positions to potentially generate hazardous waste. All hourly employees and selected job titles for salaried employees are given approximately 1 hour of awareness training annually. Topics include the nature and definition of hazardous waste, legal requirements, fines and penalties for noncompliance, aspects of the company's hazardous-waste management program, emergency procedures, and spill and leak response. Employees are also given basic training in risk assessment and hazard analysis. This training is provided to over 5600 personnel by 20 specially trained employees. Training starts in the second quarter of the year and continues until Thanksgiving. Because all the material is created internally, costs for course development and labor are minimal. This course and the structure supporting it are discussed later in this chapter.

First Responder Operations training is provided to members of the company's hazardous-waste transportation department and in ongoing training to its fire department, who are the company's designated first responders.

Hazardous-waste transportation and controlled material storage (CMS) employees have also received the 24-hour TSDF training, with a second year of 24-hour training as review. Thereafter, these employees will attend the 8-hour review sessions annually. Selected employees in the company's industrial hygiene, environmental compliance, and hazardous-waste transportation and controlled material storage (CMS) departments attend hazardous-waste specialists training as well. Environmental engineers assigned to the CMS facility also attend hazardous-waste technician and manifest training.

Sessions of 24-hour initial and 8-hour review training may be conducted by company employees. Owing to federal certification requirements, however, it is frequently contracted through vendors who specialize in this area of training. Because this course is scheduled to be held annually, budget can be allocated for it in advance. Employees whose attendance is required, and employees whose job assignments may require a company need-to-know, are scheduled to attend course sessions. By approaching hazardous-waste training in this manner, the company maximizes benefits while controlling costs.

This is one company's way of providing legally required training. This company employs over 12,500 people, and sheer size dictates many of its approaches. For example, it is able to have an in-house fire department to respond to facility emergencies and act as designated first responders. For smaller companies, however, individuals within the organization should be assigned to control the scene until help arrives. This would require First Responder Operations level training. These individuals may be company security officers, supervisors, safety monitors, or other personnel designated for the task. The number of people so designated should be sufficient to guarantee adequate coverage of the employee population and plant area.

Scenario 3

A large company is notified that state law requires employees handling and/or disposing of hazardous waste, defined as any unused or unneeded hazardous material (e.g., solvents, paints, thinners, adhesives) or anything contaminated by that material (e.g., rags, wipes, cans) to be trained in proper methods of handling and disposal. The notification stipulates the material to be covered in this training, which includes state requirements for hazardous-waste disposal, spill and leak procedures, consequences of noncompliance, and other topics. It also states that this training is to be provided in a timely manner to all affected employees. Total target population for this training is approximately 40 percent of the company work force, or roughly 5300 people. This training is to be an annual requirement, so that employees trained in any given year could expect to be retrained every year provided they remain in a job assignment requiring that they handle or dispose of hazardous waste.

The environmental training team within the environmental department at this company consists of two full-time trainers, one scheduler and record keeper, and one secretary whose job responsibilities include support for two other teams within the department. It is obvious that the personnel resources available to the team could not support this training requirement. There is also a company requirement for total quality, which is defined as continuous process improvement and universal employee participation geared to meeting customer expectations the first time.

To address these issues, each department manager responsible for any employees identified as needing this training was contacted and asked to submit the name of an employee within the department to learn how to teach the class. This training assignment was to be considered a part of that employee's work responsibilities. Certain work assignments would have to be reallocated to "free up" the employee to teach the classes. The manager was given specific criteria to use for determining the most appropriate employee to take on this assignment:

- Good communication skills (verbal and written)

- Knowledge of the work processes and materials used in his or her department
- A demonstrated commitment to completing an assignment

Once these employees were identified, they were given 24 hours of training in instructional techniques. This is a standardized course taught by the company's industrial training organization. This course is similar to many other "train the trainer" courses and covers such areas as presentation techniques, feedback techniques, and the importance of consistent application of a lesson plan. Eight hours of additional instruction was then provided by the environmental training team. This additional training was directed to the course material to be presented by the instructors and was designed to familiarize these employees with course material and anticipated questions from course participants.

None of this training was mandatory under either state or federal law. It was designed to support the legal requirement for training of hazardous-waste generators—by definition, any employee who uses a hazardous material or any item which becomes contaminated by that hazardous material and decides to dispose of it. Because this training had to be provided to so large a target population using over 20 novice trainers, certain requirements were advanced by senior management:

- The information presented had to be consistent across the company.
- The course had to be presented where employees worked, not at a centralized training facility.
- The course had to cover all required points in under 1½ hours.

To meet these standards, a 12-minute video was prepared by the company audio-video department. This video covered all the key points spelled out in the state regulation. This allowed the instructor to focus on testing the participants to determine how much of the video was retained. Initially, a multiple-choice test was administered during "pause points" scattered throughout the video. Usually the test would involve four to six questions presented by the instructor. Participants were required to circle the letter corresponding to the answer they believed to be most correct. The instructor would then call on a member of the class for the correct answer. If the answer was incorrect, another participant was called upon until the correct answer was elicited. The instructor then played the next section of video and the process was repeated until the entire video and question sheet were completed.

This process of video, question, and review had several advantages:

- It was consistent across the company. The video was the centerpiece for the course and provided for a consistent message.

- It was portable. Because of the basic video format, the class could be taught at any location (conference room, classroom, etc.) with a video player and monitor.

- It was time-efficient. The video was edited down to 12 minutes. Including question and answer, the course took a little over 1 hour to present.

This program succeeded in accomplishing its primary goal: to provide basic awareness training to over 5000 employees in a remarkably short period of time. However, in the process of administering the training, two distinct disadvantages of this format became apparent:

- It was repetitive. The structure of the course was rather rigid and did not provide for sufficient opportunity to involve participants in the learning process.

- Because of the rigid course design, the format did not make the fullest use of the instructors' experience in the work area. Some instructors grew bored with the classes they were teaching. As a result, several instructors left the program as soon as their first assignment was finished, requiring the training and development of new instructors in subsequent years.

The environmental training team addressed this situation in several ways. The instructors were recognized for their participation with a year-end luncheon celebration. Awards were given to each instructor and instructors were requested to commit to serving as instructors in the following year. In addition, the environmental training team applied company concepts of continuous process improvement and identified some areas where the course could be reformatted. Several revisions were implemented in the design and presentation of the training package:

- While the video was retained, the pause points that interrupted the flow of the course were eliminated. Additional information based on changes in legislation and company policy were incorporated on overhead transparencies.

- Instructors were encouraged to deviate from the course material to reflect issues unique to their work areas. To ensure consistency, a stipulation was made that changes had to be referred to a member of the environmental training team. The team member would then confirm the accuracy of the information with the appropriate employee in the company environmental compliance organization.

- Evaluation of the participants' retention of information was accomplished by means of a quiz-show format. Employees were broken up into teams of five or six. Questions based on information presented either on video or in the lecture were then asked of the teams in rotational order. Point values were attached to each question and the team with the most points at the end of the game won. Each member of the winning team received a pencil embossed with the inscription "I love hazardous waste...in its proper place!"

Response to this format was remarkable. The original expectation of many of the instructors was that employees would balk at playing a game in front of their peers. In actuality, quite the opposite happened. Employees really enjoyed the game. Because of the team nature of the questioning, employees could answer questions without feeling the pressure of being in the spotlight. Several employees have since revealed that morale in their work groups actually improved after the game experience.

Currently it is the company's intent to have this course serve as the basis for all ongoing training for hazardous-waste generators. Minor modifications will be made year to year to incorporate changes in regulations and to involve employees more deeply in the environmental management process. The basic format of the course, however, has demonstrated itself to be so successful that it will remain essentially in place.

These two courses, *Hazardous Waste Operations and Emergency Response* (with its annual refresher) and *Hazardous Waste Generator Training,* are the only two environmental courses taught by the company which are specifically required by either state or federal law. Other courses are provided to employees, but they are intended to ensure proper performance of legally mandated activities, not to meet government mandates. The courses to be discussed under Scenario 4 are the means applied by one company to provide its employees with the skills necessary to do what is expected of them.

Scenario 4

In order to sustain the environmental management program within the company, it has been determined that a corps of specially trained employees will be developed within each department. To be termed hazardous-waste monitors and environmental focal points, these employees will serve respectively as a shop employee's first point of contact on hazardous-waste issues and as the department resident expert on environmental affairs. Monitors will also provide employees with the requisite support materials (hazardous-waste collection containers and accessories such as funnels or bonding and grounding straps, for example), and will be responsible for ensuring that collection and storage containers are properly labeled and emptied on schedule. Focal points will have access to all levels of management within the environmental organization, and will attend quarterly meetings for updates on anticipated changes in the environmental program structure. Focal points will also be provided with a company manual and update bulletins that serve as a department's environmental reference material.

To develop this corps of employees, each manager of a department that generated hazardous waste was asked to provide the names of suitable employees for the tasks outlined in the scenario above. Criteria for selection of environmental focal points were as follows:

- Knowledge of department requirements and procedures
- Ability to effectively communicate with upper management within the department
- Demonstrated needs analysis and resolution skills

In many cases, department managers initially opted to fill the focal point role themselves. Because of the significant time commitment required, other managers assigned this function to someone reporting directly to them. For the most part, focal points also performed the role of hazardous-waste generator trainers in the program outlined above.

The focal point function was essentially a management-level activity. Another group of employees were identified to serve as hazardous-waste monitors. Essentially the department's environmental lead person, the hazardous-waste monitor required a different set of skills and was therefore identified by a different set of criteria:

- Knowledge of requirements and procedures within his or her work area
- Ability to communicate effectively with both management and hourly personnel

■ Demonstrated ability to adapt to new requirements and functions

Hazardous-waste monitors were developed at the ratio of one monitor to every 10 shop personnel. Since this constituted a sizable number of monitors, initial training became a full-time activity for several trainers within the environmental training group. The training provided to both focal points and monitors was identical in structure and content. Frequently, classes would contain both newly designated focal points and monitors. The course was structured so that focal points could obtain both the knowledge and skills necessary to do their job and be aware of monitor responsibilities as well. This was considered appropriate since the focal point became the monitor's resident expert on hazardous-waste issues.

Monitors were also treated to the same level of information as focal points. This was intended to provide them with a sense of the importance of their new function, and to obtain their "buy-in" for efficiently performing their designated tasks.

The course began with a video presentation identical to the one used at the start of the Hazardous Waste Generator class. Since monitors were intended to serve as a generator's first point of contact, it was deemed essential that they be reminded of the level of understanding of hazardous-waste issues provided to the average company employee who generates hazardous waste as an aspect of his or her work. The instructor then discussed the management structure of the company's environmental organization. Specific attention was paid to areas of responsibility within the environmental group and who a focal point or monitor could call if he or she had any questions on hazardous-waste issues. While the focal point would normally be the monitor's key resource, it was still considered important that monitors have access to as many sources of information as possible.

The focus of the course then shifted to the "bare bones" information relevant to administering or supporting the hazardous-waste management program within the company. The instructor addressed the specific responsibilities of both the focal point and monitor, spending some time discussing how the two roles interrelated. Following a directed discussion of these roles, the instructor supplied some of the terminology used within the program. Specific attention was paid to terms required for hazardous-waste labeling. This included the 40 CFR definitions for "ignitable," "corrosive," "toxic," and "reactive" materials. The instructor led a brief open discussion of these terms to ensure that all participants had a working understanding of the meanings of these terms. The terms for the physical states of waste materials (i.e., solid, liquid, gas) were also discussed.

At this point, a Material Safety Data Sheet (MSDS) was presented to the class. Using the terms already discussed, the instructor led the class through those sections of an MSDS where information regarding the physical hazards and physical state of a material could be found. Using the MSDS, the class as a group supplied the necessary information to fill out a hazardous-waste label. Additional MSDSs were then handed out, and the participants worked individually to fill out several labels.

The intent of this activity was twofold. Correctly completing a hazardous-waste label would be something most monitors and some focal points would have to do in their job, although it would not be their sole function. The second intent of the labeling practice was to acquaint class participants with the nature of hazardous materials used at company sites and to underscore the importance of proper handling and disposal requirements. The class ended with another open discussion and questions regarding specific or anticipated problems within the participants' work areas. By brainstorming answers to these issues, class members could develop responses in the classroom and became comfortable with addressing problems many had originally considered too complex. Periodic meetings with focal points and "flowdown discussions" between focal points and monitors reinforce this training on an ongoing basis. Including a 10-minute break at midpoint in the class, total running time for this course was 3 hours.

As the hazardous-waste management program became more codified within the company, other requirements became evident or were promulgated by municipal, state, or federal agencies. In many cases, focal points and monitors were used as the key personnel to implement these requirements within a department. Again, while no specific legal stipulation for training existed to support these activities, company management decided that training was an integral component for successful completion of the activities specified by these requirements. Scenario 5 describes two of these courses.

Scenario 5

The Air Quality Management District has determined that industrial emission of volatile organic compounds (VOCs) is a substantial cause for air pollution. As a result, the district creates a requirement called

Rule 109, which states that any industrial generator of VOCs must record each use of specified materials on a daily basis and must refrain from using that material on any given day when the amount used exceeds stated limits. To ensure that these records are kept, the district will conduct periodic inspections of all VOC-emitting sites to check for completeness and accuracy of use records. Fines and penalties could be imposed if records are not available, current, or accurate.

To ensure that these records were kept and logged on a daily basis, the company designated selected individuals within each department as Rule 109 record keepers. These individuals would be tasked with recording any dispensing of VOC-emitting materials to employees and record the amount used. The record keepers would retain these files in proximity to the work area and would be trained to enter this information into the company computer system on a daily or weekly basis.

As stated above, these individuals were most often employees previously designated and trained as hazardous-waste monitors. This was a great asset in implementing training because much of the initial orientation on the use, handling, and disposal of hazardous materials and wastes could be excised from course content, and the course could focus on the skills necessary to input Rule 109 records (i.e., material identification and classification, and computer and data input skills). This reduced the total time of the course and allowed a more effective use of company resources.

The course was divided into two 2-hour components. The first half of the course dealt with Rule 109 requirements, the legislation itself, the environmental impact of the regulated materials, etc. This section of the course also focused on training the participants to use company data (materials lists, usage data records, etc.) to complete the Rule 109 form. Skills practice on using these reference materials to develop accurate Rule 109 records was also part of this half of the course. Using a series of hypothetical examples, the participants would manually fill out Rule 109 records for several different materials and situations.

The second half of the course concentrated on the computer skills necessary to input electronic data using manually generated records. Each employee was given a personal password to access the computer system. The participants would use the records they had already generated by hand and input them into the computer system. Computer security was also discussed in this section of the course.

Initially, this course ran for 4 hours on one day. While this was more efficient for the trainer and allowed for easier scheduling, it had several disadvantages:

- It required that the employee be away from the work area for half of a workday.
- It limited the time of day when the class could be held (due to company break, lunch, and shift schedules).
- The fatigue factor affected participants somewhere in the third hour, limiting course-content retention.

Through an act of "training serendipity," a scheduling mix-up required that the course be rescheduled to another day midway through one session. When the class reconvened for the second half of the class the next day, they were fresher, more alert, and more receptive to the information being presented. They also noted that, with two more hours available at their workstations, they were able to cut down on the backlog of work that accumulated in their absence. This allowed them to concentrate more on the training, since they were not as worried about what would be waiting for them when they returned to their work areas.

Because of this fortunate accident, the course was structured to be presented in two 2-hour modules on different days. This resulted in a more receptive and focused class. It ultimately also allowed for easier class scheduling, since a training room would be required for only 2 hours at a time.

Scenario 6

Federal law requires any hazardous waste being transported on a public thoroughfare (air, sea, or land) to be manifested as to content, quantity, and potential hazards. Further, other laws require that any hazardous wastes destined for disposal at a TSDF be identified in writing as to whether or not it can be disposed of in a landfill. (California state law exceeds federal law in requiring the identification of those waste materials which cannot be landfilled.) The forms used to meet these requirements—the Uniform Hazardous Waste Manifest and Land Disposal Restriction or Land Ban Form, respectively—must be filled out by the waste transporter. In most instances, this means an employee of the company. Company management determined that since these forms must be accurate, the employees filling them out must do so in an error-free manner, and training was therefore necessary. The forms also had to be signed off by a company representative responsible for the site before the waste could be transported on public thoroughfares. This required that each facility have an employee designated to sign Uniform Hazardous Waste Manifests and Land Ban Forms. Deliberately falsifying information on these documents could result in criminal penalties up to and including 3 years in prison. Every company site that was geographically separate from other company sites was assigned an identification number by the U.S. EPA.

A course was developed to first train the responsible employees, in this case company hazardous-waste transporters, to accurately complete the forms. These employees had already attended the 24-hour training and annual 8-hour refreshers mandated by 29 CFR 1910.120 discussed earlier in this chapter. The training being developed to meet this new need would build on the earlier course.

The new course introduced the transporters to the requirements for filling out the Uniform Hazardous Waste Manifest. Class participants were then instructed in the specific requirements for filling out the form: what information to provide, what the terms meant, etc. Next, using real-world situations, the transporters were given blank manifests and asked to complete them. Correct examples of each manifest would then be put on a screen using an overhead projector. Participants were asked to identify any errors made in the manifest they completed and determine why the error occurred. The final test required that each employee fill out two manifests. The manifests had to be 100 percent error-free in order for the employee to be qualified to fill out manifests for the company.

Land Ban Form training expanded on the manifest training and followed the same pattern. Using correctly completed forms as examples, trainers told the employees what information was relevant for filling out the form. The employees were asked to transfer the information to a blank form to familiarize them with the contents of each section. In this instance, six forms were used to address both federal RCRA and state of California land ban requirements.

The focal point for each outlying facility was designated as the forms signer. At the company's main plant, an environmental engineer responsible for manifest and land ban compliance was also designated to sign off on the forms. While the engineer was extremely confident in his abilities to interpret these forms and identify any errors prior to signing, the focal points at outlying facilities understandably had some apprehension. Another course was therefore developed to provide employees designated to sign these forms with the requisite skills to interpret the forms and ensure accuracy.

The training was essentially the same as that provided to the transporters. Because most of the signers were focal points and had already received initial training, a certain level of competency was expected. In no way, however, could that level be equated to that of the transporters, who received 24 hours of initial training with 8 hours of refresher training every year. Also, the transporters work with these materials on an ongoing basis, receiving direction and instruction from qualified and experienced managers and leads. As a result, an additional component not included in the transporters' training was built into the course for the signers. This training included a more in-depth discussion of the nature of and terminology used for hazardous-waste disposal and transportation.

Since theirs was not an ongoing activity and questions could always be referred to environmental management before a form was signed, qualification was not required of the signers. As a result, the time spent on testing the transporters was used to provide the in-depth discussion presented in the previous paragraph. In both cases then, the training ran approximately 2½ hours. This training satisfied the management requirement that the transporter fill out the forms in an error-free way since only qualified personnel were allowed to do so, and the focal point signers' need for understanding the forms they were signing was satisfied as well.

Classes were held at the facilities where the employees were assigned to work: at the CMS for the transporters and at a centralized outlying facility convenient for the signers. This reduced total travel time for the participants, thereby reducing the total cost of the course. Training at the worksite also increased the comfort level of many employees, allowing them to encounter unfamiliar information in a familiar location.

In the scenarios already discussed, the training was provided to meet needs of the general employee population. However, in even the most efficiently run and proactive environmental training programs, advances in company culture, site reorganization, adjustment to market and business needs, etc., create the need for specialized courses. In many cases, these can be adapted from already existing material. Sometimes, however, new ideas must be implemented. Consider the next two scenarios.

Scenario 7

Closure of a company facility in another part of the state involves the transfer of several thousand management, professional, and hourly employees to another facility. The requirements in the county where the closed facility was located are less stringent than those that apply to the facility to which the employees are being transferred. As a result, a number of experienced and valued employees, some with many years with the company, are essentially unaware of the requirements encountered at their new "home." This will involve management briefings, even to the vice presidential level. It will also involve a form of new employee orientation for many of the transferees. This training must be accomplished in a timely fashion, preferably within the transition phase. Because of the complexity of the site closure, the transition will last approximately 6 months.

Training was divided into three phases. In Phase 1, senior management transferees were briefed on the environmental requirements to be encountered at their new location. This included requirements for training, record keeping, permitting, air and water quality issues, etc. Trainers distributed a list of people to contact and presented an overview of the entire environmental management program at the facility. The focal point and monitor structure was outlined, and initial delegation of focal point authority was begun. This briefing focused on acquainting these individuals with the nature of the challenges encountered at the facility and on obtaining buy-in to the requirements of the program. Without support from this group, the rest of the program would not be effective.

In Phase 2, hourly transferees from the other facility were given Hazardous Waste Generator training in the first week at their new site. Although these employees were moving into departments already in operation at the company, their work areas were still in the process of being set up. As a result, this was one of the most cost-effective times to implement the training. Since the transferees were coming into pre-existing departments, training could be provided by the departments' own Hazardous Waste Generator trainers. Because of the sudden influx of so many additional employees, support was provided by environmental training personnel, and in some cases by generator trainers from other departments. In time, additional generator trainers were developed, often from the transferee population itself.

Phase 3 involved the additional layers of training not required by law but considered necessary to adequately perform mandated activities. Once focal points and monitors were identified within the transferee population, they received this level of training. Until that was accomplished, these duties had to be performed by employees within the department already designated and trained. Training was provided in as timely a manner as possible to reduce the now-expanded workload of these employees. Since the need for focal points and especially monitors has been fairly consistent since its inception, it was easy to schedule these employees into a class.

Rule 109 training was accomplished in a similar fashion. Transferees were scheduled into one of the ongoing classes. Until these employees were trained, record-keeping tasks were performed by previously trained personnel. Since these employees were assigned to already staffed facilities, a Hazardous Waste Manifest and Land Ban Form signer had already been designated and trained, so that training was not necessary. (Retraining on these forms is provided whenever RCRA or the state of California initiates any changes on the forms.)

Scenario 8

A company has established a policy of self-governance—a concept that empowers employees to be responsible for the activities in their work areas, including compliance with all legal, corporate, and company requirements. Policies are to be established regarding conduct of work within each department, and employees are to be responsible for enforcement of these policies themselves. To support this activity, employees are designated to perform departmental self-audits. As part of this program, the environmental inspection program is being phased out and the inspectors reassigned into other departments. Environmental inspections will now become a function of departmental self-governance. In order for the department to properly conduct these inspections, it has been determined that employees performing the inspections must be trained.

To meet this new need, a course was developed in which the participants were taught by two instructors, a representative from environmental training to provide course facilitation and question-and-answer skills, and an environmental inspector to provide subject matter expertise. The inspectors required were requested for this course from the other environmental departments to which they were assigned. In this 3-hour course, participants were trained in the legal requirements for inspection, the means to conduct an inspection, and the methods for deficiency remediation.

The first hour covered the legal requirements for inspection. Participants were also provided with inspection checklists and guides. The environmental inspector also shared his or her experiences on the shop floor and gave some tips on what to look for during an inspection.

For the second hour, the participants reconvened in a shop area. Using existing conditions, the participants conducted an environmental audit of the area. (Managers and employees in the area had been previously notified of this audit and were told that it was intended as a learning exercise, not an official audit. Managers of each area were also provided with a copy of the audit findings for reference and information purposes only.) The class was divided into two teams, supervised by the inspector and instructor, respectively. For the third hour, participants met back in the classroom. An open discussion of what deficiencies were identified and what corrective actions could be taken followed. By comparing notes between teams, participants were able to benefit from other individual experiences.

While other courses can range in size from 15 (optimal for the *Hazardous Waste Generator* class) to 30 (maximum for the *Focal Point and Monitor* class) to 100 if necessary (for *Management Environmental Briefings*), the size of this class had to be limited to 10. This allowed for two groups of five to conduct the audits. Given the nature of this exercise, a group of five is the maximum number that could be effectively facilitated by one individual, whether the inspector or the instructor. Since fewer employees could be trained at once, the class is less cost-effective than other courses and should be considered only if the situation warrants.

Summary

The issue of cost has been addressed at various points in this chapter and is likely to be one of the major issues a company faces as it seeks to comply with the training aspects of environmental regulation. Quite simply, training is expensive. It costs money to hire an instructor. Outside vendors provide Hazardous Waste Operations and Emergency Response (HAZWOPER) training on either a price-per-head basis or for a blanket rate. This usually amounts to several thousand dollars per class. If a trainer is developed within the company, additional funds must be allocated to provide instructor training and, in some cases, certification by state or federal agencies. Materials and equipment must be purchased and made available to the instructor. An additional cost of training, which is frequently forgotten, is in the simple cost of the time spent by an employee in class. Since this type of training is usually provided during the workday, productivity is lost while employees attend classes and continue to receive an hourly wage and coverage by the company benefits package, savings plan, etc.

Because training is expensive, it is important to conduct an examination of the needs of the workplace before entering into an environmental training program. Figures 9-1 and 9-2 detail the environmental training program developed by one company and provide general guidance for a company seeking a program of its own. However, no program is applicable to all companies, and cost and regulatory demands dictate a careful analysis be performed of the regulations as they apply to the specific activities performed by a company.

In order for an environmental training program to be effective, support from the top levels of management is essential. This can be a simple task in smaller companies, where the people deciding on the training to be provided are often at the top levels of management. In larger companies, cost-effectiveness, minimization of downtime, and a simple cost-benefit analysis must be considered. In a case where noncompliance with an ordinance mandating training could result in severe fines and penalties, or even jail time, the benefit of compliance usually is considered to exceed the cost of noncompliance. In a company that takes a proactive environmental stance, training can be considered an essential part of the compliance program.

10

Who Should Be Trained and How Much?

John Cornelison
Manager of Safety
America North, Inc.

In the last 10 years, we have witnessed some of history's biggest environmental disasters. Negative impacts to the environment have been accompanied, in some instances, by significant loss of life. Investigators repeatedly find that inadequate training and/or unqualified personnel are a root cause for these disasters.

Every company, regardless of the industry in which it operates, should ask some fundamental questions about the training its personnel are receiving. These questions should take into account risks as well as costs. They should be directed toward answering the key question: What training must employees have to help keep them performing their jobs safely, especially in the environmental area?

Basic Questions

Question 1: What Training Is Required by Law?

Companies must, at a minimum, provide the training required by the law. Failure to do so results in increased risk of accident as well as substantial legal penalties. As a starting point, an expert in environmental regulations should perform a systematic review of all operations to determine what regulations are applicable and what training is required. This up-front investment can be very cost-effective when compared with paying for litigation and environmental restoration of impacted environment.

Question 2: Who Should Be Trained?

For training to benefit the company and employees, and to reduce risk, training must be given to the right people. The review recommended in Question 1 will identify which work processes will require training. The next step is selecting the company personnel to receive that training. On an individual basis, the trainee should be someone who has an interest in improving his or her performance as well as the performance of the company as a whole. Sometimes a company is forced to train personnel even when the training may not benefit the company's long-term goals, because they are the only people in the positions. In this instance, when changes in assignments are made, select someone who matches future training needs.

Question 3: How Much Will the Training Cost?

Training is normally considered to be an extra, something that is desirable but not required. When measured against major risk, however, and against the direct and indirect costs of an incident, training becomes highly cost-effective. All the environmental training requirements should be considered together so that risk-based priorities can be set. It's good business to allocate resources for protecting the company against the biggest projected losses and impacts.

When all the training is considered together, it may be cheaper to have consultants provide in-house training than to send personnel away from your place of business. Most of the environmental and safety regulations require refresher or maintenance training to keep skills up to the same level as the initial training.

Question 4: Is the Training Performance-Based?

Many of today's training courses are aimed at providing information without measuring how applicable the information is to a company's operations, how much is retained by the attendees, and whether it will be useful on the job. What looks good in the advertisement may not match your requirements. When embarking on a training program for more than one person, send one of your best employees to the course for evaluation of it prior to investing large sums of money. This effort will pay big dividends in meeting requirements and protecting your training investments.

Question 5: What Sources Provide Training?

There are numerous sources for training, including universities, government agencies, private companies, and consultants. The best one is the one that exactly meets your training needs and is performance-based. Cost should not be the most important factor considered in selecting a trainer. There can be major differences in quality and content. Just because a university offers the training does not guarantee the quality and content. Be selective, question references, and request samples of their training materials.

Question 6: What Training Have Employees Already Received?

This is an important question, and it can be easily answered by conducting a survey. The survey should cover the training required to perform each job, the training received by employees to date, and the training needed to fulfill the requirements identified. In terms of the training required, this question will be answered in part by the review of regulations discussed in Question 1. However, that review may not identify all the training specific to the tasks that are performed by employees. Good records must be maintained to verify training received, scheduled, and expected for the future. The training records will be invaluable when you are requested by a government agency to verify training given to employees. It will be especially valuable if training issues arise in litigation.

Training issues are complex enough that they should not be left to chance but should be assigned to a manager for developing a companywide training plan. This will reduce costs by allowing the company to be selective in the training given and by preventing different departments or groups from having different, overlapping, or contradictory training strategies.

Training is properly viewed as one of the key elements of a company's overall risk-avoidance strategy. Different categories of risk exist in any organization and can include:

- Public and environmental safety

- Public awareness through news media or public groups

- Regulatory compliance

- Employee health and safety

- Property damage

- Resources and budget

- Schedule

- Quality

- Programmatic risks

A company must decide which risks are of primary concern and publish them so that all employees are aware of these priorities.

Training Priorities

Companies are generally most concerned about the regulations specifying that a person must be "qualified" to perform the job or task. It is sometimes unclear what "qualified" means in this context. In practice, it means that if the employee fails to execute his or her job or task correctly, the authorities will first look to see if the employee was qualified or trained and, if not, why the employee was not qualified or trained. In many cases the two are linked together. When personnel in a position change, or when personnel are transferred to new positions, it is safe to assume that they will automatically need some additional training. Company personnel and training groups should be sensitive to the new training requirements.

The following risk-based decision process for selecting which training should be given first can assist management in making the right decision. There are five major training dimensions which are based on the level of potential loss or impact. As shown below, levels of priority can be assigned within each of these dimensions:

Training Priority

High for training required for job or task

Medium for training that improves job performance

Low for training that is not required but desirable

Training Frequency

Required for each task

Required daily

Required weekly

Required monthly

Required biannually

Required annually

Certification Priority

Expert

Engineer

Consultant

Company representative

Safety professional

School

Company trainer

Line trainer

Certification Priority

License for legal requirements

Certification for regulatory requirements

Certificate for verifying attendance

Attendance with no verification

Independent Review and Verification

Safety review for highest-priority training

Quality assurance review for medium-priority training

Supervisor review for low-priority training

Foreperson review for attendance only

Typically, management is faced with too many training decisions and with no method to assist them in making the right decision. The form provided in Fig. 10-1 can be used to systematically analyze training needs. The information on the form can and should be revised to reflect the constraints and risk facing a company's operations.

Training Justification

There are many justifications for training. As previously discussed, some training is required by law. Training may also be required in order for an employee to correctly perform his or her job. Training may also be justified by the need to reduce risk in the event that an incident occurs. The following examples relate to the more important reasons for training.

Example 1

A contractor working for a government agency was managing and operating a hazardous-waste storage site. A new shipment of drums containing hazardous waste was received and off-loaded into a temporary warehouse. Several days later a forklift operator was assigned to move the drums to the permanent burial site. In the process of moving the drums, the operator poked a hole in one drum with a forklift tine. The operator saw it and took no action to stop the leak. The drum was moved to the burial site and covered up.

One month later the contamination was discovered during a routine survey. In the meantime, contamination migrated throughout the site. If the leak had been corrected when it occurred, it might have cost $2000, but it was not, and cleanup costs exceeded $1 million. The follow-up investigation identified lack of training as a major contributor to the incident. There was no training on spill response for operators and no training to reinforce management's concern that all leaks be reported immediately.

RISK-BASED DECISION PROCESS FOR DEVELOPING SAFETY TRAINING

Item of Training	Assign Loss Priority	Assign Training Priority	Assign Training Frequency Priority	Assign Trainer Priority	Assign Certification Priority	Assign Independent Review & Verification
	Loss Type	Training Priority	Training Frequency	Trainer Priority	Certification Priority	Independent Review & Verification
MOST SERIOUS	Loss of Life	High (Required for Task/Job)	Each Task	Expert	License	Safety
	Serious Injury		Daily	Engineer	Certification	Quality Assurance
	Environment		Weekly	Consultant	Certificate	Supervisor
	Damage to Property	Medium (Improves Job Performance)	Monthly	Company Rep	Attendance	Foreman
	Project Delay		Biannually	Safety Pro		
	Dollar Loss		Annually	School		
		Low (Not Required but Desirable)	(Note number of training hours required)	Company Trainer		
LEAST SERIOUS				Line Trainer		

Figure 10-1. Analysis of training needs.

153

Training can be extremely cost-effective when compared with the cost of environmental cleanup. An important aspect of training is to convince every person to stop when something goes wrong and report it immediately. Regular reinforced training would have motivated the forklift operator to report the incident. An operator who understood that the company placed a higher priority on cleaning up leaks than on blaming employees for errors would have been more likely to report the incident.

Example 2

A company specialized in remediation of soils contaminated by underground storage tanks (UST). The first phase of work at an open excavation involved using a photoionization detector to sample soils for hydrocarbon contamination levels. The members of the sampling crew were experts in determining levels of contamination and the use of sampling instruments. However, they were exposing themselves to a far greater risk from the vertical walls of the excavation, which were not properly reinforced and could have instantly caused several fatalities.

In this case it is obvious that the expert sampling crew was not trained in the safety requirements for excavations. The excavation safety requirements are far more important from the risk standpoint then the level of soil contamination. It is relatively inexpensive to excavate and remove more soil. Life cannot be replaced, although it may be partially compensated for with a jury award in the multimillion-dollar range.

An important aspect of training is not to become so involved with the environmental requirements that all other aspects of the job are forgotten or overlooked.

Example 3

ABC company sent 20 people for training at a Hazardous Waste Operations 40-hour General Site Worker course. A local training company was selected based on price. Two months later the state OSHA shut down the training company for not meeting training requirements. All the people trained at ABC company had to be retrained by another company. The additional costs incurred by ABC included not only the additional training but also the employees' time away from the job.

Given the magnitude of risk and the potential for litigation, training is not one of the areas in which to save money. It sounds better to the jury to say that the company provided the best training available than to say that no training was provided or it was marginal. This does not mean it has to be gold-plated but rather that a reputable firm should be chosen and that careful attention should be paid to the completeness and appropriateness of the training received.

A good place to spend money is on training of special teams or expert teams. Select the best people and use them to train other people in your company.

Some companies send their top management to all types of training and expect top management to train the bottom-level workers. This approach is a poor investment. The quality of training is greatly reduced and the workers may not be qualified on all aspects of their job. Send the right people the first time.

If your company has the option, hire highly qualified personnel. This may mean paying top salaries, but the cost of training may cost two to four times the extra salary. In the meantime, the highly qualified person can be performing at peak level instead of in a learning mode. In today's environment, highly qualified personnel can help keep the company out of trouble, which has an intrinsic value beyond salaries.

Focus: Hazardous Waste Operations Training

Hazardous Waste Operations (HAZWOPER) training is one of the most common environmental requirements for workers. Careful attention should be paid to exactly what levels of training employees need. The following is a brief summary of the HAZWOPER courses.

Before you spend between $600 and $900 per worker for a 40-Hour General Site Worker course, stop and ask yourself if such a course is really needed. Unless your workers are in the hazardous-waste remediation business, chances are the most training you're going to need is the 24-Hour Hazardous Materials Technician course.

The Hazardous Materials Technician course enables workers to keep minor spills, leaks, and hazardous material releases from threatening the company's resources, building, inventory, personnel, and real estate. Workers trained to this level of emergency response can take "aggressive" actions such as plugging and patching drums or containers, repositioning leaking containers to minimize the volume of release, and doing minor cleaning up with absorbent pads, and booms. These workers are trained to recognize the magnitude of the risk to life and property. They are familiar with the proper selection of personal protective equipment, respirators, protective suits, gloves, and boots. Training includes the use of basic air-monitoring instruments to check for oxygen content, the presence of explosive atmospheres, and the concentration in parts per million of potential atmospheric contaminants.

Generally, most small businesses need a couple of teams of their workers trained to the Hazardous Materials Technician level. Between three and five workers on a team should be sufficient. If a business has hazardous materials on site in quantities greater than 1000 gallons, the company probably needs to outline in its spill-prevention control and countermeasures plan that a contracted off-site company will be brought in to remediate large spills. Rarely does it pay for companies to have in-house, 40-hour trained general site workers; contract this work out to the professionals.

As for other levels of HAZWOPER training, it's probably a very good idea to have your entire work force receive the First Responder Awareness level training. This training demonstrates that the employer has done the responsible thing for its workers. The payoff here is that the workers will know how to recognize a potentially hazardous situation and what to do to implement the company emergency notification system. This may save lives and property.

If all workers are trained to the First Responder Awareness level, a select group should receive First Responder Operations Level training. The operations-level workers might be the engineering and maintenance workers, plant security personnel, or perhaps the shop stewards or forepersons. The First Responder Operations level workers know defensive actions when spills occur. They know which adsorbents, pads, and booms to select and how to emplace these devices quickly and then evacuate personnel from the area and initiate the company spill response plan. Remember, no cleanup or other aggressive actions should be performed by these workers. It is the Hazardous Materials Technician who will respond to spills or releases. The technician has the appropriate training and equipment to handle small spills and release of hazardous materials.

The HAZWOPER regulation outlines the Hazardous Materials Specialist level training. Who should take this level of training? Usually, company safety personnel are the best candidates for this training. The safety personnel are already familiar with those requirements for hearing, eye, and foot protection and they probably have written the company safety plan. The role of the Hazardous Materials Specialist is to advise the Hazardous Materials Technician. In fulfilling this role, the specialist is intimately familiar with protective clothing ensembles and respirators (both air-purifying and supplied-air type) and has had an active role assessing the company's hazardous-materials inventory. The specialist compiles a list of needed spill response supplies, personal protection clothing, air-monitoring equipment, and containment and control supplies and drafts the company spill-prevention, control, and countermeasure plan. The training the Hazardous Materials Specialist receives in the 24-hour course addresses these responsibilities and actions. The specialist must also have the general skills the technician has to be able to act in this capacity.

The On-Scene Incident Commander level training should be completed by your superintendent, chief of operations, or head man or woman in charge. The objective here is to have a command center with one person in charge. This structure must ensure that your company can control this spill or release. The theory behind an incident command system is to have dedicated teams of workers responsible for operations, logistics, plans, and finance during the incident. With definite roles each worker is to perform and an incident commander in charge, the likelihood is good that a company can minimize the impact of spills or releases and recognize when outside agencies or assistance is required. The incident command system is a tested and proven system for emergency response.

11

Influencing the Legislative Process

Hank Martin
Vice President and Managing Principal Engineer
McLaren-Hart Environmental Engineering

For a number of years a small company located near what is now Giants Stadium in New Jersey operated a chemical manufacturing plant and, in the course of doing so, discharged to the site large quantities of mercury. As land values soared, it became apparent to the company that its single greatest asset was the value of its land, and the plant site was sold to a developer. The one problem: No disclosure was made to the buyer of the 500,000 pounds of mercury that also came with the land. The developer realized that no one really wanted to live or work on a mercury disposal site and demanded that the seller clean up the property. The seller, citing the "caveat emptor" (buyer suck eggs) rule of real estate, declined. After years of litigation concerning who was responsible for cleanup, the New Jersey State Supreme Court in the landmark case of *State v. Ventron* ruled that the previous owner, Ventron, should bear the liability for the cleanup.

Of course, the seller of an industrial property in New Jersey is liable for cleanup, you say. Doesn't New Jersey's Environmental Cleanup and Responsibility Act (ECRA) require it? The answer is that without the Ventron case there might never have been ECRA.

The Ventron case occurred at a time when there were no well-defined liability standards, and before environmental audits became as common as termite inspections. The case identified a problem— buyer-seller litigation over cleanup liability could seriously delay implementation of a cleanup—and ECRA became the solution, stating in essence that a seller must obtain some form of state approval before the sale could proceed.

This bit of regulatory trivia illustrates one of the basic fundamentals of public policy, and is particularly true in environmental policy: In almost every case, legislation and regulation is proposed in response to a real or perceived problem. Examples can be found at every level of government. Love Canal and Superfund, Bhopal and SARA Title III, and the above example are merely a few of the cause-and-effect relationships between a problem and the legislated or regulated solution.

This basic premise—that environmental policy results from a multitude of responses to a variety of problems—explains to some extent the general lack of coordination between major environmental protection programs. It also suggests why there has been so much new legislation and regulation in the last decade and a half. Solutions have been proposed and adopted to address a myriad of problems, from leaking underground storage tanks to catastrophic releases of toxic materials. In the absence of broader environmental goals or policy, these individual solutions often gain a life of their own and their passage becomes a high priority for their sponsors.

Given this situation, the best way an individual can influence environmental policy is to become involved in solving a problem—in making one's voice heard in the decision-making process. But influencing the outcome of a decision-making process can be difficult at best, and is impossible without an understanding of the process itself. In addition to knowing the process, it is also important to understand the role played by the professionals involved in the process, the way in which decision makers view the world, and the ways in which a position or opinion on a particular issue can be best brought to the attention of decision makers.

Understanding the Process: Civics 101 vs. Reality

As every child in America who has passed fifth grade is aware, our government is composed of three branches: legislative, executive, and judicial. At the federal level, these branches are Congress, the President, and the Supreme Court. At the state level, these are the state legislatures, governors, and state courts. At the federal level, and in most states, the legislative branch is further divided into two houses, typically a senate or "upper" house and an assembly or "lower" house. This is known as a bicameral legislature.

The process by which laws are made is also a familiar one. "How a bill becomes law," the version taught in the classroom, goes something like this:

- A bill, or someone's proposed law, is introduced in one of the two legislative houses. After a period of time for review, it is heard by a committee consisting of fellow legislators concerned with the policy aspects of the bill. At this time the public has an opportunity to comment on the bill. The committee may reject or approve the bill in its original form or in a modified (amended) version.

- If approved, the bill is then heard by a committee also composed of legislators who are concerned with the financial implications of the bill. Again, the public is provided an opportunity to comment. This fiscal committee may also reject, approve, or amend the bill.

- If approved by both the policy and fiscal committees in its house of origin, the bill will then be heard and voted on by all members of the house of origin. Again, the bill may be rejected, approved, or amended. There is no opportunity for public comment at this stage.

- A bill passed by its house of origin must then go to the other house, where the process is repeated. It must go through both policy and fiscal committee review and, if passed, a vote by all members of the second house.

- At this time, if the bill is still "alive," any differences in the versions of the bill passed by each house will be reconciled in a two-house conference committee. The agreed-upon versions are then voted on again by each house and the final version is sent to the President (at the federal level) or the governor (at the state level) for signature. The bill may be vetoed, signed, or allowed to become law without signature.

This process, as described above, conjures visions of politicians carefully weighing issues and listening intently to the opinions of their constituents on matters of great import. Does this really happen? Well, almost.

The reality of the situation is that the above process forms the framework under which decisions on major policy items are made but does not account for three major factors:

1. The influence of special interests
2. The role of legislative staff.
3. Party politics and the reelection process

Each of these factors in its own way dramatically affects the process as we learned it in grade school and serves to create an extremely complex system that is generally closed to those without the correct credentials or constituency. This process, as opposed to the one described previously, generally goes something like this:

- A bill is sponsored by a special interest group or other affected interest, such as a regulatory agency. The bill may be intended to right a perceived wrong, solve a perceived problem, or benefit a group or groups. The bill is introduced, and supporters and opponents begin their respective campaigns to either pass or defeat the proposal.

- Well before the first hearing on a bill, discussions between the author and his or her staff, and proponents and opponents of a measure begin. Many times, differences between the interest groups can be resolved at this stage and the bill, after amendment to address the concerns of the various interest groups, will begin a relatively uneventful journey toward eventual passage.

- Where consensus cannot be reached through early discussions and negotiation, the real process begins. Proponents begin to line up support for the measure, typically by dramatizing the seriousness of the problem they are attempting to solve, while opponents look for allies by describing the dire consequences of passage of the bill.

- Members and staff of the committee hearing the bill are visited by the bill's proponents and opponents, who, depending on their perspective, describe the wonderful things the bill will accomplish or the terrible pain and injustice it will inflict. Attempts are made by both sides to obtain commitments on how an individual will vote. A frequent conversation between representatives of interest groups concerns how the vote appears to be shaping up.

- The "lobbying" intensifies the day of the committee vote, with uncommitted members receiving additional attention. Meetings between interest groups, the author, and staff continue. If the bill in question is particularly important, the outcome of the hearing may be determined prior to its beginning. Both sides know how to "count," as in votes, and neither will usually fight a major battle it is destined to lose. Thus, if a bill appears, based on prehearing discussions, to be headed for passage, they will make a token opposition and look for another opportunity to stop or revise the measure. Many lobbyists have stated that, "If you don't know the vote before the start of the hearing, you're not doing your job."

- The fiscal committee is more of the same, except with all bills with any fiscal implications being considered, members rely even more heavily on the analyses and opinions prepared by their staff and the information provided by interest groups.

- If a measure makes it as far as the floor of its house of origin, it most likely will be approved. This is not necessarily due to the fact that the major issues have been addressed but rather a more practical consideration in that mounting an effective opposition movement is much more difficult when it must include all members of a house rather than only a few committee members.

- Following passage from the floor of the house of origin, the process begins again in the second house. Typically, the going gets some-what rougher for the measure since members of the second house can feel free to vote against a measure without fear of offending a close colleague. Knowing this, most authors now get very serious about the negotiations on the various provisions in their bills. For this reason, if one looks at many of the major pieces of legislation which are passed in the various state houses or at the federal level, a general trend of seeing most major changes after the bill passes its house of origin will be evident.

- Once a measure has made it through its house of origin and through the second house, an extremely interesting situation will typically be seen: The bill passed by the second house looks very little like the one passing the house of origin. For this purpose the conference committee was created.

- The conference committee is a beast whose nominal role in the process is to iron out the differences between the two versions of the measure passed by the two houses. And, in general, that is what they do. There are times, however, when the measure approved by the conference committee contains items not in either of the two bills it is trying to address. The last-minute agreements often find a conference committee in which to insert themselves.

- The beauty of the conference committee is that once a measure is reported out, it only has to pass the floors of the two houses in order to be sent to the executive branch for signature. No policy or fiscal committees are required. Since, in general, most conference committees are by their nature last-minute forums for compromise, there is often little time for detailed analysis. Thus it is very rare for an approved conference committee report to be voted down on the floor.

- Finally, the bill is sent to the governor (at the state level) or the President (at the federal level) for signature. In the Civics 101 version of the story, the President (or governor) now quietly contemplates his or her decision on the issue at hand. However, in the real world, since this is the final step in the process and the one that ultimately determines whether the measure lives or dies, the pressure from both the proponents and the opponents intensifies.

- In 1991, Governor Wilson of California faced a decision on the passage of a bill providing for protection from discrimination based on sexual orientation. The lobbying for and against the bill became a story unto itself, with demonstrations, promises, and threats by all sides. So much for quiet contemplation.

In summary, the real process is much more of a continuum of negotiation and persuasion, rather than the series of finite decision points that is typically taught in government class. The stakes are high and those with interests in the outcome utilize every moment to ensure that the outcome is most beneficial to their cause.

Politicians as People

It is often easy to forget that elected officials are human and possess the same attributes and failings as other individuals. This is particularly true when the papers report the more blatant abuses of the position, such as free use of government aircraft by the President's chief of staff and the cashing of bad checks at Congress' own bank.

Despite these testaments to the lack of reality in high political circles, it is a fact that most did not start out as politicians (although a greater number of career politicians are now being seen) and once had a "real" job. Most entered politics with truly admirable goals and have a genuine desire to do the "right" thing. All have friends and family who are important to them. Finally, as a group, most of our elected officials are generally well educated and are extremely capable communicators.

Given an ambitious and laudatory beginning, what happens after election to our elected officials to create the headlines that become more common each day? The answer to this question is an important consideration as one begins to investigate the process of influencing the legislative decision-making process.

After election, these individuals find themselves in a position in which the demands of their role create priorities and perceptions which differ radically from those of the average person on the street. Among the factors that color the way in which a legislator will view the world around him or her:

- The need to deal with and make decisions on a vast array of issues, from interstate banking to criminal justice to environmental affairs to insurance reform, which they, like you and me, cannot be experts on

- A constant demand for their time and favor

- A general detachment from their constituency, due to the need to spend large amounts of time in a state or federal capital.

- The ever-present specter of the next election

- A continuous reinforcement of the importance of the office, and therefore the individual, by supporters, special interests, and others

The result of the new set of circumstances is the creation, in all but the most resistant, of strains of the "beltway mentality." This insidious disease is marked by a number of symptoms, easily recognizable once one begins to look. These include:

- An increasing belief that the universe revolves around the actions in the capital and that the sun really does rise and set at their doorstep

- A decreasing trust in those from the outside and not part of the process, based on the perception (which is generally true) that everybody wants something

- The emergence of maintaining the position as the top priority in life, since "I can't do any good unless I'm here"

- A growing perception that many of the general rules of conduct are inapplicable to their actions, because of the import of their duties

The disease is as subtle as it is relentless. Most are not even aware that they have been infected. But, given the pressures, demands, and altered perceptions of the world, it is more a wonder that anyone can resist for any length of time (do I hear a call for term limits?) than it is that anyone succumbs.

What these factors translate to in terms of influencing the process is the more obvious conclusion that only "insiders" are really effective on an ongoing basis, and the not so obvious one that given a high-visibility issue, such as environmental protection, reelection requirements demand some sort of action.

Special Interest Groups: Why Are They So Special?

Did you know that in the state of California if a firefighter contracts cancer, and it can be demonstrated that he or she was exposed in the course of duty to a carcinogenic substance, there is a presumption for the purposes of worker's compensation that the illness is occupational? Were you aware that even in the face of billion-dollar-plus deficits in 1991, New York City teachers received pay raises averaging 5 to 10 percent? What about the fact that New Jersey has two different forms of automobile insurance, one that allows the holder the ability in the case of an accident to receive pain and suffering damages, while the other, and somewhat cheaper, version allows only actual damages?

What do California firefighters, New York City teachers, and New Jersey lawyers and insurance companies have in common with doctors, senior citizens, environmental groups, and real estate agents everywhere? Each represents a very powerful special interest group.

Contrary to popular belief, the term special interest does not only apply to the "usual suspects" such as big oil, banks, and the National Rifle Association. Rather, special interests can be found in the most unlikely of places, such as the environmental groups identified above, churches, homeless advocates, and the SPCA. Any group with an issue for which it wishes to see governmental action is in fact a special interest.

This is not to suggest that special interests should not pursue their individual agendas. To the contrary; without the participation of these groups with a vested interest in the passage or rejection of various proposals, many of the good ideas for solutions to problems would not be identified, and the level of effort needed to mold these ideas into workable laws would not be put forth.

Special interest groups serve as one of the primary sources of information for decision makers. Although, as would be expected, interest groups provide the information that best suits their position on a particular issue, the aggregate effect of all sides to an issue providing exhaustive analyses of the good and bad on a given issue is an understanding of the issue which would not have been achieved with only a third-party review.

Take, for example, the issue of regulating underground tanks used to store hazardous materials. There is undeniable evidence that some tanks have leaked and contaminated soils and groundwater. Should all underground tanks be banned? Should all existing tanks be immediately removed? Who is going to oversee all of this? Who is going to pay for all of this?

When faced with these questions in 1984, the state of California found that there were more opinions on the "right" way to solve this tank problem than there were tanks. Local government, as local government is known to do, wanted autonomy to do whatever it saw fit. State government wanted control of the program but wanted local government to do the dirty work. Environmental groups wanted a strong state standard with the ability for local governments to get tougher. Oil companies wanted special provisions for tanks at service stations. Others just wanted the problem to go away.

In the center of the storm was the author of the measure, a junior assemblyman from California's Silicon Valley, where many serious groundwater problems had been linked to leaking tanks. Representing a constituency consisting of all the identified interest groups, his responsibility was to craft a program which solved the problem but which was not so overly onerous as to severely affect the ability of the area's major industries to continue in business.

In a textbook example of how special interest groups can be used to develop acceptable, if not actually good, public policy, the author utilized the resources of each of the groups to develop a program which, some 7 years later, is still functioning relatively smoothly. Compromises were reached on how authority for program implementation would be split between state and local agencies. Modifications to compliance time lines were included. Special procedures for addressing the thousands of gasoline and diesel fuel tanks were provided.

It is doubtful that, without the participation of the many groups involved in the development of the program, as workable a solution to a real problem could have been obtained. The usefulness of special interest participation is demonstrated over and over as complex issues and problems are addressed in public policy decisions.

What is it that these groups provide? The answer is specialized expertise and a unique perspective on the implications of a proposed measure. In the above example, only local governments could know the issues concerning funding and management of the program. Likewise, those involved with underground tanks on a day-to-day basis were best prepared to present the difficulties of implementing some of the proposed actions.

Special interest groups, because of the potential economic implications of some of the proposed policy measures, can also dedicate substantially more resources to researching issues than can legislative bodies. The information generated by these groups is often the only real data available upon which to base important policy decisions.

Finally, and most importantly, special interest groups represent real constituencies. Teachers, doctors, firefighters, policemen, and even labor unions and oil companies are part of the American landscape and, within our process of policy development, have a right to make their views known. So, even though the general perception of special interest groups is that they exert too much influence on policy development, consider that those making the claims are usually also special interests and that one group's idea of undue influence is another's idea of how the democratic process functions.

Arguing the Point: What Works, and What Doesn't

As discussed previously, it is a general premise of the public policy process that a given law or regulation is a solution proposed in response to a problem. Whether it is an environmental problem, a problem with crime in the streets, or a state budget problem, each and every proposed law or regulation is designed to solve a real or perceived concern.

Since most of the major pieces of legislation result in a choosing of sides between support and opposition, it can be generally assumed that there must be a reason for the opposition. Looking at the types of arguments made against proposed measures, they can be put into three simplistic categories. These are:

1. It's not a problem.
2. It's not the right solution; and, as a corollary to number 2,
3. The solution is worse than the problem.

Each of these arguments is used every day in Washington, at various state houses, or before regulatory bodies. Each argument can be made on every issue; the key is knowing when to use the right argument.

The "it's not a problem" argument is often the initial reaction to most proposals. It is frequently the easiest to voice and requires the least amount of consideration of the other side's perspective. It is also the argument least likely to be listened to and is the one most difficult to make convincingly.

If one again considers the basic premise that all proposals are intended to address somebody's idea of a problem, and realizes how difficult it is to bring a perceived problem to the attention of a regulatory or legislative body, then a logical, and practical, assessment is that enough people consider the issue to be a problem to make this an unworkable argument. In "realpolitik" terms, it will matter little how correct the no-problem position is if enough people perceive a problem to exist. The argument can be used, however, as an initial position from which to negotiate, or in conjunction with other arguments to successfully address a proposed initiative.

An example of this can be seen in an issue which came to light in the mid-1980s. Claims began to be made that the use of plastic pipe for drinking water systems resulted in the leaching of organic chemicals into the water and created a threat to the public health. As can be imagined, plastic pipe manufacturers took issue with this and flatly asserted that this was not true and that the driving forces behind the argument were metal pipe manufacturers, for obvious reasons, and plumbers' unions, because it took less time to assemble plastic pipe and their members were losing work.

This position, as meritorious as it may have been from the perspective of the plastic pipe manufacturers, was not, from a strategic point of view, going to win the day. A strong constituency did exist which claimed that there was a problem (and yes, plumbers' unions and metal pipe manufacturers were part of that constituency). In addition, enough sympathy for this position had been generated to effectively eliminate the plastic pipe manufacturers' ability to merely argue that it wasn't a problem.

Recognizing this fact of life, the group modified its approach to one of advocating additional research on the subject to determine whether in fact a problem did or did not exist. This approach was acceptable; it demonstrated adequate concern on the part of the manufacturers to look further into the issue, and gave the decision makers an acceptable course of action to approve.

The "it's not the right solution" argument is both the most difficult to construct and the most effective when posed correctly. It is particularly difficult in the corporate world because inherently by admitting that a problem exists, one becomes committed to buying into a solution. When faced with the decision of returning to management and saying "I fought all I could, but look what those ____ politicians did," or "I've come up with a compromise solution that will only cost $$$," the safest position is often the former.

The safest position, however, is often not the smartest. As a wise man once said, "I know enough not to stand in front of a speeding freight train." Environmental policy measures are frequently the legislative version of a freight train. Rather than trying to stop the train, it is wiser to try to have some influence—or, to complete the analogy, to send the train to a more favorable destination.

Take, for example, a bill in New Jersey in 1990 mandating that industry in the state implement programs to minimize their generation of hazardous waste. The safest position would have been to cry that there was in fact no problem and that the business community had already begun these programs. In all probability, the measure would have passed and would have contained extremely onerous penalty provisions, mandatory reduction goals, and direct governmental involvement in process and operational changes. Instead, bowing to the inevitable, the business community worked within the process to identify real operational and logistical problems and solve them. The outcome was a measure which, although not something the business community would have asked for, was livable.

Again, the approach of developing and proposing an alternative solution to the identified problem is one which will not always bring favor with others who would just like to see the thing go away. However, when the problems are real, or are very visible in the public's eye, and a legislative solution appears inevitable, it is the prudent, and responsible, approach.

Working within the Process: Options for Success

How do individuals make their views known on an issue of concern? Does a phone call to a local assemblyperson or senator do the job?

To answer this, consider four points made earlier:

1. Each decision maker faces literally hundreds of measures per year and is often unable to give detailed attention to specific measures.
2. "Special interest" representatives are constantly involved in making their views on key issues known.
3. The process, while not necessarily closed, is one where those who are a part of the network have access to and sometimes the trust of decision makers.
4. Much of the actual work done on a day-to-day basis is not public.

On the surface, these facts seem to indicate that it is extremely difficult, if not impossible, for an individual to have any real effect on the decisions made on major environmental issues. Without "portfolio," an individual and his or her opinions would appear to carry little weight. The key is in obtaining access to the ongoing activities within the decision-making process.

Trade associations are by far the most common avenue for most business groups to make known their opinions on important policy matters. From chambers of commerce representing a wide range of businesses to associations representing a narrow niche of businesses and interests, if a business provides a product or a service, there is likely to be a group to represent their interests.

There are distinct advantages and disadvantages associated with the use of trade groups. The most obvious advantage is that a trade group speaks for a number of businesses and as such will generally be viewed by decision makers as reflecting the opinion of those businesses. One disadvantage is that any position taken by a trade group will likely be one that reflects a consensus of the entire membership and therefore may suffer the "least common denominator" disease. That is, only plain vanilla positions will be agreed upon by the entire membership.

Other advantages to trade groups are their ability to address many issues with a relatively knowledgeable staff. As discussed previously, a wide range of issues will arise in the course of a year and it is doubtful that any one individual can be an expert on all of them. Most trade groups maintain a staff with expertise in a number of policy areas. And, since a number of companies support an association, the resource commitment required of the individual member business will be limited.

Another method of gaining access to the system is to hire a professional lobbyist. Lobbyists provide the capability for a single firm to make its interests known and to participate in policy development. An advantage to the use of a lobbyist is that the individual or firm will be responsive to the individual needs of the client and will not be constrained by the need to reach agreement on an issue among a group, as is the case in a trade group. Individual lobbyists will be more responsive on issues which may affect only their client, while trade groups may be more interested in issues of broader application.

A disadvantage to this alternative is that, in general, lobbyists are expert in the process and not in technical issues. Without strong technical support from the client, it is highly unlikely that the full benefit of lobbying will be obtained. For example, few professional lobbyists are fully knowledgeable concerning all the issues that a major oil or aerospace firm may face in the course of a legislative session. Yet it is usually not practical for a company to hire one lobbyist to work on tax, another on the environment, and yet another on labor-management issues (although specialists are sometimes utilized). Rather, the lobbyist will be hired for access, credibility, and knowledge of the process, and experts within the company will be called on to provide the lobbyist with guidance.

A final alternative is to commit an employee to serve as the company's lobbyist. There are many advantages to this approach in that the employee will likely know the company and its operations and management and will be responsive to only one client, the company itself.

The disadvantages are cost, access, and consistency. An office in a capital city costs money for rent, salaries, benefits, and expenses. A small operation can easily run well over $100,000 per year, a figure which likely won't hurt any of the Fortune 100 but makes this option out of the question for most midsized to small companies. In addition, the individual selected by the company to perform this function, unless hired from inside the political system, will have a substantial amount of catching up to do in order to be fully effective. Finally, most employees look at career paths and are not likely to remain in the position until the day they retire. Therefore, it is probable that there will be a significant amount of turnover in the position.

Regardless of the option chosen, it is critical to realize that value obtained from trade associations, lobbyists, and even internal personnel will only be as great as the effort made to utilize them effectively. For example, merely attending a trade group meeting on an infrequent basis, or when you need something from them, will not be particularly effective. Likewise, the best lobbyist will not be able to represent the interests of his or her employer unless adequate guidance is provided.

Can One Voice Make a Difference?

The surprising answer to this question is yes. As ironic as it may seem, the very same factors which would argue against individual influence—the generally closed nature of the process, the influence of insiders, and the ivory tower mentality of which most elected officials are accused—create demand for ideas and concepts from the outside. The issues are complex, and often there is an information vacuum that can only be filled by someone from outside the process.

The important factors in making a difference can be summarized in three simple guidelines:

1. Understand the realities of the process and allow the professionals within the process to do what they do best: Provide counsel on possible strategies, obtain access, and deliver the message.
2. Recognize that, to someone somewhere, the problem for which a solution has been proposed is real. Be reasonable in addressing the issues and, if a solution is needed, look for the one least painful to you and your company.
3. Understand that regardless of the effort and appropriateness of the actions taken, there is no certainty that factors beyond your control will not determine the outcome of a particular measure or issue.

Finally, those frustrated with the inefficiencies of our system should remember the words of Winston Churchill:

> Indeed, it has been said that democracy is the worst form of government except all those other forms that have been tried from time to time.

12

Environmental Regulation: A View from the Legislature

The Honorable Cathie Wright
California State Senate

As most people in business and industry know, the state of California leads the nation in programs to protect the environment. This distinction comes a result of a decade-long effort to create a regulatory structure that prevents the wanton destruction of our land, sea, and air, and to protect the lives and lifestyles of our citizens. As a member of the State Assembly for many years, and currently as a State Senator, I have taken part in these efforts, which no doubt have benefited California and have blazed the trail for other states in the years to come.

But just as California has been the first to take on the environmental challenge, it is the first to see the negative effects of significant environmental legislation on the business community. This issue has emerged as a priority in recent years, as the national recession persisted and California absorbed the effects of defense cuts and other impacts on its economic health. State legislatures are charged with protecting the well-being of their citizens in all respects—not just their health, and not just their pocketbooks. This chapter outlines how one state legislator sees this balancing act is working out, highlighting some notable successes—and failures.

The Education of a State Official

I guess the best way to start is with a little background on how I got involved with toxic legislation. From 1978 to 1980, I sat on the City Council of the city of Simi Valley in Ventura County, California. At that time, the city was a member of the Ventura Regional Sanitation District. Those of us on the council believed—as we had every reason to—that we were handling the toxic and hazardous waste problem very efficiently and certainly in tune with what was the state of the art at the time.

We oversaw the Simi Valley landfill, which at the time was a Class 2 dumpsite. Strenuous measures were taken to ensure that any materials believed to be hazardous waste would not come into the landfill as a mix of the household garbage brought in by the haulers. We limited the times that suspected hazardous materials could be brought into the facility. Such materials were accepted for several hours a day on only two days of the week. We required that a hazardous-waste manifest be submitted to us before the waste was delivered to the site. We made sure that, upon inspection, the items listed on the manifest were the same items received at the site. We ensured that the waste was immediately taken to a far end of the site and disposed of in an acceptable manner.

In the early 1980s, through discovery and investigation, and due to fears expressed by members of the community, the portion of the landfill that was designated for toxic and hazardous waste was closed. Later in that same decade, the landfill was sold to private industry and now accepts only household waste. This was my first lesson in the complexities of toxic and hazardous waste. It taught me about the business of waste disposal and the demands that are placed on those responsible for handling hazardous materials. It also showed me that even aggressive compliance efforts may not protect a business if environmentalists and public opinion are opposed.

I came to the California State Legislature in 1980. At the beginning of the session in January 1981, a committee was established to deal with the issues of environmental programs and toxic waste. I joined the committee and served on it for the next 12 years. In that time I have seen changes, not the least of which has been a vast increase in the volume of legislation directed at environmental problems. Appendix A provides a summary of the legislation introduced in just a single session of the California Legislature. Unfortunately, not all of the legislation has been based entirely on scientific data. In many instances it has been what I would call a knee-jerk response to the fears that environmentalists have built up in our communities. The compound effect over 12 years is that the members of our business community, not to mention our citizens in general, are entirely confused and highly skeptical as to whether or not we are protecting them from dangerous substances.

In some ways, the problem lies in technology. Methods of measuring environmental hazards are so much more refined than they were 12 years ago. As a result, we now hold businesses and companies responsible for contamination that could not have been accurately detected or analyzed in the past. Even worse, companies find themselves liable for damage that occurred 20 or 30 years ago when, in some instances, they were simply following the mandates of government and were using state-of-the-art practices for that era. The legislation I have carried has attempted to reach a balance between what is necessary to preserve life, lifestyle, and jobs, and yet protect the environment and our people from environmental hazards.

Environment vs. Economy

I'll give you one example that I thought was extremely interesting—peanut butter. I think there are few mothers in the United States who haven't raised their children on peanut-butter-and-jelly sandwiches. Yet peanut butter could be considered a natural carcinogen because of how peanuts grow (that is, underground) and because of the materials they absorb as they grow. So, are we to outlaw peanut butter? Are we to outlaw peanut farming? Are we to say that people can no longer eat peanuts? Legislation could take many forms, and some laws will harm one class of citizens without benefiting anyone else. In environmental legislation, as in medicine, the strongest remedy is not always the best remedy, and in fact it is sometimes more harmful than the original problem itself.

In reality, what we should be looking at is: What volume of peanut butter does someone have to eat for it to endanger his or her health? I think the same logic applies when we talk about pesticides. We should be aware of exactly how much of a substance our body can be exposed to before it becomes a danger.

Much legislation has been directed at restricting what a farmer can do in raising crops. Today, California produce is considered among the finest, if not the finest, in the world. Our environmental friends contend that vegetables and fruits should be grown without the use of pesticides, when in fact we would not be able to grow the volume or quality of foodstuffs that is required for our state, let alone the nation, without them. Go to any market and look at the section displaying produce grown without insecticides. See which of the oranges, apples, potatoes, carrots, asparagus, or Brussels sprouts you would select for your table. Opposition to pesticides is often based not on science but on the assumption that what is bad for bugs must be bad for people. Many farmers believe that the public has not been well informed on the subject of pesticides, and they are probably right.

One piece of legislation that I was proud to carry was the "Home Collection Program," an effort for the collection of hazardous waste, typically paint and used oil, found around the house. The legislation enabled people to safely dispose of household hazardous wastes at facilities managed by the county. Such a program is a large undertaking because of the liability that is always present with handling hazardous materials.

I later carried legislation to allow small businesses with limited amounts of waste to participate in the Home Collection Program. This law, for example, would enable a jewelry store that has a small container of jewelry-cleaning solution to dispose of it in the Home Collection Program instead of participating in expensive commercial waste programs. Such laws protect small businesses from regulations aimed at high-volume hazardous-waste generators.

Permit by Rule and Assembly Bill 646

In 1991, I came across an issue that I think epitomizes the way in which a desire to protect the environment can lead to laws that stifle business. It began with a piece of legislation that stated that California could not, in any way, shape, or form, continue the current trend of increasing the amount of toxic waste produced in the creation of products for market. To reverse this trend, the legislation required companies to reduce, recycle, or reprocess the toxic wastes created in the production process.

Assuming that the required technology is available, this sounds like a good idea. But there was a catch. If your business complied with the law, it would be subject to regulation not only as a hazardous-waste generator but also as a hazardous-waste treatment facility. In this dual role, you would be subject to all the permits, regulations, and inspections applicable to a generator, as well as those applicable to a treatment facility. Your business would be in the same position with city or county government as with the state. So, in the name of protecting environmental health and welfare, the state created a no-win situation. How could you comply with the law—again, if the technology was available—and yet avoid a situation in which you had to double your regulatory responsibilities?

In 1989, the Department of Health Services, which had previously concentrated its permitting efforts toward large hazardous-waste facilities, began to look for an approach for handling smaller facilities. The approach developed was known as the Permit by Rule, or PBR. The aim of the PBR process was to exempt low-volume hazardous-waste treatment operations installed by small businesses from the lengthy and expensive permit process that applies to full-fledged toxic-waste treatment facilities. Although Health Services described the process as simplified, it in fact placed an extremely heavy burden on businesses that had installed treatment units. The worst of the provisions concerned liability insurance and public notification requirements.

The PBR required that toxic-waste treatment facilities carry $1,000,000 in liability insurance in case of a spill. Health Services later modified that requirement to $500,000, $300,000, or $100,000, depending upon the volume of waste treated. Still, it was very, very difficult for small businesses. In fact, a photo lab in West Los Angeles estimated the insurance, even at the lower coverage of $100,000, would cost $20,000 if it was available—and it wasn't available.

PBR would also require businesses to publish a notice in the local newspaper that the business is a toxic-waste treatment facility. Can you imagine what would happen to a nice, friendly rural community if the doctor's office had to put out a notice that they were operating as a toxic-waste treatment facility? Businesses felt the notice would raise undue fear in the public and in some cases threaten their very operation.

Businesses would also have to maintain voluminous records subject to random audits by Health Services, even though such records are inappropriate for an in-house pretreatment operation. The businesses are already regulated by the local health department, federal Environmental Protection Agency, Air Quality Management District, and other city or county agencies.

These in-house treatment operations are not hazardous-waste treatment facilities as we normally think of them. They would include doctors' offices, dentists' offices, and one-hour photo labs. Other businesses that were included, such as small circuit-board manufacturers and metal finishers, pretreat their wastewater, removing chemicals and solvents before the water is released into the sewer system. The pretreatment concentrates the chemicals and solids into a sludge that is then taken to a licensed dump site by a certified waste hauler.

Many businesses have made large investments in pretreatment equipment. According to Mark P. Johnson of R & R Industries in Brea, California, that company spent over $100,000 to install pretreatment equipment and meet the compliance requirements. Now this same equipment would represent a severe liability if the Department of Health Services proceeded as they had intended under PBR. Companies that had not yet invested in treatment equipment could decide it was just simpler to place the waste in a truck and let it be hauled off to some facility. Why get involved with treating waste when it meant additional expense, additional liability, and an additional burden of keeping up with the technology? Businesses who spent heavily on environmentally sound wastewater treatment equipment objected that they now were subject to unreasonable regulations and additional expense simply because they were more conscientious.

In response to this situation, in February 1991, I introduced a piece of legislation, Assembly Bill (AB) 646. The purpose of this law was to enable small businesses to comply with hazardous-waste regulations on an economic basis.

AB 646 modified the regulatory requirements applicable to two types of hazardous-waste treatment operations: silver reclamation from film processing waste, and treatment of industrial wastewater containing metals. The industries impacted were film processors, including doctors, dentists, chiropractors, radiologists, one-hour photo labs, metal finishers, and circuit-board manufacturers. The groups opposed included Sierra Club and other environmental organizations, who saw it as weakening the basic law in regard to toxic materials.

The bill gradually assumed its final form through the various stages of the legislative process. For photo finishing, for example, we started out with a cutoff point of 1000 gallons of waste solution a month; that is, businesses producing more than that amount would be subject to the more strenuous regulations. In addition to a variety of informal meetings and discussions, the bill was discussed in a number of hearings. On the Assembly side, it was first in the Toxics Committee, then Ways & Means, and finally floor debate. When we reached the Toxic Committee on the Senate side, it was clear that we were going to have to tighten up the 1000-gallon limit in order for the bill to pass. There was no way we could get the bill passed as is with the environmentalists so opposed. Through research, we discovered that we could reduce the amount from 1000 to 250 gallons and still take care of 90 percent of the minilabs, most of the radiologists, and all of the doctors' and dentists' offices. But even this was unacceptable to opponents of the bill. Finally, we reduced the amount to 150 gallons, which basically took care of 80 percent of the businesses.

It's interesting to note at this point that California is the only state in the United States where silver halide is considered a hazardous material. There was absolutely no chance, however, of getting silver removed from the list of toxic materials. So we reduced the amount to 150 gallons. The legislation was finally passed and signed by the governor.

In addition to the waste volume, AB 646 also addressed the liability insurance question. AB 646 requested that the State Insurance Commissioner report to the Legislature on the availability and affordability of liability insurance. In that way, it gave businesses a 1-year moratorium before they would be subjected to the liability insurance requirement.

Other provisions of AB 646 addressed public notifications, inspections, record-keeping requirements, and permit fees. Waste generators will still be required to notify newspapers but can use an affirmative statement that they are pretreating wastewater rather than saying they are dealing in hazardous materials. Businesses will be subject to inspections by the Department of Health Services only every 2 years. They will not be required to keep the extensive records required of large hazardous-waste treatment facilities and they will still pay the lower $1000 permit fee.

We are still trying to help business deal with other aspects of PBR, which is still in operation, and our own legislation. We constantly hear from small businesses who find that, because they go just a little over 150 gallons, they become involved in the full-blown PBR process. The costs of compliance really impact these businesses, and in many instances, I don't see where their practices in any way, shape, or form endanger the health of the people of the state of California. In fact, I've had to introduce another piece of legislation because I think it is very difficult for businesses like one-hour photo shops situated in shopping centers to suddenly be flagged to the community as dealing with a hazardous-waste substance. I don't think anyone would say this is the way that they envisioned their health and safety being protected.

Nevertheless I have to admit we were fortunate to get environmental groups to go neutral on this piece of legislation. But that doesn't mean that they aren't constantly monitoring it and watching very closely what we are doing. More and more legislation seeks to eliminate the use of toxic and hazardous materials altogether.

As a practical matter, I really don't know how we could get around the use of these materials given today's technology. So much of it goes into medical research and the manufacturing of pharmaceuticals that save lives and prolong life. If we had been as restricted as we are today, would penicillin have been invented? Would some of the inoculations that save children's lives ever have been invented or discovered? I think we must think through what we consider to be an environmentally safe workplace, an environmentally safe lifestyle, and an environmentally safe nation.

The Future Challenge

Over 50,000 of California's small and medium-sized businesses were relieved of a new round of heavy-handed environmental regulations with the passage of AB 646. Yet to this day, I don't feel that we have accomplished everything we can to help businesses—and particularly small businesses, because they are the heart of our economy—fulfill the mandate for a cleaner environment and yet continue to prosper and create jobs. As we try to achieve a balance between the necessities of business and the demands of environmental protection, it becomes more and more difficult because it appears that the basic demand is, and evidently will continue to be, that hazardous materials must be entirely eliminated, while preserving the comforts and benefits of technology. It is mind-boggling that anyone believes this can be accomplished.

Today, with the benefit of more than a decade of experience, we can and should reevaluate the environmental, toxic, and hazardous-waste legislation that has been written to see where this legislation works and does not work, where it conflicts and how those conflicts can be resolved, and what overall principles and structure, if any, are reflected in this body of work. We can then, in turn, ensure that we have the ability to prioritize what regulation is necessary at any given time and still have the flexibility to make exceptions to those cases and those areas that really are not life-affecting and in some way help those industries to improve.

I do not believe that business and industry—our very economic base—wants to be injurious to the health of the people of the state of

California. We must give them the time and make it economically feasible for them to turn around many of the systems that are being used and many of the products that are being developed and to find substitutes. We must give them the time to do that. We cannot demand change by any given date. I don't believe deadlines affect or improve upon the system. I feel very positively that we can change the way we do business in California and change the way that we manufacture as we move into the next century. I think that everyone—those who represent industry, the environment, and government—has to learn that we must work together to do what is necessary to make it possible without making it economically prohibitive. Cost is important, the safety of our people is important, and a balance must be achieved.

What I am striving for as a legislator is to see that we fulfill our responsibility to oversee and to guide; that changes, when necessary, are made, and made in a timely and less costly way; and that we simplify our regulations so that everyone can live with them.

13

Effective Environmental Communications

John E. Mullane
Vice President and Director,
Division of Scientific, Technical
and Environmental Affairs,
Hill and Knowlton, Inc.

Edward O. Raynolds
Senior Vice President,
Hill and Knowlton, Inc.

It is obvious to anyone who picks up a newspaper or turns on a television set that we live in an era of heightened environmental awareness. Names like Three Mile Island, asbestos, Bhopal, and Valdez are embedded in the public consciousness, stirring fear and anger.

Concern about the environment has reached such a pitch that the public's reaction to a new environmental crisis often is to (1) assume the worst has happened, and (2) pronounce an immediate guilty verdict on whoever appears responsible.

It is in this arena that organizations today must communicate. It is a thorny, tricky field in which events move with lightning speed. An organization caught flat-footed in an environmental crisis often finds itself behind the media curve and is able to gain control of the communications process only with great difficulty. Under these circumstances, poor communications will only exacerbate an already serious crisis.

What is reported by the news media has a powerful influence on legislators, regulators, the courts, and others who affect an organization's ability to succeed. Because the organization's main audiences obtain most of their basic information on a crisis from the news media—particularly in the early stages—the media represents the company's most critical means for rapidly conveying its side of the story to the outside world.

In fact, an organization's reputation with its key publics will rise or fall depending on the skill with which it handles its media relations during a crisis. Getting clear, accurate information out through the media must therefore be at the top of every organization's agenda for dealing with environmental issues.

Five Principles of Crisis Communications

Seize the Initiative

A central principle for any organization involved with environmental concerns is: *Seize the communications initiative.* We will see that principle at work throughout this chapter. Organizations must seize the communications initiative

- In environmental crisis response planning
- In communications during a crisis
- In siting new facilities
- In day-to-day communications about environmental issues

Prepare for a Crisis

The best thinking in communications situations comes when the time is taken for cool, rational reflection. But when an environmental crisis strikes, often there is no time at all. The news media get word of the crisis just about as quickly as an organization's managers do and begin flashing bulletins on it immediately.

It is the news reports that go out in the first few hours of a crisis that form the public's attitudes about what happened and who is to blame. In countless crises, organizations have been frozen with indecision about how and what to communicate in the early hours of an event.

This usually means they have lost the communications initiative and allowed others to fill the information vacuum—with speculation, hearsay, and out-and-out inaccuracies—often causing irreparable damage to their reputations.

Consider what happened at Three Mile Island. Early in 1979, the nuclear reactor at the power generation plant near Middletown, Pennsylvania, failed to cool properly. No one knew exactly why. There was no official spokesperson, and speculative news stories were breaking in Washington, D.C., Bethesda, Maryland, and Middletown and Harrisburg, Pennsylvania. Panic and controversy followed. Because the public—and the news media—lacked background knowledge about nuclear power issues, the often conflicting reports fueled rumors, speculation, and general confusion.

Eventually, President Carter visited the site and restored a semblance of calm. Harold Denton of the Nuclear Regulatory Commission was designated the official spokesperson, and a public relations firm was brought in to develop a communications plan. Communications at Three Mile Island began to take a positive turn.

But it was too late. The credibility of the Metropolitan Edison Company, the operator of the Three Mile Island facility, was shattered in 7 short days and took years to rebuild. Even more important, public perceptions of the accident set the cause of nuclear power in the United States back decades.

How do you make the right communications decisions when there is no time to think? The best way is to have a crisis response plan in place so that the major decisions are made in advance.

Such a communications plan must be linked closely to the organization's operational crisis response plan. Both plans should flow from an overriding *policy* that the organization has adopted for handling an accident or other crisis.

The purpose of such a policy is to provide a standard that the organization's management can turn to in order to act both responsibly and in the organization's best interests. The elements of some of the better crisis policies that organizations have in place today include:

- Accepting appropriate responsibility for an accident involving the organization's facilities

- Committing to compensating accident victims for damage caused by the organization

- Doing whatever is needed to remedy the crisis situation (i.e., clean up the oil spill, recall the contaminated product, etc.), regardless of cost

■ Communicating all information about the accident openly and accurately, as soon as it can be verified

Such a unified response system—policy, operating response plan, and communications response plan—enables an organization to act positively and decisively in an environmental crisis. The need for debate and discussion is eliminated.

Experience shows that the treatment the organization receives in the media and from public officials and other opinion leaders in a crisis will be a function of two related factors: (1) whether the organization accepts responsibility for its actions, and (2) whether it is perceived to have acted responsibly. Both will be a function of the organization's crisis policy and its communications plan—and how well they work together.

Build a Communications Plan

An effective crisis communications response plan can be activated instantly once triggered. It normally kicks in when the organization's officer with day-to-day communications responsibilities is alerted to the crisis by an operations person.

From that point on, much of what happens on the communications side is automatic. Members of the communications staff go to preassigned posts. A designated officer of the organization steps into his or her role as primary media spokesperson. Other staff people support that chief spokesperson, taking media phone calls, issuing news releases as called for, and tending to the minute-by-minute needs of the news media.

Frequent elements of crisis communications response plans involve:

■ Creating a system for the communications staff to be constantly updated by senior operating people

■ Establishing a method (data fax, electronic bulletin boards, etc.) for getting news out quickly to all organization employees

■ Setting up a media station to which all media arriving at the scene are directed and where they receive periodic briefings on the emergency

■ Arranging to provide communications assistance to the media, such as word processors, extra telephone lines, and staff assistants to handle ongoing needs

■ Logging information released and tracking questions received

Perhaps most important, a mechanism should be in place for integrating all these functions.

Simulate a Crisis

An invaluable way for preparing for communications in any crisis is to simulate an actual emergency. This kind of scenario is a role-playing exercise in which the communications team is taken through a crisis simulation step by step and responds to the media at each stage. The simulation works best when the participants are prepared and critiqued by professional communicators and media trainers. The various sessions may involve any combination of typical media situations, including ambush interviews, news conferences, and interviews by the print media, television, and radio.

Such a simulation exercise gives the organization's staff a firsthand idea of what they will face in the event of an actual emergency. Should a real crisis occur—complete with fast-breaking events and the stress of competing pressures—the communications team will have the benefit of having undergone a similar experience before. To make the simulation realistic, it is useful to make the crisis communications exercise be part of an operating crisis response drill involving the entire crisis team.

Be the Main Information Source

When a crisis strikes, the goal of the organization must be to take control of the communications process and keep control of it. It can achieve that only by seizing the communications initiative so that the organization strives to become a primary source for information throughout the crisis—often along with government agencies.

If an organization closes the gates in a crisis—or if it gives only warmed-over information or speculative or inaccurate information—then the media turn to other sources. Once the organization has allowed others to fill the communications pipeline with inaccuracies, speculation, and editorializations, it has embarked on a slippery trail.

But when the organization takes the lead in communicating and becomes an open, credible source, it soon finds it is providing much of the media's information. The organization is then in control, and the media has far less need to turn to outside sources.

The attitude an organization projects is a key factor in the crisis communications process. That attitude will serve the organization well when it shows concern for the public interest, rather than the organization's immediate financial interests. Thus the communications process is the company's chance to rebuild confidence and respect.

While a plant community may be seriously concerned about a company's financial pain, the world doesn't care how much it is going to cost the organization to clean up a problem or how much production is going to be lost. It wants to know how the organization feels about the people or the environment that have been harmed and what it is going to do to help them.

Showing a public-interested attitude means not minimizing an emergency but acknowledging its seriousness and committing to doing everything humanly possible to repair the damage. The organization must show its sincere concern for:

- Anyone killed or injured

- The environment

- Learning the cause of the emergency in order to prevent a recurrence

Communicating these concerns places the company on the same side of the issue as the general public. The kinds of public attitudes an organization communicates will be a function of its overall crisis policy, described above.

At the same time, in order to protect its own interests, the organization may have to make special efforts to place information it communicates in accurate perspective. That will certainly be the situation when activists or other adversaries interpret information inaccurately and in a way that harms the organization.

Often, a respected scientific authority, either inside or outside the organization, will be the most credible person to issue technical information in the proper context. That person should also have gone through the crisis-simulation exercise set forth above.

Because of the nature of the news media today, organizations will have to work extra hard to communicate the scientific nuances of a situation and place the event in perspective. Donella H. Meadows, coauthor of the watershed work, *The Limits to Growth,* and an adjunct professor of environmental studies at Dartmouth College, lists the following as among the difficulties in the media's reporting on complex issues:

- They [the media] are event oriented and shallow; they do not report underlying structure, historical context or long-term implications.

- Their attention span is short; they create their own fads, follow them and tire of them...
- They simplify issues; they have little tolerance for uncertainty, ambiguity or complexity.
- They love conflict and controversy and find harmony boring; they portray the world as a set of win/lose, right/wrong situations.
- They operate from skepticism; they have been manipulated so often that they don't believe anyone; therefore they convey a lack of trust in all information.
- They report through unconscious filters of helplessness, hopelessness, cynicism, passivity and acceptance. They describe problems more than solutions, obstacles more than opportunities. They systematically unempower themselves and their audience.

Even when the physical damage in an environmental crisis is substantial, an organization's reputation can emerge intact when its policies are constructive and its communications are handled effectively. The rupture of an oil tank owned by the Ashland Oil Company in Pittsburgh is a case in point.

On New Year's weekend 1988, an above-ground storage tank holding 4.3 million gallons of diesel fuel suffered a massive failure. A tidal wave of No. 2 oil surged over retaining dikes, carrying about a million gallons into the Monongahela River just east of Pittsburgh.

The resulting oil slick killed birds and fish and sullied the shoreline, as it rushed westward toward Pittsburgh and the confluence of the Ohio River. Cleanup efforts began, but little could be recovered from the moving waters.

Fresh water intake pipes bringing supplies to Pittsburgh and surrounding communities had to be closed for several days. Factory workers took forced holidays; small businesses reliant on fresh water were closed; and residents carried jugs and pails to obtain water from tank trucks.

The media quickly established several awkward facts:

- The failed tank was erected just a week before using 40-year-old steel.
- The tank was not tested according to industry standards before being filled.
- The tank lacked a key construction permit.

The local and national news media focused sharply on the story. More than 100 reporters were covering the spill by day three. It was the lead story on national television and played on page one of every major daily newspaper.

Early on, Ashland adopted a policy of open communications with the news media and accepted responsibility for its actions. Assisted by a crisis communications team from a firm with a Pittsburgh presence, the company established a system for bringing information quickly to the table for discussion and action.

In its active public communications effort that went forward, Ashland:

- Held frequent media briefings

- Appeared before community meetings

- Conducted editorial briefings

- Opened and maintained effective lines of communications with local and state government officials

- Obtained video and still photography to document the crisis

- Performed extensive monitoring and evaluation of ongoing media coverage—essential to gauging public reaction and adjusting strategy as events progressed

The story of the Ashland oil spill left the front pages almost as quickly as it arrived, and without leaving a bitter aftertaste. The media itself cited effective communications as one of the reasons why.

The Pittsburgh *Press* and *Post-Gazette* ran their first editorials on the spill on day four of the crisis. Both editorial lamented the spill but credited the company and its executive officers for their responsible handling of the crisis. In fact, the Ashland spill is often cited as a model for effective crisis communications.

Public Attitudes as a Critical Factor in Siting Facilities

Public communications also have become an indispensable part of the process of siting new industrial facilities. Environmental concerns have reached a stage where negative public attitudes can stop the siting of a new facility or new technology dead in its tracks. But even when no permits or approvals are required, public acceptance may be needed for a successful siting.

Public opposition to sitings is mobilized quickly, often by attention-seeking activists, creating a climate that can make it politically hazardous for legislative and regulatory bodies to grant their approval.

An organization wishing to site a facility that requires federal, state, or local approval will have to lay a careful communications groundwork to accomplish its objective. It must first have environmental impact studies and other scientific work done and have people in place who can be trained to communicate the results clearly and positively in public meetings and to the media.

It will need to keep community leaders, as well as state and federal legislators, informed about the siting plans, carefully explaining why these plans have the best interests of the community and locality at heart. In doing so, it will need to calculate the economic benefits to the area and present them *credibly* in terms of jobs, payrolls, tax revenues, and dollars pumped back into the economy.

The organization must show that it wants to become a positive force in the community, perhaps even listing the kinds of civic and monetary contributions it is prepared to make.

This story should be taken to community groups in informal meetings in which the organization shows concern for people's fears and a willingness to compromise on nonessential issues. The organization should also brief the news media in advance on its intentions, attitudes, and plans, to encourage sympathetic reporting as the siting approval process unfolds.

A key tactic is to preempt activist adversaries by getting the organization's positive story out to the media and to the community first, so the activists can't say, "We told you they'd say that."

In one siting instance, a municipality had spent 7 years studying and planning the purchase and installation of a refuse-to-energy plant. The facility was to play a key role in the locality's overall plan to deal with a growing trash crisis. At a late stage in the siting process, powerful opposition crystallized around questions of environmental impact and safety.

Suddenly, a story that had received little attention was page one news. The community was aroused by false and exaggerated charges. An upcoming hearing—originally seen as a perfunctory part of the process—suddenly loomed as a major battle that could prove decisive. Coming to testify for the opposition would be the leaders of three national environmental groups who opposed incineration.

The municipality recognized that it quickly needed to build a better understanding of the project among the press and the public. Aided by a firm with crisis communications capabilities, the locality developed a strategy for dealing with both the hearing and the community relations aspects of the situation. It launched a communications effort that included:

- Preparing and disseminating background papers both on the various emissions and discharges (lead, cadmium, dioxin, dibenzofurans, wastewater, and ash) and on the trash crisis itself, including the landfill situation, health hazards associated with landfills, and the future scope of the trash crisis
- Training spokespeople to address key issues in various forums
- Conducting briefing sessions with community leaders, and with civic and social groups
- Producing a video program for community dissemination and airing it on the local television station
- Identifying and briefing third-party experts to testify in support of the government's plant

By intelligently challenging the misstatements and exaggerations of its opponents, the municipality was successful in bringing good sense to bear on the garbage crisis. The media briefings and community meetings played a major role in educating the public to the facts and placing the environmental health issues in perspective. Editorial and public opinion soon took a perceptible turn in favor of the proposed incinerator. The incinerator was approved and successfully sited.

Environmental Communications—A Daily Need

Time was when organizations' interactions with the environment were the last things they wanted to communicate publicly. Why lay yourself open to criticism by bringing up subjects like discharges and emissions when you could avoid the issue, confident that no one else will raise it, either?

The days when an organization could lie low on environmental matters are gone. Environmental concern has reached a point where an organization that wants to minimize the risk of damaging public criticism had better be ready to communicate about its relationship with the environment on an ongoing basis.

One factor in creating this need is that federal and state laws have significantly stepped up the public reporting requirements on an organization's environmental activities. Those statutes are covered in greater detail in other chapters of this book.

One federal requirement we will mention here, however, because of its direct relationship to the communications process, is for the mandated filing under Title III of the federal 1986 Superfund Amendments and Reauthorization Act (SARA). Title III requires affected facilities to report on (1) release of toxic chemicals above certain levels, (2) hazardous chemical inventories, (3) emergency releases of certain kinds of hazardous substances, and (4) the facility's emergency response planning.

The fact that this Title III information is on public file means the news media can access it at will—and it does so in researching "round-up" stories about environmental problems in its locale and in reporting on a specific incident or controversy. The availability of these new data is one reason why it is in organizations' interests to communicate environmental information regularly, taking the opportunity to place the data in perspective.

The best place to begin regular communications about the environment is in a facility's own community. Experience shows that maintaining an open door to the community on environmental matters serves an organization best. In fact, it is usually best for the organization to seize the communications initiative, going out actively with its story. The goal is to let the community know that the organization is its partner in acting responsibly toward the environment and wants to keep the lines of communications open.

A useful step many organizations have taken is to establish advisory groups composed of community leaders, which meet regularly with the organization's officers to discuss and advise on environmental issues. In that way, the organization has a mechanism in place for keeping the most influential members of the community informed about what it is doing—and keeping itself informed about what is happening in the community. Forming such a group also gives the community leaders a stake in the organization's actions.

It is often beneficial for a local facility to invite the community in from time to time for an open house in which company officials talk about the organization's relationship with the community—including its environmental activities. Facilities tours and audiovisual displays can be effective in getting the facility's environmental story across. Of course, questions should be encouraged and answered candidly.

Creating a speakers program, in which organization officers address service clubs (Rotary, Kiwanis, etc.) and civic groups about the organization's environmental record and policies, can also be helpful in getting its message out.

Positive relationships with the local news media are essential in this kind of community relations effort. Organizations should create opportunities to brief the media on their activities—environmental and otherwise—even when no story or editorial is being written. With hometown newspapers, combined meetings with editors and reporters can be extremely valuable. Should an environmental accident occur, the quality of existing media relationships will be critical to securing sympathetic coverage of the event.

One of the most powerful influences on opinion within the community is the organization's own work force. Because employees speak informally as organization "insiders," what they say is believed. Employees can either be tremendously helpful or harmful to an organization's interests, depending on what their attitudes are and how they express them to others. In carrying out its day-to-day activities, the organization naturally also wants to motivate its employees positively and have them support management.

It follows that an organization needs to see that its employees are well informed about its policies and its record on environmental matters (as well as other subjects). Obviously, management's messages must have credibility with employees if its communications are to succeed.

Enlightened organizations today pursue ongoing programs of communicating with their employees. Face-to-face meetings conducted by supervisors and management are the most direct, natural way of reaching an organization's employees and establishing a dialogue. Organizations can also use techniques such as newsletters and magazines to reach their work forces, as well as videotaped messages and electronic bulletins.

Organizations need to communicate on a broader scale about their positive environmental activities, as well. Certainly, they will want to keep legislators and executive branch officials at the state and national levels informed. Depending on an organization's size and scope, it may also want to reach opinion leaders on a national scale, through speeches before national forums, op-ed-style columns, appearances on television discussion programs, and occasionally, paid advertising.

If the organization is a publicly held company, it has another crucial audience to reach: investors. Of course, both the professional investment community and individual shareholders are primarily interested in a company's financial performance and prospects. However, they will also focus on the company's environmental behavior as it affects their investment.

Increasingly, institutional investors today are evaluating their investments from a social performance point of view. Some institutional investors will take public positions about social issues in an effort to influence actions by management and the board of directors. A company's annual shareholders meeting can also become a forum for investors (including activists who have bought only a few shares) to air their positions on such social issues as the environment, often to attract media attention.

Public companies, then, have strong needs to tell their environmental stories to the broad business and investor audience. They will want to be sure they report effectively on their environment-related activities in their annual reports and other communications to shareholders. They will also want to deal with the environment in their investor meetings and in their relations with the national business media.

In all the above communications, organizations will want to discuss their environmental behavior in terms of *costs versus benefits.* In a world of limited economic resources, it makes little sense for an organization to pretend that its goal is 100 percent protection of the environment, no matter what the cost.

Instead, an organization serves its interests best when it presents its performance in the context of what constitutes a sensible balance between benefits to the environment and costs to the organization's customers, shareholders, employees, etc. (as appropriate). Given the nature of media reporting and the reluctance of the public today to accept compromises on environmental issues, this can be a formidable task. But it is one that organizations must undertake if they want to communicate credibly and in their long-term interests.

The Chemical Industry
Launches an Initiative

Following the tragic 1984 accident in Bhopal, India—as well as several highly publicized incidents in the United States, the creation of "Superfund," and a growing fear of chemicals in general—the Chemical Manufacturers Association (CMA) began studying how it could reassure the public about the safety and integrity of the U.S. chemical industry. The industry should not have been surprised to learn through extensive public polling that the man in the street ranked the industry next to last in terms of credibility (the tobacco industry trailed the list).

The chemical industry realized that the public had achieved a high degree of influence over chemical companies' basic business activities.

For example, adverse public opinion could stop the construction of a new plant, stymie a plant expansion, restrict or veto a critical operating permit, and limit the disposal or transportation of wastes. The industry further understood that the only way to influence this potent force was by improving performance and being more open and accessible to the public.

In its own words, the chemical industry determined that "long-term fundamental commitment and action to improve the industry's management of chemicals was the best way to deal with the public's widespread concern over chemicals and chemical operations."

In 1988, the CMA adopted such a comprehensive program, calling it Responsible Care. To give the effort teeth, the CMA's board of directors made carrying out the Responsible Care mandates a condition for companies' continuing membership in the CMA.

The basis for Responsible Care is a set of guiding principles regarding health, safety, and environmental quality, and codes of management practices based on the guiding principles. The codes of management practices state their intended results and define quantitatively what is expected of CMA member companies.

To assist CMA, an advisory panel of "informed citizens and environmental and community leaders from across the country" is in place to see that public concerns are understood and that the member companies act in a way that responds to those concerns. The panel reviews all proposed codes of management practices and provides an early warning on issues of public concern.

One feature of Responsible Care is member self-evaluation. Each management practice code requires a member company to conduct an annual evaluation of its progress on implementing each element of that code. The results must be reported to the CMA. For example, under one sample practice code, companies must evaluate their progress in such specific areas as:

- A clear commitment by senior management through policy, communications and resources, to ongoing reductions, at each of the company's facilities, in releases to the air, water, and land in the generation of wastes.
- A quantitative inventory at each facility of wastes generated and released to the air, water, and land, measured or estimated at the point of generation or release.
- Establishment of priorities, goals and plans for waste and release reduction, taking into account both community concerns and the potential health and safety impacts....

The companies must report their progress in meeting these prescribed practices according to six implementation stages:

Stage I—No action

Stage II—Evaluating company practices against code practice

Stage III—Developing action plan to implement code practice

Stage IV—Implementing action plan

Stage V—Code of management practices in place

Stage VI—Implementation reviewed and reaffirmed this year

The Responsible Care program also states that "periodically, progress will be measured and reported to key external audiences." As Robert D. Kennedy, chairman and chief executive officer of Union Carbide, said: "We don't expect them [the public] to trust us. We ask them to *track* us. If we continue to make progress...we believe we can earn their trust."

The most progressive element of Responsible Care was its stated commitment to communicate directly with chemical plant neighbors. In some parts of the United States, the trend has been to buy out adjacent property owners and create a liability-free moat of isolation. That trend probably won't stop, but in many older sites it isn't practical, and Responsible Care holds great promise for building bridges to the community.

To truly appreciate the radical shift Responsible Care was proposing, one needs to realize that most chemical plants were off-limits to the public. Responsible Care calls for opening the plant gates, bringing people in, and telling them candidly about their operations, even including the use of potentially hazardous chemicals on the site (though perhaps not on the first visit!). Responsible Care actually charges CMA members with explaining the specific risks that the plant presents because of the types of chemicals used, emissions, potential explosions, and the transportation of either products or wastes.

A radical challenge, indeed, and one that has been embraced by a majority of chemical companies. The growth of community advisory panels and other outreach efforts makes it clear that a new day is dawning—a day of greater openness and candor between the chemical industry and the public.

The chemical industry further recognized that to be fully useful, Responsible Care needed to be evaluated periodically and redirected as needed to assure that it remained credible and was achieving its objectives. CMA had begun such a review of Responsible Care as this book went into publication.

Environmental Marketing: It's Not Easy Being Green

"Green marketing"—citing environmental benefits to sell products or services—emerged in the 1980s, primarily in the United States and Europe.

Green marketing developed in response to its counterpart, green consumerism—consumers' heightened awareness of the effects of products and packaging on the environment. In the 1980s, environmentally oriented consumers began factoring this raised consciousness into their choices in the marketplace. Some of these consumers even reported paying more for products they saw as better for the environment than a competing brand.

A survey conducted in Britain by MORI, a market research group, found that between November 1988 and May 1989, the number of consumers who said they had chosen a product because of its environmental friendliness rose from 19 to 42 percent. A poll of Americans in 1989 by Michael Peters (MPG), a product-development consultancy, found that about three-quarters of that sample said they were willing to pay a little more for a product with biodegradable or recyclable packaging. True or not, the green marketing craze had begun.

Many marketers were quick to use this new marketing tool—in some instances, too quick. Environmental communications were often simplistic, incomplete, and sometimes blatantly deceptive. Products touting environmental benefits ranged from environmentally friendly socks to nuclear-free light bulbs. Consumers reacted with confusion and skepticism, governments with lawsuits and new laws.

Among the more prominent lawsuits was one filed against a well-known national corporation with billions in sales. A minor product line was green plastic bags, which the company touted as "biodegradable." Six states sued when the bags did not biodegrade as claimed in the "real world" conditions of a landfill.

A second suit was against an oil company who, in advertising its unleaded gasoline, made the remarkable claim that it caused "no pollution of the environment."

Other green marketers have run aground on trickier issues, such as that faced by a large chemical company who introduced a line of household cleaners, claiming they were "environmentally friendly."

An activist group alerted the media that while the cleaners themselves might be innocuous, manufacturing them created water pollution and consumed considerable energy.

In the United States, dozens of states introduced legislation in the early 1990s to regulate environmental marketing claims. By early 1992, laws had been passed in Rhode Island, New York, and California, among others. Each state has taken its own approach to environmental marketing regulation—yielding a jumble of conflicting regulation that is anathema to a national market.

Anticipating this Balkanization of the U.S. market, a group of trade associations led by the National Food Processors Association petitioned the Federal Trade Commission early in 1991 to promulgate national guidelines for environmental marketing claims. The FTC held public hearings on the issue and in the summer of 1992 issued its guidelines.

The guides describe what types of environmental claims the commission is likely to find deceptive under Section 5 of the Federal Trade Commission Act. While they do not preempt state laws or regulations, the states were expected to conform to the FTC guides.

The guides apply to environmental claims included in labeling, advertising, promotional materials, and all other forms of marketing. They embrace four general principles requiring that:

1. Qualifications and disclosures be sufficiently clear and prominent to prevent deception

2. Environmental claims make clear whether they apply to the product, the package, or a component of either

3. Environmental claims not overstate the environmental attribute or benefit, especially when the benefit is insignificant

4. A claim comparing the environmental attributes of one product with those of another product make the basis for the comparison sufficiently clear and can be substantiated

The guides provide direction on specific types of claims, including general environmental benefit claims, as well as degradable/biodegradable/photodegradable, compostable, recyclable, recycled content, source reduction, refillable, and ozone-safe/ozone-friendly claims.

Generally, unless there is adequate substantiation, the commission guides discourage unqualified claims such as "environmentally friendly," "recyclable," or "contains no CFCs," stating that such claims are likely to mislead consumers about the extent of the environmental benefit.

The guides state that claims should be qualified as necessary to prevent consumer deception, and the FTC provides examples of how specific claims might be presented in order not to mislead reasonable consumers. Marketers must be able to substantiate all claims—expressed
or implied.

In the midst of these legal and regulatory intricacies, can or should
responsible marketers use environmental claims as a marketing tool?
The answer is, perhaps.

A seemingly compelling argument for a company to embark on
green marketing is: "If you're benefiting the environment, why not get
credit for it in the marketplace?"

But the situation is never simple, as the FTC guides recognize. One
difficulty is that many times it may be impossible to know whether
one product or process is more or less beneficial to the environment
than another. There are, for example, no definitive answers as yet to
such questions as: Are phosphate substitutes in detergents less harmful than the original phosphates? And, does mercury in discarded bat-
teries cause water contamination?

Another complication is that a company who wants to laud a product for having environmentally harmful substances removed may be
vulnerable to attack over the damaging ingredients it has left in.
Environmental watchdogs will more than likely spot the contradiction
and alert consumers through a cooperative news media. The FTC and
other regulatory agencies are also likely to act—perhaps even at the
instigation of the competitor.

How, then, should a would-be green marketer proceed? First, they
must make sure that their claims comply with the regulations in all
states in which the products are to be marketed. Second, they must
make sure that their environmental claim can be substantiated, is
clearly communicated, and can be readily understood by the consumer. Third, they should think twice about making environmental
claims that apply to only a small portion of the product or package or
communicate "half-truths" (i.e., "no CFCs," but still contains ozone-
depleting chemicals). The most successful environmental claims are
likely to be those that communicate a real product benefit and/or provide useful information to the consumer.

The most important question of all for a marketer is, will green marketing make a difference? Despite the surveys suggesting that consumers do factor environmental "friendliness" into the purchase decision and that they are willing to pay somewhat more for a product
with environmental benefits, the evidence of actual buying behavior is
less clear. According to a May 1992 article in *The Wall Street Journal,*

while "survey after survey indicates consumers' overwhelming willingness to pay...more for environmentally friendly products, retailers and manufacturers say that sentiment hasn't held up at the cash register."

However, the same article reported that Procter & Gamble's Ultra Tide refillable line—"great Tide cleaning, less to throw away"—had been a marketing success. The reason, according to one retailer, is "not because [it's] marketed as environmentally friendly. There are savings for the retailer, manufacturer and consumer."

Over the foreseeable future, the environment will likely continue to be an important issue for consumers. But that concern will not necessarily translate broadly into a new market for goods and services. Environmental claims in and of themselves are unlikely to be a major selling point for most products. However, all other things being equal, where a marketer has clearly made a real difference—through the use of refillable, source reduced, or recycled and recyclable packaging, for example—environmental communications can be a powerful marketing tool.

Environmental protection remains an issue of active public debate. While some factions argue that not enough is being done to protect the earth, others claim that stringent measures will stifle economic growth and development. But signals from the 1992 Rio Earth Summit and elsewhere suggest that over the long term, policies will move inexorably toward requiring stronger environmental protection. It is also becoming clear that industry will shoulder much of the burden.

Organizations today, then, have no option but to establish constructive environmental policies and communicate about their interactions with the environment. To the extent that they do so actively, intelligently, and credibly, they will benefit not only their public image but their very ability to survive and achieve their business goals.

14

Dealing with the News Media

Richard Varenchik
Public Information Officer
State of California Environmental
Protection Agency

The most compelling story to emerge from southern California during the torrential winter rains of 1992 was that of a teenaged boy being swept to his death in a raging Los Angeles river. A picture of the boy, as he was swept under bridges while crying out for help, was shown on virtually every television station in the nation and appeared on the front page of countless newspapers.

"Don't they have to get his family's permission before they can print a picture like this?" one of my coworkers asked as he studied the boy's image on the front page of the *Los Angeles Daily News*.

The question is one I have been asked many times in more than 20 years as a working journalist and public information officer. My answer—"No, they can print anything they want and they don't have to ask anyone's permission"—is only a slight exaggeration.

Within that answer lies the answer to another question that affects any manager working today in the hazardous-waste industry: Why should I care about the news media? Because the news media has the power to say just about anything it wants to concerning your company.

Remember that credibility and a good image have tremendous value to your company. The news media can help you build that credibility and good image—or totally destroy it. Generally, however, if the media is going to destroy your company's public image, it will be able to do so only with a great deal of help from you. To this day, officials at Exxon probably feel they got a bum rap from the news media. But the *Exxon Valdez* did run aground and dump 11 million gallons of oil in Alaska's Prince William Sound. Any inaccuracies or mistakes or unfairness or outright lies the media told about Exxon after that were overshadowed by televised film of birds and sea otters dying slowly in a dark sea of Exxon crude.

An interesting footnote to this story arose about 2½ years after the spill. Studies showed that wildlife recovered faster in beach areas that were not steam-cleaned than in areas that were, probably because steam cleaning had virtually sterilized areas where it was used. Will the oil firm involved in the next big spill, from a public relations point of view, dare to face the media and say it is better to do nothing than to steam-clean oil-soaked beaches?

Different Media, Different Messages

Is the asbestos you are removing from the third floor of a building going to affect workers on the first floor? Will it drift to the elementary school across the street? Will the people living in surrounding apartments breathe lead-contaminated dust from the old dump you are remediating? Were you following proper safety regulations when your worker fell and broke his neck? Why did your truckload of hazardous waste crash on the freeway at rush hour?

The list of possible questions the news media may ask you—with little or no advanced warning—is endless. The most important question is: how well prepared are you to answer?

Before you can tackle that question you need to understand that the "news media" are not one homogeneous lump. Television, radio, newspaper, magazine, and trade journal reporters all have varying needs. They will make different demands on your time, and they also vary in the amount of the information they require and how they want it presented.

Of the different news media reporters, radio reporters are probably the easiest to deal with. They usually want someone to say a few sentences into a microphone so they can tape a "live" voice to run with their story on the next hour's news broadcast. Frequently, they will ask for a paragraph or two to be read directly from a previously prepared press release.

Television is a different story. It's a visual medium—reporters generally are as interested in good pictures as they are in solid information. (Thus, for example, many southern California television stations fill their summer newscasts with stories about meaningless brush fires. Spectacular, leaping flames compensate for the fact that the fires have no news value.)

The last resort for a TV crew is the "talking head" shot, film of a company spokesperson talking into the camera. It's not great, but at least it's film. They would much rather have shot some film of workers in "moon suits" cleaning up spilled asbestos, or of children crying as they were evacuated from school, but if your "talking head" is all they can get, they'll take it. This should also give you a hint about expanding the amount of time you get on camera to give your side of the story. If you are doing something that makes good film footage while you talk, or at least standing in front of something photogenic, you will probably get a little more time on the evening news.

The bottom line is, even though some people go nearly catatonic when faced with a TV camera, TV reporters are really not all that hard to deal with. Later, we'll talk about some ways of getting your point across when the reporter is asking tough, nasty questions.

Depending on the situation, a good newspaper reporter can be among the best or the most troublesome of the newspeople you encounter. Reporters covering environmental affairs for large newspapers like the *Los Angeles Times, Washington Post,* and *New York Times* are often experts in their fields. More than one executive for a hazardous-waste firm has started an interview with one of these reporters and quickly learned that the reporter knows more about the subject than he or she does.

Obviously, explaining a complex subject is easier when dealing with a person who has extensive background in that subject. However, the reporter's background knowledge will put you at a disadvantage if your company has fouled up or done something that you are not eager to talk about.

The expertise of the reporters in a particular subject generally decreases with the size of the paper they represent. This is not because reporters on smaller papers are less intelligent. It simply reflects the fact that smaller papers hire "general assignment" reporters who cover a wide variety of areas such as police, school board, and city council. Small papers do not have the money to hire reporters who cover nothing but toxic wastes, air pollution, water contamination, etc.

Is it your responsibility to educate reporters who come to you without the technical knowledge to understand the work your company is doing? The answer is yes. Many will argue that newspapers should hire reporters with the knowledge to write about any story they are assigned to cover. This is good theory, but it is not the way the world of journalism works. In my last years of reporting I became very knowledgeable about California's criminal courts. I gained this knowledge by asking endless questions of attorneys, policemen, court clerks, judges, and anyone else who worked in the courts. My education took place after I was assigned to cover the legal system. This is the way most reporters learn.

If you refuse to educate the reporters who write about your company, you guarantee one thing: The public will read inaccurate stories about your company and the work it is doing. Keep in mind, though, . that inaccuracies can creep into the best of stories written by the best of reporters.

Magazine and trade journal writers are interested in some of the same things as newspaper reporters. However, they tend to write in more detail. Trade journals particularly can be interested in esoteric subjects that are meant for a very small and select audience. "Avoiding Lawsuits through Proper Placement of Spa Drain Covers" may seem boring to you, but it will be avidly read by those who build or install spas for a living.

While reporters for the various news media differ in many respects, they all have two things in common—editors and deadlines. Deadlines are the answer to the oft-asked question: "Why was that reporter so damn rude?" Answer: "Because he was on deadline."

On a daily newspaper, the word deadline means just about what it says. Your story has to be in by a certain time or your editor will kill you. (Actually, he or she might be nice and just fire you.) There is no adequate excuse reporters can give to explain why they missed a deadline. A reporter with a 4 P.M. deadline who is on the phone with you at 3 P.M. trying to get information may get a bit rude if you seem evasive. Imagine what it is like to live like this each and every day of your working life.

Aside from the fact that they will accept no excuse for missed deadlines, editors are horrid people in other ways: An editor once assigned me to track down and interview the jurors from a murder trial. I reached 11 of them, but number 12 had gone to an island off the coast of California and was staying in a home with no telephone. "Only 11 out of 12?" my editor groused when I turned in the story.

Keep in mind that reporters never write the headlines that go on top of their stories in the newspaper. Editors write the headlines; an interesting point since I always received more complaints about the headlines (which I hadn't written) than the stories (which I had).

What Is News?

While most people agree that murders and wars are news, the definition of news becomes less clear as events diminish in importance. When I was a reporter, we had a joke that news was anything that happened to or near an editor or a member of his or her family. One friend of mine ended up doing a five-part series on bad backs after our editor injured his back. A story on boating safety was in order when an editor witnessed an accident while water skiing.

In other words, news is what editors and reporters say it is. You may think nothing about the bag of asbestos that didn't even break open when it fell off one of your trucks, but the local editor thinks it would make a great story to fill that big hole on the front page of the paper. And you can save your breath if the editor thinks your company has done something seriously wrong. (Whenever I was doing a story that was going to cause someone grief, I would sympathize with them and agree that it was not much of a story. But then I'd add that my editor insisted I do it.)

Another word about television news. It generally tends to have a memory about 24 hours long. If you can survive today's interview, it is very unlikely that the television people will be back tomorrow or the next day unless there are continuing developments or good new pictures for them to broadcast.

Look at the example of Watergate, one of the biggest news stories of the 1970s. Even though it was a story that continued month after month, television never did very much with it because it was a complex subject that did not offer much in the way of pictures.

But while television was ignoring Watergate, the *Washington Post* and eventually other newspapers kept the story alive. God help you if a really sharp, dedicated newspaper reporter who has editors' backing decides your company is involved in a dishonest or environmentally unsound practice. You'll find that the stories just keep coming until the day your company is forced to radically change the way it does business—or you are on your way out the door without a job. Just ask former President Richard Nixon.

Planning for Media

In the face of all this, it is amazing how few companies have a plan for responding when the news media comes calling. There's a "good news, bad news" joke about the corporate executive whose secretary told him he was about to become famous. "The good news is that there's a camera crew here to put you on television. The bad news is they're from *60 Minutes*."

What type of plan does your company have for dealing with anything from a camera crew at the front door demanding to know if your new use of ultraviolet light in groundwater cleanup is going to kill kids at the neighboring elementary school, to the local newspaper wanting an interview with your new executive vice president? If you don't have a plan, put one together.

Start by designating two or three people in the office to take calls from the news media. Don't be like the sheriff's department that designated one deputy to handle the news media. The plan worked great until he went on vacation at the same time the sheriff was out of town and no one else would talk to reporters.

If your firm is large enough, you can think about hiring a full-time public information and community relations officer. This person should have a news media or public relations background; a person who was once a reporter and has worked a few years in public relations is ideal. Aside from dealing with the news media, your PR person can do things like respond to inquiries from the public and elected officials, implement an outreach program to try to make the public aware of the good things your company is doing, help your technical staff write reports that are more readable, and be proactive in putting out good news stories to the public.

If you don't have the financial resources to hire an outside person, you must designate one or more of your existing staff to be company spokespersons. In either event, the person designated should have direct access to the president or other top management in your company. It should be very apparent to your staff that the company spokesperson speaks with the total backing of the company's top management. If this is not the case, your staff will tend to shrug off or ignore the spokesperson's sometimes inconvenient and annoying requests for quick information (remember the reporters' deadlines) and your goal of quick and accurate responses to news media questions will fail.

Training for your spokesperson is available through a variety of college classes and extension courses. There also are public relations, communications, and media relations firms that offer classes or seminars on how to do a television interview, how to deal with the news media, and related topics. Books are available on topics such as dealing with the media and crisis communications. Video and audio tapes on media relations are available through some public relations firms.

The quality of the programs and the tapes varies greatly—be selective before committing your company's money.

Make sure everyone in your office knows who the media spokespersons are, and be sure they are aware of how important it is to route all media calls to the spokespersons. Reporters enjoy calling a half-dozen people in the same office and asking them all the same questions. When they get different answers, it makes a great news story.

Find out what the reporter wants to know and then decide if the company spokesperson or someone else on the staff is going to do the interview.

Handling Interviews

Here are some rules for handling media interviews.

Be Prepared

The reporter has already told you what he or she wants to talk about. Try to anticipate specific questions and be ready to answer them. Figure out what points you want to get across and be proactive in pushing them. You don't have to simply sit there and respond to questions. Push the particular points that make your organization look good. Pick three points you want to get across and repeat them in slightly different ways several times during the interview.

This is very easy to do, particularly in a television interview. It is more difficult but possible in interviews with print media reporters. To see how it is done on television, watch one of the Sunday morning interview shows like *Meet the Press* or *Face the Nation*, particularly when they are interviewing political candidates. The reporter will ask a question like: "When you were governor twenty percent of your state's aerospace firms moved to other states because your environmental laws were too strict. With a record like that at a time when the nation's economy is in bad shape, why should voters vote for you?"

To which the candidate will answer: "Overall economic growth in our state was as healthy as in any other state in the union during my term as governor. We had satisfactory growth and protected the environment too." In other words, the candidate never answered the reporter's question but simply gave a little campaign speech. Knowing that he was vulnerable on the economic question, his staff had briefed him on how to reply to economic questions if they were asked. Of course, if you know for a fact that there has been growth in aerospace firms you quickly point that out and quote the relevant statistics.

If you don't know an answer to a question (during a print media interview), admit it but offer to find out and telephone the reporter as soon as possible. Speak, as much as possible, in plain English. Avoid jargon and technical terms, which tend to sound evasive to the general public.

Trick Questions

During the interview, the reporter may use a number of different trick questions which you should learn to recognize and avoid. They include:

- The false premise: "This chemical spill is the latest in a series of similar incidents that gives Support Environmental a very poor environmental record. Why should anyone believe you will do a good job on the cleanup?" If you have facts to show that Support Environmental has an environmental record as good or better than similar firms, now is the time to politely dispute the reporter's statement and put the facts on the table.

- The invisible man: The reporter quotes someone who is not around as saying something bad about your company or project. "The mayor says dust from your project is causing lead contamination to those living nearby." Don't call the mayor names—you have no idea what he really said. Stick to the facts and say something like "our work on this project exceeds all state and federal standards. We will wet the soil hourly. We will shut the work down when the wind blows."

- The hypothetical: "Won't this contaminated soil be a threat to children if one of your trucks crashes into the elementary school during recess?" Don't respond to the speculation. Say something like: "We have an excellent safety record and have not had a serious trucking accident in more than 15 years."

Never say "no comment." It makes you sound guilty or as if you are trying to avoid something. Instead, say, "I'm not sure. Let me check and get back to you." Or, "That is a legal case and I'm not permitted to comment on such matters."

And forget about "off the record" too. The federal Environmental Protection Agency tells its staff to think how they would feel if their words appeared on a freeway billboard the next day. Keep that in mind and remember that you are never off the record.

Remember too that the interview is never over until the reporter is gone. Putting away the note pad means nothing. Turning off the lights and packing up the camera equipment mean nothing. The interview is over when the reporter is out the door and can't hear you anymore. If you doubt this, just remember the experience of then presidential candidate Jimmy Carter who told a *Playboy Magazine* interviewer (after the interview was over) that "I have lusted in my heart."

The interview picture, however, is not totally bleak. You do have rights that most major news media will respect in an interview. While the reporter can ask tough questions, he or she should be courteous. The reporter should be prepared to tell you the general content of the story and what slant it will take.

You have the right to admit you don't know the answer to a particular question and ask for some time to get the information and get it to the reporter. You also have the right to be quoted accurately and to have the general tone of what you said reproduced accurately in the story.

A few other points about interviews: Dress correctly for television interviews. This means conservatively! Loud or flashy clothing will call attention to themselves and away from what you are saying. Very loud clothing will make you look like a buffoon and destroy the credibility of your message.

Expect the television reporter to blindside you with a really loaded question once the camera starts rolling. They won't always do it, but you should be prepared for it. Remember, you don't have to reply to the loaded questions. Use them as a bridge to get across the prepared points you want to make.

Reporter asks: "This is the third oil spill your company has caused in two months. How do you respond to people who are calling for your refinery to be shut down?"

You reply: "The Econo Oil Company's refinery has an environmental record that ranks in the top 5 percent of refineries in the state. We had cleanup crews here within 45 minutes of the spill and we'll stay here as long as we are needed."

An interview technique called the "softball lob" was one I used as a newspaper reporter when I was interviewing someone I was pretty sure had done something wrong or illegal. To relax them and soften them up I'd lob them a really easy question to start the interview. They'd respond by bashing an answer right back at me. I'd lob in a few more really easy questions and the person being interviewed would respond by bashing answers back at me. I'd let them really get confident and then I'd slowly start asking more and more difficult questions. Not one time did I encounter a person who would simply stop and refuse to go on as the questions got more difficult and incriminating. When good reporters are working on stories about illegal activity, they already know the answers to the questions they are asking.

Demanding (and Getting) a Retraction

This having been said, when should you call and demand a retraction or correction if a story is inaccurate in stating information you provided? This is a judgment call.

If a newspaper is printing a story that portrays your company in a negative light, asking for a correction or retraction gives them a chance to reprint, along with the retraction, the original negative message about your company.

A good philosophy is: "Don't sweat the small stuff." I frequently do interviews where I say something like "we will take 15 soil samples and also sample the liquids in 25 of the drums." The next day the paper reports that the investigation will include "25 soil samples and samples from 15 of the drums." Sure it's an error, but how much does it really matter?

On the other hand, if you say that the lead-contaminated soil is no danger to children at the neighboring school and the paper quotes you as saying it could be a real danger to the kids, you should ask for a correction. You can't ask for a correction, though, if you say it is no danger and someone else is quoted disagreeing with you. The news media almost always ask for other opinions to balance out what you say because there is a self-serving interest to your statements.

Keep in mind that while the negative story about your company may run across the top of page one, the correction will usually run in a little box buried somewhere inside the paper. Unless the original error is one that can be considered criminally libelous, the paper has no obligation to run the correction in the same place it ran the original story.

There is one area where you should feel totally free to pick up the telephone and scream long and loud at the editor of your local paper.

This is when the paper runs a story that portrays your company in a negative light and makes no attempt to call you and ask for your side of the story. It is a fundamental rule of journalism that a person or company being attacked in the paper has a right to make a reply if negative things are being said.

But this only means that a reporter must try to contact you for comment. If one tries but cannot reach you, the paper has the right to say you could not be reached for comment and go ahead with the story. (Reporters have been known to wait until 8 P.M. before calling for comment, knowing full well that the company will be closed and everyone gone home by then.)

Seek Out Positive Stories

Fortunately, most of us have done nothing wrong and we deal with small to medium-sized papers in the cities and towns where our companies are located. The good things your company is doing can be news to a small or medium-sized newspaper.

Papers love stories that deal with "firsts," "lasts," "biggests," "smallests," "most expensive," "least expensive," and other superlatives. If your company is the first in the area to use a new form of technology for dealing with an environmental problem, then by all means telephone the local paper and let them know. If you have developed a new method for dealing with a problem or something that is different from solutions tried in the past, let the local paper know.

If your company or someone in it wins an award, tell the local editor. If you have something that would make good pictures, contact the local television stations.

15

Financial Decision Making in the Environmental Age

W. Gordon Wood
Vice President, Finance (CFO)
Facilities Division, Fortune 100 Company

The process of financing environmental management programs begins by comparing the difference between success and failure. You may already have won $10 million in cleanup and regulatory liabilities. The only assured means to avoid consequences of such magnitude is to prepare. A business needs credible knowledge of the nature and cost of mistakes. Expect to remedy past mistakes, postpone inevitable accidents, and prevent disasters.

Change in Traditional Role of the CFO

The modern history of environmental disasters and the associated liabilities has resulted in a significant change in the role of the chief financial officer. In the not-too-distant past, the financial information required for entering or retaining businesses included little more than answers to these basic questions:

- How much will labor and materials cost?
- What should be spent on plant and equipment to minimize economic cost?
- How should the product be priced to maximize market share and economic return?

These questions were challenging enough, and they continue to eliminate most potential competitors from the marketplace. Unfortunately these questions vastly oversimplify the responsibilities of the CFO in analyzing the financial position of a firm today. A new array of environmental responsibilities requires satisfactory answers to questions that are technical as well as financial. These questions include, at a minimum:

- What are the environmental issues impacting price and the availability of materials?
- What are the environmental issues governing price and liabilities of transportation of materials to our plant?
- What are the potential material- and waste-handling costs, risks, and liabilities with regard to the work force and the environment?
- What are the regulatory requirements of operation, and what are their associated costs?

In the past these questions were not necessarily part of the financial data that were reviewed in the decision process. Few if any texts would have included environmental management concerns within the scope of "due diligence" of a CFO. Most financial executives have become aware of these issues only after an event, not through their academic training.

Environmental liability has become so material to the basic costs of operation that many apparently profitable businesses have never been economically viable. Comprehensive financial analysis must include the costs of cleanup, decline in property values due to residual damage, and effective prevention systems. Unfortunately, these factors have not been adequately understood, nor have they been included in either financial or operating decision models. As a result, the role of the CFO has expanded to include comprehension of environmental technology.

At a minimum, financial executives require some scientific training in order to adequately appraise financial conditions and to properly advise operating executives. This training is necessary to integrate the essential range of cost factors into each financial recommendation. This presents a significant challenge to the traditional role of operational accounting. The effect of including another significant cost and risk factor is to decrease the approval rate of proposed ventures. This meets with great resistance from other business disciplines. To overcome this resistance, the CFO must comprehend and effectively communicate the relevant financial impact of expenditures for environmental remedy and risk management.

Competing for Resources

Every firm has its own list of demands on resources, but none is without the requirement to evaluate and prioritize. The following environmental tasks are components of the decision equation with differing potential to be accomplished with the available funds:

Prevention Investments

1. Technology evaluation expenditures including literature searches, technical consultation, legal advice, and surveys.

2. Operating system development expenditures including software acquisition or development, preparation of procedures and training literature, and data acquisition and assimilation (relevant MSDSs, etc.).

3. Capital system development expenditures including alternatives in manufacturing and handling equipment sources, and environmental engineering alternatives (both regulatory and evolutionary).

4. Product component source alternatives (e.g., potential risk and investment aversion through vertical disintegration).

5. Development of long-term regulatory compliance planning.

Risk-Weighted Liability-Limiting Investments

6. Insurance premium expenditures for liability in the event of accident.

7. Retainers and contractual relationships with legal counsel, public relations representation, and expert environmental technologists to help operate in the event of incident.

8. Business operating structure to limit personal liability of investors and principal owners (incorporation, subsidiary shell structures, etc.).

These financial resource–consuming tasks compete with other more traditional demands on the firm's available funds such as employee salary and fringe benefits, human resource development, process development investments, capital equipment for operating capacity, horizontal and vertical integration investment, and return on the owner's investment.

Evaluating Cost of Environmental Programs

The true cost of environmental programs can only be determined with an accurate assessment of the risks. Very few business owners, whether stockholders in the investment market or hands-on owner-operators, have taken the time to evaluate the potential for either past, current, or future environmental conditions to demand material amounts of their resources. The potential is great even for a firm that has no direct involvement in the utilization of environmentally harmful materials. The following hypothetical case examples illustrate some of the risks that may confront the financial executive.

The Plant Lease Bargain

In 1970, the We-Make-It Company (WMI) is lucky enough, during a period of growth, to find an empty manufacturing plant available for long-term lease (i.e., more than 50 years with the exercise of option periods) at a very attractive rental rate. In fact, the rental rate contractually declines over time owing to an assumption of depreciation and obsolescence by the initial lease negotiators. The location is in an industrial park with many varied businesses ranging from "environmentally clean" financial services to heavy "smokestack" manufacturing. The location is further enhanced by being near a large, moderately priced residential community, a favorable source of employees to staff the facility. The plant has previously been occupied by a now-bankrupt combined machine shop and development laboratory. WMI proceeds to utilize the facility for machining and engineering metal products.

During the past 20 years, WMI has invested heavily in improvement to the leasehold for the following apparently good business economic reasons:

- Characteristics of the site were consistent with growth requirements.

- Alternative sites reflected higher initial costs of development due to inflation of land and construction costs.

- The sufficiently long lease term provided adequate time to fully amortize costs of development against projected production.

- Changes in manufacturing and operating technology continued to drive development of facilities.

The improvements include new buildings, major renovation of existing structures, and the near-permanent installation of heavy machining equipment. Much, but not all, of the equipment is modern and relatively new. The acquisition planning for the new equipment includes substantial consideration for the proper care of the environment. Recent equipment designs incorporate such criteria as low consumption of electrical power and minimization of historically required chemicals (lubricants, cleaners, coolants, etc.). Owing to ·evolutionary demands of the various regulatory agencies governing environmental and safety compliance, installation permits require careful control of materials and waste. However, at no time during the financial and operation evaluations done prior to investment did any consideration focus on preexisting site conditions. Each of the prior investments ignored the potential for the value of the new and future investments to be offset by the cost of environmental damage cleanup.

Governmental regulatory discovery processes have evolved over the last 10 years to include a number of means to open a case. In this example, an inspector observes surface discoloration on paved grounds as an indicator that illegal dumping had potentially occurred. Without further conclusions being drawn as to the cause and effect of the surface stain, a specimen sample of the pavement is tested. Evaluation indicates that the material is a well-known and commonly used machine shop chemical and that the chemical is listed as a hazardous material. The site is then excavated. The pavement is removed and disposed of in an allowable manner. (There remains much question about how to dispose of mixtures of inert and hazardous materials and how much disposal will cost.) A sample of the subsoil is taken to determine if the chemical has penetrated the paving and contaminated the ground. Once it is determined that the subsoil contained at least surface residue of the chemical, drilling is begun for the purpose of obtaining soil core samples for analysis.

From the perspective of a CFO, it is important to note at this point that:

1. All of the expenses incurred in the above-described discovery process were not included in the annual operating budget commitment of business performance.
2. As such, the owners have had the value of their investment diminished without their knowledge, but within the fiduciary responsibilities of the appointed operating officers.
3. The owners will not receive operating profits as great as projected and upon which they based their approval of existing business plans.
4. The owners are not best served by replacing the management staff due to the following factors:
   a. The staff has become unusually experienced with the handling of an environmental incident.
   b. The staff's prior ignorance was not unusual and was probably within the range of performance standards.
   c. Few competent managers would want to join a business with the future problems that can be anticipated in resolving the site conditions.

The results of initial drilling indicate that traces of the previously identified chemical are present in the subsoil to a depth of 10 feet. The situation is further complicated by the fact that many other contaminants are also found in the core samples. These other contaminants are found to continue to much greater depth than the contaminants initially discovered. Further drilling away from the excavated spill site is ordered and completed. Analysis of these core samples indicates that the newly discovered contaminants are abundant throughout a significant area of the leased grounds.

Further discussion of the eventual technical resolution is irrelevant from a financial perspective. WMI has incurred millions of dollars in testing, analysis, legal representation, and cleanup expenses. Since the additional contamination problem is pervasive, there is a strong possibility that Superfund contributions may be assessed.

The financial officer has a responsibility to the owners to perform an ongoing evaluation of the value of the business. This evaluation must include consideration of the following range of potential additional liabilities:

1. Plant closure expenditures including employee severance pay, local regulatory demands for job retraining and outplacement services, and lease payments required under the terms of the lease agreement

2. Manufacturing equipment relocation expenses, and the cost of finding and developing suitable facilities in another location

3. Lost production capacity during shutdown

4. Contractual liability for product delivery delays under contract terms with customers

The financial officer is faced with the enormous burden of evaluating the quality of the evolving compilation of information. Professional ethics and regulations compel disclosure to both owners and prospective investors (for a publicly traded company) in periodic reports. Initially the disclosure may be contained in a footnote to the balance sheet until the liability can be accurately computed and recorded.

In retrospect, the problem began in 1970 when the leased site was selected as a viable location to operate. The preexisting subsoil contamination was begun by the previous occupant and was possibly compounded by other surrounding businesses. These conditions made the plant site location unsuitable for the investments which were to follow. WMI followed the then-accepted financial analysis procedures by preparing a return-on-investment analysis (ROI) for the decision process before making each subsequent investment on the site. Assumptions in assessing the ROI for each prospective new building, building improvement, equipment installations, and local area staff development decision were erroneous. The ROI analyses were based on the assumption that at least a minimum profit would result after inclusion of all the substantial and relevant costs of operation. The cost to remedy environmental damage due to WMI employees was ignored in the decision process. The further complication of the previous tenant damage was far from consideration. The financial question becomes whether these costs are avoidable. Can the funds drain end by simply writing off the remaining value of the plant investment?

WMI's escape from incurring growing costs is further complicated by a number of other factors:

1. WMI faces liability based on its commitments to customers for the products that are manufactured on the site.

2. Regulatory agency demands may pierce the corporate veil (due to

legislative impact) in the event that the remaining assets are insufficient to pay for the cleanup.

3. Employees of WMI may desire and act to preserve their personal livelihood by keeping the company operating, even at a continuing loss. This behavior could increase the long-term losses of stockholders and owners. The actions can take the form of erroneous estimates of lower future costs of remediation and operation and/or higher than realistic income (price) projections.

The WMI example is obviously an extreme case, but owing to accumulation of accidents, calculated permissible emissions, and intentional acts of environmental murder, many otherwise desirable business properties may have potential problems of this nature. Another common type of problem that has impacted the ability of financial officers to assess the condition of the firm involves the apparently minor businesses that have resulted from vertical integration efforts.

The Incidental Business

In 1974, the Rent Equipment to Anyone Company (REA), a large multibusiness supplier of goods and services, feels a very severe financial pinch from the oil crisis. A shortage in gasoline is keeping REA's trucks and power equipment from being available for its customers. The rental business by its nature is a very competitive business with easy entry from many lightly capitalized and small operators. Seeking to obtain an advantage over these smaller firms through a small venture into vertical integration, REA decides to strike a deal with a major oil company (MO) to inventory and dispense gasoline and diesel fuel from tanks and pumps to be located on REA's premises.

A construction contract is negotiated with another firm to excavate, provide, and install underground tanks, pumps, and plumbing to provide safe storage and dispensing of the fuels. The installation is completed and operation begins without incident.

This new venture is not intended to contribute a significant profit from the fuel business but only to assure that a ready supply is available to keep the fleet of trucks and power equipment in service. REA sets prices based on a formula that provides gross margin sufficient only to cover ordinary maintenance of pump equipment and labor to service and manage the fuel operation. REA maintains the relationship with MO throughout the years.

Prices from MO are not particularly favorable owing to REA's independent status, relatively small volume, and exclusive vendor relationship with MO. REA's customers mistakenly believe the fuel prices to be highly profitable to REA but are satisfied with the associated convenience.

By the early 1990s many and varied horror stories of gasoline contamination of groundwater and subsoil are known. By this time routine procedures for evaluating, monitoring, and periodic replacement of pumping and storage systems are in practice. Under those procedures, the tanks are scheduled for replacement with newer technology double-walled, leak-sensor-fitted equipment. During the excavation process, contamination is found. The problem is isolated to a defective plumbing connection, but it is one that has probably existed from the first day of operation. The continual leakage of small amounts of gasoline has contaminated the soil. Only traces of the fuel are detected in core samples taken from a depth of 10 feet. This depth is far above the current groundwater depth of 40 feet. The following critical technical questions remain:

1. What was the rate of descent through the subsoil of the gasoline contamination?

2. What was the highest level of the groundwater during the period of the leakage?

3. Was there a period when the water table reached a height great enough that it could have contacted the continually dropping contamination level?

4. If the worst conditions have occurred, how much has the contamination spread?

Additional testing wells will need to be drilled, at substantial cost. The cost to date has deeply impacted the operating performance of the rental business. Cost of cleanup for the worst-case scenario will exceed the profit made in gasoline sales for the entire period of operation.

Contamination of this nature is all too common throughout the cities and towns of the United States. Many past environmental acts of irresponsibility have yet to be uncovered. Some current costs of development have been substantially increased because of acts of prior occupants. An example is the case of the healthful land redevelopment.

Healthful Land Redevelopment

A company called Health Services (HS) has received the donation of a vacant lot located in a prosperous and active business and residential community in southern California. The benefactor hopes that HS will utilize the lot to build a medical facility for the treatment of children's diseases. HS would very much like to develop such a facility in the community.

The past uses of the site are undocumented and uncertain. Standards for the building of health care facilities since the Olive View Hospital disaster during the 1971 Sylmar earthquake are stringent. Structural engineering requires that the subsoil be compacted to the very high density that is natural to the area and that the foundation engineering assures integrity against great seismic forces.

The process of development begins in 1990 with the drilling of core samples to determine the existing density of the subsoil. The findings are that the soil is not in its natural state and that substantial debris has been buried in the distant past. Further tests determine that the debris included lead from paint, and other undesirable and potentially harmful materials. Initially it is thought that soil removal and replacement to a reasonable depth of 2 to 3 feet would be an adequate safeguard for the future use of the site. The subsequent decision is, however, to replace all the soil with clean fill that will compact reliably and assure that the healthiest soil conditions will remain.

These predevelopment activities have increased the cost of construction by adding engineering tasks, construction permit approval, and the excavation, removal, replacement, and compaction of soil. Funding for the project continues to increase but results in the curtailment of other desirable efforts of HS, which relies on funding from various benefactors. The initial simple intent to provide a desirable location has resulted in a long-term financial entanglement and has consumed much of HS's available operating management resources.

Each of the case examples has demonstrated that the evolution of environmental management responsibility has compounded the elements of concern that financial management must contemplate. These compounding concerns have challenged the basic concepts upon which basic business operating theory is founded.

Key Accounting Concepts

The accounting profession has a number of key concepts upon which the consistent reporting of assessed conditions is based. These concepts have a profound effect on the role a CFO must take in the event of a discovery of an environmental incident or the implementation of a major operating system for environmental management.

The Going Concern

One concept that has a major bearing on financial reporting responsibilities is known as the "going concern" concept. The concept requires that reporting of financial information be based on the presumption that the business is intent on continued operation. In practice, this generally affects the valuation basis of assets and liabilities.

Assets under the going concern concept are always carried at original cost net of amortization through the period just ended. The amortization rate is predicated on the expected economic useful life of the business less any reliably assessed residual value. The assets are not appraised for the potential resale value, if liquidated. There is also a presumption that the original cost of assets is a fair and reasonable assessment of their base economic value to the business. No comparison is made to apparently similar assets operated by other businesses or available on the open market.

Liabilities under the going concern concept are recognized on the basis of contractual obligations and reasonably assessed identified demands. An evaluation may be made to determine that the periodic payment requirements can be met from the business' operating return. No effort is made to compute whether the potential liquidation value of the assets will return enough to meet these obligations. The assessment of potential liquidation value is left to the lenders and their appraisers.

Consistency

The going concern concept is elemental to the assumption of consistency when providing financial information related to the previous year or years. The owners or potential investors have been considered to have a right to be assured that the figures on each succeeding annual report have been prepared on the same basis. Any change is required to be reported in footnotes or other more overt presentation.

Insolvency

The accounting profession does not engage in speculation or supposition reporting for the potential winding down of a business. The process of compiling market value assessments of a business does not influence operating statements or public reporting until a statutory definition of insolvency has been determined. The definition of insolvency varies from state to state, and state law varies from federal law as written in the National Bankruptcy Act. Insolvency is deemed by most states to occur when a business is unable to meet maturing fund obligations. Under the National Bankruptcy Act, insolvency occurs only when the assessed fair valuation of assets is less than liabilities. Insolvency or bankruptcy are not further defined in Generally Accepted Accounting Principles (GAAP). At the time of the statutory determination of bankruptcy, the accounting profession begins a separate process of report preparation to formulate a statement of affairs. It is noteworthy that it is very possible for a business to reach statutory bankruptcy without meeting the federal criteria for bankruptcy. It is also possible for a business to meet its obligations while operating with negative net worth. The fact remains that a business in this condition needs to be examined in a different and more intense light. Unlike the ordinary public income statement and balance sheet, the statement of affairs is directed to inform and protect the creditors rather than the owners. The essence of the change is that the creditors have become the owners upon the event of insolvency.

Matching

Another example of an accounting concept that has an effect on environmental management costs is that of matching costs with revenue. This concept is intended to provide a mechanism to associate the relevant costs of units of output with the realized equivalent unit revenue. In the case of environmental management we are confronted with situations in which the costs of remediation may have no related (matched) unit of output. One alternative to matching units of output is "period costing," wherein the matching is with a fiscal period of time. The costs are presumed to relate to that period of time.

Typical period costs are those operating expenses that do not vary based on business levels and that fall into each accounting cycle (e.g., executive salaries, property taxes, fixed rentals). The concept also has been applied to situations in which the discovery of liability related to closed prior benefiting periods. This is due to the fact that the information value of the reported performance of prior periods cannot actually be affected without the availability of time travel. A certain amount of these transactions are inevitable in the imperfect world of information. To the extent that the total impact is similar and ordinary between comparative fiscal operating cycles, highlighting is not required. However, when these events are significant to the business performance of a specific period's financial statements, a complete and clear disclosure is required in the form of a footnote.

In addition to the reporting aspect of period costs is the assumption that there remains no residual value to the expenditures. This aspect has very significant impact on the process of continued operation of a business that has major remediation to accomplish and may be inappropriate in many circumstances.

Capitalization Policy

In the case of investments to remediate environmental damage, we may be dealing with the creation of new assets. The function of these assets may be to retrieve the utility of existing assets. Correction of discovered hazards is required to continue operations. In either instance, the costs may be of sufficient magnitude to question the merit of period costing. It is likely that, as in the example of The Incidental Business, no economic value was derived in the past due to the incident. However, continued economic utility may be derived in the future. When the events of REA are applied to a privately owned service station, remediation could represent an investment with long-term impact on operations (including insolvency). The remediation circumstances may dictate installation of wells and equipment. The actual investment, if paid entirely from available operating funds, may exceed the short-term cash generating capacity of the business. The business may, however, have the capacity to produce operating cash flows sufficient to meet all the current and prospective obligations if the necessary incremental funds are borrowed. This requires the expenditure for remediation to be reflected on the balance sheet as a liability to the extent of the debt. Therefore, the investment decision rests at least partially on the accounting treatment that is justified under the circumstances.

There are a number of justifications for the capitalization of remediation expenditures. In the example of the Plant Lease Bargain, it remains possible that remediation costs may constitute leasehold improvements. This could be the case if the combined amount of lease payments and amortization of capital costs over the remaining period of the lease is at or below market value for similar facilities. The nature of the improvements is also an important element. An examination beginning with the following questions must be conducted:

1. Will durable assets be created? If yes, what is the estimated useful life?
2. Is there potential residual value of the assets upon completion of the planned remediation?

3. Is there a projection of positive business operating return after inclusion of interest on any additional debt, depreciation and amortization of the remedy assets, and other incremental costs?
4. Answers to the above questions can be further compared with the following aspects of potential alternative decisions such as:
   a. What is the cost of unavoidable liability (regulatory and contractual)?
   b. What is the potential loss in capital value of the owner's interest?

All these considerations are relevant when land appreciation could justify incremental investment. Current appraised value may justify a prudent lending institution to provide mortgage funding. It is important to note that these concepts represent a very broad and liberal interpretation of GAAP and may meet with resistance.

Interaction with Public Accountants

A broad interpretation of capital assets and depreciation policy must be taken to treat remediation assets as value added. This interpretation may first meet stiff opposition from the auditors of the company's financial statements. It is very important to prepare a well-founded position before beginning an interim or year-end audit activity. This effort is necessary in order to present the liberalized treatment from a position of strength and knowledge. This liberalization will likely be regarded as an accounting change. Any such change is generally presented in a footnote to the financial statement.

There are many theoreticians in the accounting profession. The arguments may be apparently logical and very intense. The result of a business firm's accepting an audit position of inflexible treatment may precipitate a statement of affairs. The fact remains that there is no clear definition within the literature to stand firmly against the position to capitalize remediation assets. If the position of the auditors is entirely unyielding, fire them. The intent of the accounting change is one that can be expressed clearly and openly in any news release. Finding another public accountant to assume the audit will not be difficult. The concept of capitalizing environmental remedy assets is destined to become an ordinary accounting treatment.

16

Federal Facilities Compliance Act

Major John Gunderson
United States Air Force

On October 6, 1992, President Bush signed into law the Federal Facilities Compliance Act (FFCA). The act is intended to eliminate the double standard that generally was acknowledged between federal and privately owned facilities regarding the management and disposal of hazardous and solid waste. It does so by increasing the power of state agencies and the U.S. EPA over federal installations.

The passage of the act is likely to bring about major changes in environmental efforts at federal facilities. Many of the changes involve the resolution of relatively high-level questions such as the effect fines and penalties will have on the federal budget, and the myriad legal questions involved in changing traditional relations between federal and state bodies. Other changes, however, will directly affect how compliance activities are run at the line level. Environmental managers at federal facilities—as well as contractors and consultants conducting work on site—will need to be aware of the new regulatory environment they face, and the ways in which their practices must be tailored to the new situation.

The FFCA as currently enacted deals primarily with regulation and enforcement under the Resource Conservation and Recovery Act (RCRA). However, compliance under the Clean Air Act and other federal environmental statutes has been also subject to scrutiny, and developments similar to those reflected in the FFCA are likely to occur

with other federal environmental statutes as well. The time environmental managers devote to understanding and addressing the implications of the FFCA will therefore bring benefits that go beyond present-
day needs.

Following is a discussion of the rationale behind the act, a review of
the act's provisions, and a summary of how the act may affect those
with direct responsibility for environmental matters on a day-to-day
basis. The purpose is to provide a starting point for environmental
managers in their efforts to proactively address the problems and
opportunities posed by the FFCA.

Rationale

The FFCA is designed to address a situation that has garnered increasing attention in recent years at both the local and national levels. Some
private companies that have incurred significant costs to comply with
hazardous waste regulations have noted that nearby federal facilities
were apparently not subject to the same scrutiny from the state and
federal agencies. Statistics brought forward in the Supreme Court case
involving the Department of Energy's Fernald uranium-processing
plant in Ohio indicate that this view may be true of federal facilities
throughout the nation. The numbers indicate that federal facilities fail
to comply with the Clean Water Act far more often than private firms,
and also that the Department of Defense and Department of Energy
show a compliance rate 10 to 15 percent lower than private industry.

Why the disparity? Under the principle of "sovereign immunity,"
the federal government is not subject to the dictates of state or local
authorities except where specifically set forth in federal law. Federal
agencies took the position that such immunity protected them from
the civil fines and penalties levied by state agencies under RCRA.
While RCRA included a waiver of sovereign immunity, this waiver
did not explicitly allow for monetary penalties for past violations. The
Supreme Court's interpretation of waivers of sovereign immunity
have traditionally been extremely narrow. Supreme Court rulings
have established that such waivers will be considered to cover only
those areas specifically spelled out, and any ambiguity will be
resolved in favor of the federal government.

Federal agencies maintained their immunity from fines on legal
grounds, but they had other reasons as well for a narrow interpretation of the immunity waivers in RCRA. Federal agencies were concerned that states might not act reasonably in enforcement actions.

States like California with a history of aggressive environmental regulation could be viewed as unreasonable in comparison with states less active in the environmental arena. The federal agencies were also concerned that having to respond to the unique enforcement environment in each state would preclude them from pursuing a consistent approach to environmental problems nationwide, and effectively eliminate the agencies' ability to prioritize their efforts. For those reasons, among others, federal agencies maintained their immunity from fines and penalties.

Complicating matters was a complex legal history regarding the question of whether existing law provided for civil penalties for past violations. Did federal law provide for punishing past offenders, or merely for coercing compliance now and in the future? In two cases, the Supreme Court found that past violations were not covered in existing law.

Gwaltney v. Chesapeake Bay Foundation, 108 S. Ct. 376 (1987), decided by the Supreme Court on December 1, 1987, concerned an environmental group that brought a citizen's suit against the holder of a national pollutant discharge elimination system (NPDES) permit. The suit maintained that 1981 to 1984, the permit holder, Gwaltney of Smithfield, Ltd., had repeatedly violated the conditions of its permit by exceeding authorized effluent limits. Due to installation of new equipment, the last reported violation occurred in May 1984. In June 1984, the foundation announced its intention to file suit based on its belief that Gwaltney would continue to violate its NPDES permit.

A federal district court in Virginia granted a partial summary judgment against Gwaltney and established an amount for civil penalties. Hearing the case on appeal, the Supreme Court found that the Clean Water Act did not provide for civil penalties for wholly past violations, but that penalties could be assessed based on good-faith allegations of "continuous" or "intermittent" violations.

Gwaltney clarified the law regarding the provisions of the Clean Water Act as it applied to a private company. In *U.S. Department of Energy v. Ohio,* 112 S. Ct. 1627 (1992), the Supreme Court considered a related question in a case involving RCRA and a federal facility. The case centered on violations at a uranium-processing plant operated by the Department of Energy in Fernald, Ohio. The State of Ohio sued DOE for violation of federal and state hazardous waste and water discharge pollution abatement statutes in its operation of the plant. A consent decree entered into by Ohio and DOE covered all counts except for civil penalties for past violations. DOE maintained that the waiver of sovereign immunity under RCRA did not permit penalties for past violations.

The Supreme Court's decision supported DOE's position. The Court found that the waiver did not permit state imposition of civil penalties for past violations under RCRA or the Clean Water Act. The Court's decision drew a distinction between "punitive" penalties (that is, those intended to punish for past actions) and "coercive" penalties (that is, those a court may impose to enforce its orders governing actions now and in the future). It concluded that existing law permitted only coercive penalties.

Ohio made clear the necessity for a federal law allowing the imposition of administrative fines under RCRA. The conference report accompanying the legislation explicitly addressed the ambiguities the act was intended to resolve: "This waiver subjects the federal government to the full range of available enforcement tools...to penalize isolated, intermittent, or continuing violations as well as to coerce future compliance."

Summary of the Act

The FFCA's amendments to RCRA reflect the dual thrust of the act: first, to apply the same standards to federal facilities that apply to private industry, and second, to provide an enforcement framework to penalize noncompliance and encourage the rapid resolution of environmental problems. The provisions of the act are summarized below, with an emphasis on items of interest to those with compliance responsibility.

Scope of the Act

The FFCA is intended to subject government agencies to the full range of enforcement tools for regulations pertaining to the management and disposal of hazardous and solid waste. The scope of the act is limited to RCRA. Not included are the Clean Water Act; the Clean Air Act; the Comprehensive Environmental Response, Compensation, and Liability Act (CERCLA); underground tank regulations; and regulations pertaining to the disposal of medical waste.

One of the most important clarifications made in the act is the inclusion of hazardous waste management. The waivers previously in place in RCRA specified only disposal—creating confusion as to whether management was or was not subject to immunity.

Penalties and Fees

The act states that it is intended to waive sovereign immunity for violations of federal or state requirements, including "all administrative orders and all civil and administrative penalties and fines." It is important to note that the waiver has not been extended to local law, but only to federal and state law. The act goes on to specify that fines and penalties can be imposed for either "coercive" or "punitive" purposes, and for isolated, intermittent, or continuing violations.

The provision for punitive damages means that federal facilities may be penalized not only to encourage future compliance but also as punishment for past actions. Federal facilities will be subject to the full range of monetary sanctions for noncompliance. RCRA fines for noncompliance can be as great as $25,000 per day for each violation.

With regard to individual liability, the act holds federal employees immune from federal, state, and local civil fines for acts or omissions that occur in the performance of official duties. However, the act states that federal employees and agents remain subject to criminal penalties, which can include fines or imprisonment. Federal departments and agencies are immune from criminal sanctions.

The amendments covering fines and penalties are likely to be the most closely scrutinized by personnel charged with compliance. The waiver of immunity from civil penalties is not likely to bring any surprises to a federal facilities manager, since most federal facilities understand current exposure based in penalties assessed (thought not paid) in the past. (States have historically levied fines and penalties on federal facilities despite the fact that these facilities have not recognized their right to do so, and consequently have not paid them. The act is not retroactive.) However, considerable confusion still exists with regard to how the facilities will fund payment of these sanctions; how penalties will be computed, and how the waiver on civil penalties will affect the likelihood of criminal charges against individuals. These issues are examined briefly below.

Funding. Almost no legal precedent exists for the payment by federal agencies of environmental fines levied by the U.S. EPA or state authorities. The President's Signing Statement accompanying the act indicates that fines and penalties should be paid for by agency appropriations, not from the Judgment Fund. The underlying assumption is that if the agency pays fines from its own funds, it will have a greater incentive to comply with regulations and avoid the penalties. It seems likely that each agency will carry payment responsibilities as far as possible down to the operating level, so that the department or unit responsible for the activities resulting in the fine will be responsible for paying for it.

Making lower-level organizational units responsible for the payment of fines will help ensure that pressure for compliance reaches that level. But, it will not ensure that individuals in their day-to-day activities will be motivated to exercise care in hazardous waste management and disposal activities. Ultimately, federal agencies will have to assign compliance responsibility to individuals in a manner specific enough to allow an evaluation of their performance. This effort is likely to change the way environmental responsibility is distributed in the organization.

The effort to assign specific compliance responsibility to line personnel, combined with the uncertainty about where funds to pay fines will come from, may also have an impact on consultants and contractors. Consultants can expect increasing scrutiny about their activities in connection with noncompliant conditions. And unlike federal employees, consultants and contractors are not immune from civil fines and penalties.

Computation of Penalties. Another area of uncertainty is penalty computation. The U.S. EPA currently considers, among other factors, economic benefit when determining the magnitude of the fine to be levied. The fine is increased to the extent that the business has profited from avoided costs or taxes. This factor is clearly inapplicable to federal facilities. Size is another characteristic that distinguishes federal installations from their private counterparts. Other factors in penalty computation, such as the gravity of the violation, compliance history at the facility, and evidence of good faith efforts can be directly transferred from the private sector. RCRA gravity-based penalties are determined by the use of a matrix:

Potential for harm	Extent of Deviation from Requirement		
	Major	Moderate	Minor
Major	$25,000 to $20,000	$19,999 to $15,000	$14,999 to $11,000
Moderate	$10,999 to $8000	$7999 to $5000	$4999 to $3000
Minor	$3999 to $1500	$1499 to $500	$499 to $100

Facility managers should keep in mind, however, that the amount of a fine or penalty can often be negotiated. In fact, in most cases a letter from the agency concerning civil penalties should be viewed as an invitation to dialogue rather than as the final word on the subject. Increasingly, environmental authorities are approving schemes in which services, labor, or other items can be offered to reduce or elimi-nate the cash amount of the penalty. Known as "supplemental envi-ronmental projects," such efforts are now official policy of the federal EPA and many states.

Effect on Criminal Penalties.   One possible benefit of the waiver of immunity on civil penalties concerns the effect on criminal actions. Until the passage of the FFCA, criminal penalties were the only option avail-able to address ares of serious noncompliance in the management and disposal of hazardous waste at federal facilities. Because the FFCA opens the avenue of civil measures, the likelihood of criminal penalties in all but the most egregious instances of noncompliance is greatly reduced. However, the real effect of the act will not be known for some time.

Department of Defense Provisions

The federal agencies that are affected the most by the FFCA are the Departments of Transportation, Energy, and Defense. A number of provisions are directed specifically at the military. These include amendments on military munitions and public vessels, as well as regu-lations governing federally owned treatment works (FOTWs).

The FFCA orders the EPA to promulgate regulations specifying when military munitions may be considered hazardous waste. Confusion currently exists as to whether excess munitions should be considered hazardous waste. As recognized expert in this area, the Department of Defense is working with the EPA to clarify this matter and to establish standard procedures for the safe transportation and storage of munitions that are considered hazardous waste.

In response to concerns expressed by the Navy regarding the appli-cation of RCRA to naval vessels, the FFCA establishes that "public vessels" are not subject to RCRA's storage, manifest, inspection, or recordkeeping requirements. Hazardous wastes on the vessel become subject to regulation once they are onshore. This provision addresses a concern that ships would require permits under RCRA, a situation that may be untenable when ships sail from port to port.

Finally, the act adds a new section to RCRA on FOTWs. Formerly, federal facilities were not governed by the domestic sewage exclusion, a rule that applied to privately owned treatment works (POTWs). The rule excluded from the definition of solid waste (and therefore of hazardous waste, since the latter is a subset of solid waste) any solid or dissolved material in domestic sewage, subject to some conditions. RCRA's "mixture rule" previously required all sewage sludge to be treated as hazardous waste. The majority of FOTWs handle domestic sewage flows.

Other Provisions

The FFCA contains several provisions not discussed above. An amendment to the "Inspections" section of RCRA requires the U.S. EPA to conduct annual inspections of federal facilities, with the cost to be borne by the facilities. The same amendment allows, but does not require, the state to perform similar inspections.

A mixed waste amendment requires the Department of Energy to prepare a report on hazardous waste management and disposal in the United States. Designed for submittal to the U.S. EPA and state authorities, the report is intended to provide specific data on the volume of mixed waste on a state-by-state basis, and on the available mixed waste treatment capacities and technologies. A section is also added to RCRA Section 3021 that requires the Department of Energy to develop comprehensive plans to treat mixed wastes, and provides a detailed requirements for these plans.

A section on U.S. EPA enforcement activities indicates that the authors seek to have federal facilities treated in a manner identical with private parties. The section specifies that the U.S. EPA may initiate administrative enforcement actions under EPA's RCRA against any federal agencies or bodies, including the Congress and the judiciary. The amendment also establishes the right of the federal agencies to consult with the U.S. EPA before the administrative order can be finalized.

Other provisions limit the use states can make of income derived from civil penalties collected from federal agencies, and establishes ground rules for the payment of fees or service charges to states.

Effects at the Line Level

Line managers charged with environmental compliance responsibilities will be directly affected by the FFCA now and into the future. Following is a brief summary of the impact of each area.

Sovereign Immunity

Overall, the revised waiver of sovereign immunity means that a great deal of the ambiguity that existed with regard to U.S. EPA and state authority over federal facilities has been eliminated. Line managers should therefore work with facility environmental law specialists to become thoroughly familiar with the act and state administrative processes. This is necessary so that line managers can assess the appropriateness of actions taken by enforcement personnel and decide on appropriate responses.

Fines and Penalties

The firm establishment of the right of states and the U.S. EPA to levy fines and penalties means that the old methods of evaluating compliance performance will be replaced by the dollar value of penalties assessed. When faced with a potential or action compliance problem, the manager should coordinate immediately with the environmental laws specialist and the local Staff Judge Advocate to ensure that legal advice will be available through every stage of the process.

Inspections

The new requirement for annual U.S. EPA inspections of federal facilities raises the question of what happens to current internal audit functions. Since some suspect that the U.S. EPA will only inspect facilities where they have some suspicion of noncompliance, internal audit teams should continue to be a part of business. However, when an EPA effort takes place, departments will be required to provide funding, and, as a consequence, may not be able to continue with their own inspection efforts due to budget constraints.

Appendix A

California Environmental Legislation

The following is a summary of the environmental legislation under consideration in the 1991–1992 session of the Legislature of the State of California. The summary was prepared by the Office of Legislation of the California Department of Toxic Substances Control.

Assembly Measures

AB 181

Would have exempted local municipalities from liability for incidental solid waste handling services, as defined, provided before January 1, 1990. Would have required the trier of facts to consider specified criteria when apportioning liability for sites where a municipality performed nonincidental solid waste handling services. Would not have effected local municipalities' potential liability for negligent acts. Vetoed.

AB 143

Allows community facility districts to finance the acquisition, improvement, rehabilitation, or maintenance of any real or other tangible property for the purpose of hazardous substance release cleanups. Chapter 29, statutes of 1991.

AB 151

Requires the PUC to identify rail track that poses a local safety hazard and to report on those sites to the Legislature. Requires the PUC to propose regulations to reduce those safety hazards and to establish an inspection program for railroads. Chapter 763, statutes of 1991.

AB 158

Requires the Department to prepare a report stating all of a hazardous waste facility permit applicant's convictions, judgments, or settlements concerning violations of hazardous waste control law which occurred within the previous three years, excluding administrative or civil penalties of $1,000 or less. Requires local air pollution control or air quality management districts to review a permit applicant's compliance history as part of their permit approval process. Chapter 1209, statutes of 1991.

AB 189

Requires the DTSC and the SWRCB to each develop policies and procedures for oversight of the investigation and cleanup of hazardous substance releases by July 1, 1992. Chapter 292, statutes of 1991.

AB 213

Revises the definition of mining waste and clarifies the criteria used to define mining waste as hazardous waste. Chapter 174, statutes of 1991.

AB 240

Allows Native-American tribes to enter into cooperative agreements with Cal-EPA for the purpose of siting solid and hazardous waste facilities on Native-American lands. The intent of the bill is to provide for the full regulation of such facilities in accordance with state and federal law without directly addressing the issue of Native-American sovereignty. Chapter 805, statutes of 1991.

AB 260

Authorizes CIWMB to reduce the source reduction, recycling, and composting goals for a city or county that, on or before 1/1/90, disposed of 75% or more of its solid waste by transformation, if either of 2 specified conditions are met. Makes technical and clarifying changes in these provisions. Chapter 736, statutes of 1992.

AB 304

Replaces language relating to variance fees, permit modification fees, and postclosure fees that was chaptered out last session from AB 2794 (Chapter 1267, statutes of 1990). Replaces language that provided an exemption from variance fees for local agencies to transport waste from a household hazardous waste facility that accepts waste from small quantity commercial generators that was chaptered out last session from AB 2641 (Chapter 1266, statutes of 1990). Also conforms language relating to small quantity commercial generators with federal regulations. Chapter 1124, statutes of 1991.

AB 375

Reaffirms a public agency's obligation to follow through with mitigation measures identified as necessary to compensate for the negative impacts of a project being approved by the agency. Chapter 1070, statutes of 1992.

AB 420

Would have enacted the Local Toxics Enforcement and Training Act of 1991 to provide financial assistance through the Surveillance and Enforcement Branch of the DTSC for local agency training programs in enforcement of hazardous materials laws for peace officers, local public health officers, and public prosecutors. Would have repealed the existing Hazardous Material and Waste Enforcement Training Fund under Health and Safety Code Sec. 25515.2 and established the Hazardous Materials Enforcement and Training Account in the General Fund. Penalty moneys collected pursuant to Health and Safety Code Chapter 6.95 would have been placed in this account, and made available, upon appropriation by the Legislature, to the DTSC to implement the provisions of the bill. Would have established the Advisory Committee on Toxics Enforcement and Training within the DTSC.

AB 473

Authorizes additional expenditure of existing funds for operation and maintenance costs of a water treatment system for the Valley County Water District in the San Gabriel Valley. Chapter 447, statutes of 1991.

AB 476

Provides that fees and taxes local agencies receive from hazardous waste facilities shall not be required to meet the state's "maintenance of efforts" requirements. Chapter 1073, statutes of 1991.

AB 604

Exempts government agencies from fees related to hazardous waste cleanups performed by the agency. The fee exemptions would not apply to hazardous waste spills caused by the agency. Chapter 1122, statutes of 1991.

AB 646

Provides special conditions for the management of dilute aqueous waste containing metals and provides that effluent from silver processing shall be excluded from full regulation as a hazardous waste if specified conditions are met. Chapter 1125, statutes of 1991.

AB 684

Requires the safety division of the PUC to inspect and investigate railroads and public mass transit guide-ways, to advise the PUC on its findings, to propose measures to reduce railway accidents, to enforce state and federal rail transportation law, and to report annually to the Legislature on its activities. Chapter 764, statutes of 1991.

AB 715

Authorizes specified hazardous waste transporters to inspect and self-certify their rolloff bins. Outlines inspection criteria, requires the

California Highway Patrol to conduct random inspections of at least 25 percent of all rolloff bins to ensure compliance, and imposes penalties for violations of the program. Chapter 1084, statutes of 1991.

AB 736

Would have required railroads to have in the engine a Secondary Emergency Response Materials packet containing specified information on all hazardous materials being transported, as well as providing the same to local emergency response agencies. Would have required railroads to notify immediately the appropriate local emergency response agency in the event of an accident. Vetoed.

AB 754

Requires the East Bay Regional Park District to acquire property for and plan for development and operation of the East Bay Shoreline State Park. All costs necessary to test for the presence of toxic wastes and hazardous wastes or substances associated with the appraisal and acquisition process will be paid from existing bond funds designated for park acquisition. Gives the district immunity from "liability and responsibility" for existing and potential environmental cleanup costs and activities. Chapter 2054, statutes of 1992.

AB 869

Requires Cal-EPA to provide local governments with lists of contaminated sites and requires that development permit applicants provide specified information to the lead agency if their proposed development is located on a site included on these lists. Chapter 1212, statutes of 1991.

AB 903

Authorizes the Controller to reimburse counties with a population under 1,750,000 from the Clandestine Drug Cleanup Account for the costs of prosecuting or investigating specified controlled substance clandestine laboratories, or for the costs of removing, disposing of, or storing toxic waste from these laboratories. Chapter 929, statutes of 1991.

AB 908

Requires each planning agency and the legislative body of each county and city to adopt a comprehensive, long-term general plan for the physical development of the county or city and land outside its boundaries that, in the planning agency's judgment, bears relation to its planning. Requires the general plan to contain, among other elements, a safety element for the protection of the community from seismic and other geological hazards, floods and fires. Chapter 823, statutes of 1992.

AB 928

Prohibits a school board from approving the acquisition of a new school site, or the construction of a school, or the approval of an EIR or negative declaration for a school project, on any property within ¼ mile of a facility which handles hazardous substances. Requires an owner or operator of a development project within ¼ mile of a school site which handles hazardous substance to submit an RMPP, or exemption to RMPP requirements, pursuant to a specified procedure, to the lead agency for permit approval. If it is determined that the RMPP is deficient, the operator is required to submit a corrected RPM within a specified time or may be granted a one-time extension of 30 days prior to resubmittal. Chapter 1183, statutes of 1991.

AB 937

Would have required permit applicants for specified potential high-impact development projects, such as hazardous waste treatment facilities, to provide demographic data with permit applications and would have prohibited approval of permit applications if the required information was not provided. Vetoed.

AB 1024

Provides mechanisms for school districts to recover costs for the cleanup of hazardous substances on property acquired through eminent domain proceedings. Chapter 814, statutes of 1991.

AB 1131

Sets a new requirement for submission of an RMPP by handlers of acutely hazardous materials within 12 months following the request for the RMPP by a local agency. Adds a requirement for inclusion in the RMPP of a clearly prepared map noting the location of the facility in relation to specified populations and the zone of vulnerability including the levels of expected exposure in each zone. Sets public noticing and public review requirements for local agency's determination that the RMPP is complete. Requires the local agency to consider public comments in their review of the RMPP. Chapter 816, statutes of 1991.

AB 1475

Requires persons managing more than 100 kg a month of recyclable materials, which are excluded from the hazardous waste control law, to provide specified information to local agencies. Chapter 715, statutes of 1991.

AB 1519

Prohibits the Department of Transportation, when acquiring property for the Cypress freeway reconstruction project, from deducting costs for hazardous substance removal from the compensation paid for the property to the owner of a small business. The prohibition only applies if DTSC, the San Francisco Bay Regional Water Quality Control Board, and the Alameda County Department of Health all make specified determinations. Chapter 1228, statutes of 1992.

AB 1520

Requires the CIWMB to consult with various agencies, including the DTSC, for concurrence with a finding that a specific sludge could be counted towards solid waste diversion requirements. Chapter 718, statutes of 1991.

AB 1613

Phases out interim status for non-RCRA offsite hazardous waste facilities. Provides that a permit to modify a land disposal facility or offsite large treatment facility is a discretionary project subject to CEQA and requires an EIR or negative declaration. Chapter 7-19, statutes of 1991.

AB 1639

Requires asbestos or hazardous substances found by a general contractor on a worksite to be removed under separate contract before work in the area can be continued. Chapter 789, statutes of 1991.

AB 1642

Requires a lead agency to independently review and analyze any draft EIR, EIR, or negative declaration and, prior to adoption, find that the report or declaration reflects the independent judgment of the lead agency. Modifies the procedures for lead agency response to comments from public agencies. Chapter 905, Statutes of 1991.

AB 1713

Allows the DTSC to reclassify a site as to size during an ongoing mitigation phase for the purposes of adjusting (up or down) the oversight fee. This would enable the DTSC to more accurately assess fees for site mitigation oversight activities. Also contains RCRA conformity language. Chapter 1126, statutes of 1991.

AB 1731

Eliminates an obsolete provision of current law which provides a categorical variance from regulation by the SWRCB for specified underground hazardous waste tanks. This variance has not been used in eight years. Chapter 724, statutes of 1991.

AB 1735

Amends foreclosure law to allow lenders to waive their lien as an alternative remedy to foreclosure when the secured property is environmentally impaired due to actions by the borrower or a related party. Allow lenders to bring an action against borrowers for breach of any environmental provision in a contract relating to the real property security. Gives lenders entry and inspection rights on contaminated or potentially contaminated property. Chapter 1167, statutes of 1991.

AB 1760

Requires, after January 1, 1994, solid waste facilities to refuse to accept major appliances or other metallic discard which is economically feasible to salvage, as determined by the facility operator. Prohibits any person from disposing of metallic discard mixing metallic discard with solid waste, excepting by a solid waste facility that complies with specified conditions. Requires the CIWMB, in consultation with the DTSC and other agencies, to conduct studies on possible uses of metallic recycling residues and to develop a plan on metallic discard recycling. Chapter 849, statutes of 1991.

AB 1772

Establishes a five-tiered program for authorizing treatment at most hazardous waste facilities that do not require a permit under federal law. The five tiers, in descending order of regulatory burden, are: (1) the federal-equivalent "full" permit tier, (2) the "standardized permit" tier, (3) the "permit by rule" PBR tier, (4) the "conditional authorization" tier, and (5) the "conditional exemption" tier. Requires that most of these facilities be inspected within two years of their entering that tier and be inspected every two years thereafter. Chapter 1345, statutes of 1992.

AB 1899

Allows used or spent etchants, stripping solutions, and plating solutions to be excluded from regulation as a hazardous waste. Allows an exclusion to specified contaminated fuels provided they are processed into fuels at a refinery. Repeals the requirement for an annual report from the DTSC to the Legislature listing the recyclable hazardous wastes, and instead requires the DTSC to include any additions or deletions to the existing list in the DTSC Biennial Report. This bill is double joined with AB 1713. Chapter 1173, statutes of 1991.

AB 1991

Eliminates the reduced fee for disposal of hazardous waste in state or out of state for generators that use specified treatment methods. Chapter 1127, statutes of 1991.

AB 2076

Requires oil manufacturers to pay quarterly $0.04 to the CIWMB for every quart of lubricating oil sold or transferred in, or imported to California. Requires the CIWMB to pay a recycling incentive of $0.04/quart to certified used-oil collection centers, curbside collection programs, and industrial generators for every quart of lubricating oil collected and transported to a used-oil recycling facility. The recycling incentive received by the centers would subsequently be refunded to consumers who return used oil to the centers. Requires the DTSC to annually inspect used-oil recycling facilities. Chapter 817, statutes of 1991.

AB 2092

Extends the date when the city source reduction and recycling plan and the HHW plan to the county must be prepared and adopted to 7/1/92. Specifies related duties if the city determines it is unable to comply with the deadline and requirements of CEQA. Chapter 105, statutes of 1992.

AB 2178

Specifies conditions under which (1) any location may accept recyclable paint for eventual recycling, (2) any person can transport recyclable latex paint without the use of a manifest, and (3) any person can recycle latex paint. Chapter 364, statutes of 1991.

AB 2277

Would have repealed section 6434 of the Labor Code, which grants governmental entities immunity from civil penalties when worker safety violations have been identified. Vetoed.

AB 2280

Enacts the Local Toxics Enforcement and Training Act of 1991 to provide financial assistance through the Surveillance and Enforcement Branch of DTSC for local agency training programs in the enforcement of hazardous materials laws for peace officers, local public health officers, and public prosecutors. Chapter 743, statutes of 1992.

AB 2292

Existing law authorizes a county to establish and operate a collection program for farmers with specified unregistered or outdated agricultural pesticides until January 1, 1993. AB 2292 extends this authority until January 1, 1994 and includes participation by: (1) agricultural pest control businesses, (2) agricultural pesticide dealerships, (3) other agriculturally oriented businesses, (4) parks, cemeteries, and golf courses, and (5) specified government agencies. Chapter 591, statutes of 1992.

AB 2299

Allows DTSC to extend the exempt holding time for hazardous waste to be kept at the transfer station. Such an extension could be granted only to a public agency or a response action contractor in case of an emergency release. Chapter 293, statutes of 1992.

AB 2370

Establishes the California Dry Cleaning Industry Task Force. Requires the Task Force to prepare a report on prescribed matters relating to the effect of dry cleaning industry practices on the environment. Requires submission of the report to the Governor and the Legislature by February 28, 1993. These provisions become inoperative on March 31, 1993, and are repealed on January 1, 1994. Chapter 347, statutes of 1991.

AB 2456

Revises the definitions of "owner" and "property" to include owners of common areas within a residential common interest development for purposes of a rebuttable presumption against liability for a hazardous substance release. Chapter 859, statutes of 1992.

AB 2472

Requires responsible agencies and public agencies under CEQA, with jurisdiction over natural resources affected by projects that are held in trust for the people of the state, to respond to a notice that an environmental impact report is required for the project. Chapter 1201, statutes of 1992.

AB 2481

Consolidates several reporting requirements in its biennial report. Repeals the requirement that the SWRCB submit an annual report on an agricultural drainage project loan program and on agricultural drainage problems. Chapter 321, statutes of 1992.

AB 2497

Would have exempted dry cleaning operations from hazardous waste treatment facility requirements. Vetoed.

AB 2500

Would have repealed the requirement that DHS develop a plan for the management, treatment, and disposal of low-level radioactive waste (LLRW) and submit elements to the legislature. Would have provided that, if the operator of a LLRW facility fails to maintain the minimum nuclear liability insurance, DHS would have been required to suspend immediately the license issued to the operator of the facility. Would have set fees on generators of LLRW to fund the Low-Level Radioactive Waste Facility Environmental Cleanup and Liability Response Fund and would have set specified requirements for operation of LLRW facilities. Vetoed.

AB 2589

Allows the Director of DTSC to release from liability those who provide financing for removal/remedial costs at the site of the former Kaiser Steel Mill in Fontana or those who acquire an interest in the hazardous substance release site under specified conditions. Chapter 1209, statutes of 1992.

AB 2618

Makes technical and nonsubstantive changes to existing statutes regulating the permitting of hazardous and solid waste facilities in Native-American lands, and the definition of a permit. Chapter 113, statutes of 1992.

AB 2750

Makes minor changes to the definitions of "release" and "real property security," effecting no real change to law. Chapter 167, statutes of 1992.

AB 2824

Exempts state and local agencies from preparing and submitting written reports to the Legislature or the Governor until January 1, 1995, except under specified conditions. Chapter 710, statutes of 1992.

AB 2874

Requires state agencies to make specified interest payments on overdue payment of contracts for property or services. A payment becomes overdue the day after the due date provided for in the contract, or 51 calendar days after the postmark date of the invoice. Chapter 711, statutes of 1992.

AB 2967

Requires DTSC to prepare a plan by January 1, 1994 to survey urban counties for abandoned sites. Chapter 550, statutes of 1992.

AB 3024

Would have required permit applicants for specified potential high-impact development projects to provide demographic data with permit applications and would have prohibited approval of permit applications if the required information were not provided. Vetoed.

AB 3043

Would have required rail transporters of hazardous materials operating on any route deemed to pose a local safety hazard, to include a "Secondary Emergency Response Materials" packet in the engine of any train carrying hazardous materials, as well as a 24-hour emergency response number. Vetoed.

AB 3078

Relates to CEQA, which requires state and local lead agencies to prepare an environmental impact report on projects that may have a significant effect on the environment. Limits its application, in any development, to effects upon the environment that are peculiar to the parcel or the project and were not addressed as significant effects in the prior environmental impact report. Chapter 1102, statutes 1992.

AB 3089

Makes technical amendments to the underground tank law, which is administered by local governments with guidance from the State Water Resources Control Board. Chapter 654, statutes of 1992.

AB 3172

Expands the "recyclable materials" exemption for on-site recovery of oily waste and conditionally exempts treatability studies. Chapter 1343, statutes of 1992.

AB 3173

Makes technical changes to the Lempert-Keene-Seastrand Oil Spill Prevention and Response Act. Chapter 1313, statutes of 1992.

AB 3180

Creates the Leaking Underground Storage Tank Cost Recovery Fund in the General Fund, and would authorize SWRCB to expend the money in the fund, upon appropriation, for specified activities relating to underground storage tanks containing petroleum, and for administrative expenses related to carrying out these activities. Requires that all money recovered pursuant to that federal law be deposited to the Fund. Chapter 1215, statutes of 1992.

AB 3188

Requires that the provisions regulating underground storage tanks are to be known as the Barry Keene Underground Storage Tank Cleanup Trust Fund Act of 1989. Establishes the Underground Storage Tank

Cleanup Fund in the State Treasury, rather than the General Fund. Revises the requirements for a tank owner to be eligible for payment of a claim without certain funding being made and declares that these changes are declaratory of existing law. Chapter 1290, statutes of 1992.

AB 3222

Requires each state agency using any automated voice system to require, during normal business hours, a human operator option and the routing of rotary telephone callers to live persons. Vetoed.

AB 3348

Loans $3 million from the Solid Waste Disposal Site Cleanup and Maintenance Account (SWDC&MA) to the California Used Oil Recycling Fund, appropriates $2.5 million to SWRCB for completion of review of specified solid waste landfill facilities under the Solid Waste Assessment Test program, makes specified changes in grant funding from the SWDC&MA, and allocates $60,000 to DTSC for the development and maintenance, jointly with the CIWMB, of a database on all HHW collection events, facilities, and programs within the state. Chapter 1218, statutes of 1992.

AB 3427

Requires DHS to adopt regulations to establish standards to carry out the Medical Waste Management Act and to issue permits for offsite medical waste treatment facilities. Requires the regulations that the Department is directed to adopt to promote waste minimization and source reduction. Revises the definitions for the terms "biohazardous waste," "common storage facility," "container," "medical waste generator," "onsite," and "sharps waste." Chapter 878, statutes of 1992.

AB 3511

Requires that if a state agency, in proposing to adopt or amend any regulation, determines that the action may have a significant adverse economic impact on any business enterprise, the agency is required to include specified information in the notice of proposed action on the regulation. Requires state agencies proposing to adopt or amend any regulation to assess the potential for adverse economic impact on California business enterprises and individuals. Chapter 1306, statutes of 1992.

AB 3541

Allows DTSC to enter into agreement with owners and operators of hazardous waste facilities to provide consultative services, including limited on-site inspections. Authorizes the DTSC to sell, lease, or license products, including videotapes, audiotapes, books, pamphlets and software. Chapter 1117, statutes of 1992.

AB 3631

Authorizes arson investigators to enforce hazardous waste control laws and regulations. Chapter 1231, statutes of 1992.

AB 3690

Clarifies DTSC responsibility to update its regulations related to chronic toxicity hazards. Chapter 1058, statutes of 1992.

AB 3694

Provides the Attorney General or a district attorney, if approved by the Attorney General, with the power to sue illegal dumpers for costs to be incurred in repairing the environmental damage arising from the crime. It applies to illegal hazardous waste disposal cases but not to state Superfund cleanup cases. Funds may be collected before doing the work and held in a special deposit trust fund or the Fish and Wildlife Pollution Cleanup and Abatement Account. Chapter 1123, statutes of 1992.

AB 3765

Authorizes Cal-EPA to call together permit-writing teams of DTSC and Regional Water Quality Control Board staff to develop consolidated permits when an applicant so requests. Chapter 952, statutes of 1992.

AB 3789

Requires Cal-EPA to contract for a study on the application of hazardous waste testing criteria for corrosivity of cementitious wastes, including, but not limited to, portland cement and cement kiln dust (CKD). The study will be paid for by private industry at a cost not to exceed $100,000. DTSC will suspend regulation of cementitious wastes for corrosivity until completion of the study, or until January 1, 1994. Cal-EPA must appoint a technical advisory committee to assist in selection of a contractor to perform the study, and to provide technical assistance during the study. Chapter 1125, statutes of 1992.

ACR 62

Declares that no state agency shall accept financial liability or responsibility for environmental damage originating from operations at three specific California laboratories. Chapter 110, statutes of 1991.

Senate Measures

SB 48

Requires railroad corporations to pay a fee to the PUC for purposes of being regulated by the PUC, and establishes an article to specifically address "Railroad Safety and Emergency Planning and Response." The article requires the PUC to report to the Legislature concerning railroad sites that pose a risk and to adopt regulations providing for enhanced railroad safety. Creates the "Rail Accident Prevention and Response Fund" which funds various studies and costs associated with implementing the article. Creates a Cal-EPA deployment force to develop a plan to prevent railroad spill accidents and deploy resources to mitigate spills. Enhances current enforcement mechanisms related to hazardous material spills and establishes penalties for violations. Chapter 766, statutes of 1991.

SB 50

Repeals the presumptive classification of solid waste incinerator ash and residues as nonhazardous under H&SC Sec. 25143.5, but retains the presumptive nonhazardous classification for biomass incinerator ash and residues if specified conditions are met. Removes a pre-1985 preemptive classification of solid waste incinerator ash and residues from waste-to-energy facilities as nonhazardous. Chapter 1218, statutes of 1991.

SB 152

Requires railroad corporations having a gross intrastate revenue of $10 million or more to pay a fee for purposes of funding a rail safety program. Requires the PUC to submit a budget for the rail safety program for the Legislature for approval. Chapter 767, statutes of 1991.

SB 194

Makes a technical change to include hazardous waste property and border zone property determination fees within Hazardous Substance Tax Law. Allows liable persons to "recover costs" rather than "seek contribution or indemnity" from other persons for cleanup costs, and corrects chaptering-out problems from last year's fee bills. Chapter 1123, statutes of 1991.

SB 260

Would have required courts to place corporations on probation for specified felony or misdemeanor convictions. Would have provided an exemption to nonprofit and professional corporations. Vetoed.

SB 442

Would have included the existence of lots or other areas which contain hazardous waste or a hazardous substance within the factors whereby land could be characterized as a "blighted area" for purposes of redevelopment and would have set special reporting requirements concerning the costs and funding sources of hazardous substance cleanup. Vetoed.

SB 428

Exempts businesses handling lubricating oil, including motor oil, transmission fluid, and hydraulic fluid, from the requirement of establishing and implementing a business plan for the emergency response to a release of the hazardous material. The exemption only applies if the lubricating oil is stored in quantities of 55 gallons or less at any time. Chapter 1123, statutes of 1991.

SB 611

Authorizes DTSC to grant variances from land disposal restrictions for wastes that were receiving a variance from the original 1990 land disposal restriction deadline. The extension ends on January 1, 1993. Chapter 33, statutes of 1992.

SB 669

Requires the DTSC (upon request by the person issued an order under Sec. 25187 who chooses to resolve the order directly with the Department and does not file an administrative or judicial appeal) to prepare a written statement explaining the violation and the penalties applied as specified. Requires the DTSC to amend the written statement into the order. Chapter 885, statutes of 1991.

SB 711

Would have prohibited post-trial confidentiality agreements regarding specified information in court actions based on fraud, personal injury, or wrongful death alleging damages caused by a defective product or an environmental hazard unless a final protective order is filed and entered by the court. Vetoed.

SB 846

Allows public utilities to backfill excavations with native soil if, among other conditions, a local agency has not provided (within 30 days prior to compaction), the public utility or its contractor with physical evidence of, or substantial reason to believe that there has been, contamination of the soil from hazardous wastes. Chapter 1060, statutes of 1991.

SB 966

Establishes a 5-year pilot program in not more than 8 counties to allow the Department to delegate its authority to carry out specified hazardous waste administrative enforcement actions under H&SC Secs. 25187 and 25189.2 to an authorized local health officer through a negotiated delegation agreement. Fifty percent of the collected penalties would go to the DTSC (to be deposited in the Hazardous Waste Control Account) and 50% to the local agency imposing the penalty. Makes a clarifying amendment to the definition of "each day of violation" pursuant to H&SC Sec. 25189.5. Makes a number of amendments conforming the provisions of the bill to the Administrative Procedures Act. Chapter 886, statutes of 1991.

SB 1021

Requires the Governor by March 15 of each year to prepare and transmit an annual report to the Legislature entitled "Environmental Report of the Governor." The report is to be prepared by the Governor, utilizing the staff and resources of state agencies. The report shall broadly review environmental developments and trends and summarize state policies and actions relating to environmental developments and trends. Chapter 777, statutes of 1991.

SB 1133

Changes the method of calculating the major hazardous waste streams that must be addressed in the plans and reports required by the Hazardous Waste Source Reduction and Management Review Act of 1989 (SB 14, Chapter 1218, statutes of 1989). Chapter 538, statutes of 1991.

SB 1143

Requires DTSC, in cooperation with the CIWB, to develop and maintain a database of all HHW collection events, facilities, and programs within the state. Raises certain volume and weight limits for specified HHWs transported to household hazardous waste collection facilities (HHWCF), and would authorize curbside collection programs to transport specified HHW wastes to HHWCF. Chapter 1346, statutes of 1992.

SB 1197

Sets fines and penalties for knowingly depositing hazardous substances (including radioactive materials) into or upon any road, street, highway, alley, or railroad right of way or upon the land of another (without permission of the owner), or into the waters of the state. Chapter 1120, statutes of 1991.

SB 1346

Would have allowed DTSC to consult with the CIWMB on a study of the handling and disposal of discarded fluorescent light bulbs. Vetoed.

SB 1410

Appropriates $1.4 million from the general fund to DTSC for use in cleaning up the ASARCO hazardous substance release site. Chapter 891, statutes of 1992.

SB 1469

Creates and revises several fees supporting DTSC. Combines the funding of the Hazardous Waste Control Account (HWCA) and the Hazardous Substances Account (HSA), and requires the DTSC to develop a plan to charge hourly rates for several of its activities. Chapter 852, statutes of 1992.

SB 1489

Would have required the Secretary of the Business, Transportation, and Housing Agency, using existing resources and personnel, to study the feasibility of establishing a one-stop permit system for state permit applicants at convenient locations throughout the state. Vetoed.

SB 1524

Makes several changes to hazardous materials manifest and hazardous material reporting requirements. Requires OEHHA, in consultation with administering agencies, to adopt a single hazardous materials reporting form for businesses. Requires ARB to streamline emissions reporting. Allows Cal-EPA to request specified information as found in the federal toxic chemical release form and requires them to create a standard facility identification provision for use by the regulation community and the agencies within Cal-EPA. Requires DTSC to: (1) make specified changes to annual hazardous waste facility report requirements; (2) revise the California Hazardous Waste Code Numbers to include only non-RCRA hazardous wastes; (3) eliminate the requirement that specified small-quantity generators obtain a California EPA ID number; (4) simplify the generator notification form for non-RCRA hazardous waste generators; and (5) establish a mechanism to enable DTSC to use the automated hazardous waste manifest data to assist generators in completing the federal biennial report. Chapter 684, statutes of 1992.

SB 1535

Would have repealed DTSC authority to plan and construct a model incineration facility for the disposal of hazardous waste. Would have required DTSC to prepare and submit to the legislature by 6/1/93 a report on statewide capacity for the incineration of hazardous wastes. Vetoed.

SB 1679

Creates the San Gabriel Basin Authority and authorizes it to assess taxes on groundwater users with the Basin. The funds generated will be used to construct and operate groundwater treatment facilities. Chapter 776, statutes of 1992.

SB 1726

Delays the imposition of treatment standards upon hazardous wastes for which incineration is a treatment option or for which the waste is a solid hazardous waste containing metals, and requires DTSC to reevaluate the treatment standards for which incineration is an option. Broadens the applicability of the Hazardous Waste Source Reduction and Management Review Act (SB 14, Chapter 1218, statutes of 1989) by including generators of more than 5,000 kilograms of hazardous waste per year. Chapter 853, statutes of 1992.

SB 1731

Amends the Air Toxics Hot Spots law; imposes new requirements on the Office of Environmental Health Hazard Assessment and the Air Resources Board. Chapter 1162, statutes of 1992.

SB 1832

Would have extended certain reporting requirements for the Public Utilities Commission relating to railroads and correct deficiencies in SB 48 (Chapter 760, statutes of 1991). Vetoed.

SB 1985

Exempts HHW collection programs from liability for cleanup oversight fees and defines "household hazardous waste collection program." Chapter 363, statutes of 1992.

SB 2056

Allows a responsible party who is in compliance with a DTSC cleanup order or agreement to seek, in addition to contribution, treble damages from noncompliant responsible parties (RPs). One-half of any treble damage award will be paid to DTSC, for deposit in the Hazardous Substance Account. The remaining one-half will be shared by each contribution plaintiff in proportion to their agreed upon cleanup cost responsibility. Explicitly authorizes DTSC to intervene for cost recovery in contribution lawsuits between RPs. Chapter 1237, statutes of 1992.

SB 2057

Clarifies the definition of "waste," excludes from regulation as hazardous waste chlorofluorocarbons (CFCs) that are recycled, allows DTSC to order RPs to pay for cleanups, and establishes penalties for intentionally or negligently releasing hazardous substances. Chapter 1344, statutes of 1992.

Acronyms

AA	Attainment Area
ACL	Alternate Concentration Limit Act
AHERA	Asbestos Hazard Emergency Response Act
AIA	Asbestos Information Act
AIHC	American Industrial Health Council
AMSA	Association of Metropolitan Sewerage Agencies
ANPR	Advance Notice of Proposed Rulemaking
ANSI	American National Standards Institute
AOC	Administrative Order on Consent
APCA	Air Pollution Control Association
ARAR	Applicable or Appropriate Relevant Requirement
ASHAA	Asbestos School Hazard Abatement Act
ASIWPCA	Association of State and Interstate Water Pollution Control Administrators
ASTM	American Society for Testing and Materials
ASTSWMO	Association of State and Territorial Solid Waste Management Organizations
ATSDR	Agency for Toxic Substances and Disease Registry
AWMA	Air and Waste Management Association
AWT	Advanced Wastewater Treatment
BACT	Best Available Control Technology
BAT	Best Available Technology
BATEA	Best Available Technology Economically Achievable
BCT	Best Conventional Technology

BDT	Best Demonstrated Technology
BMP	Best Management Practice
BOD	Biologic Oxygen Demand
BPJ	Best Professional Judgment
BPT	Best Practicable Technology
BTEX	Benzene, Toluene, Ethylbenzene, and Xylenes
BTU	British Thermal Unit
CAA	Clean Air Act
CAP	Corrective Action Plan
CDC	Centers for Disease Control
CDE	Control Device Evaluation
CEPP	Chemical Emergency Preparedness Program
CERCLA	Comprehensive Environmental Response, Compensation, and Liability Act (Superfund)
CERCLIS	Comprehensive Environmental Response, Compensation, and Liability List
CFCs	Chlorofluorocarbons
CFR	Code of Federal Regulations
CMI	Corrective Measures Implementation
CMS	Controlled Material Storage
CMS	Corrective Measures Study
CO	Carbon Monoxide
CSGWPP	Comprehensive State Ground Water Protection Program
CTG	Control Techniques Guidelines
CWA	Clean Water Act
CZM	Coastal Zone Management
DEC	Division Environmental Coordinator
DMR/QA	Discharge Monitoring Reports/Quality Assurance
ECRA	Environmental Cleanup and Responsibility Act (New Jersey)
EFT	Effluent Toxicity Testing
EGD	Effluent Guidelines Division (EPA)
EIR	Environmental Impact Statement
EOP	End-of-Pipe Treatment
EPA	Environmental Protection Agency
EPCRA	Emergency Planning and Community Right-to-Know Act

ERC	Emissions Reduction Credit
FACA	Federal Advisory Committee Act
FDA	Food and Drug Administration
FFDCA	Federal Food, Drug, and Cosmetic Act
FGD	Flue Gas Desulfurization
FIFRA	Federal Insecticide, Fungicide, and Rodenticide Act
FIP	Federal (Air Quality) Implementation Plan
FOTW	Federally Owned Treatment Works
FS	Feasibility Study
GC/CD	Gas Chromatograph/Conventional Detector
GC/MS	Gas Chromatograph/Mass Spectrometer
GLP	Good Laboratory Practices
HAP	Hazardous Air Pollutant
HAZWOPER	Hazarous Waste Operations and Emergency Response
HC	Hydrocarbons
HCS	Hazard Communication Standard
HHW	Household Hazardous Waste
HMTA	Hazardous Materials Transportation Act
HMTUSA	Hazardous Materials Transportation Uniform Safety Act
HRS	Hazard Ranking System (Superfund)
HSWA	Hazardous and Solid Waste Amendments
IERL	Industrial Environmental Research Laboratory (EPA)
ITC	Interagency Testing Committee
LAER	Lowest Achievable Emission Rate
LDR	Land Disposal Restriction
LQG	Large-Quantity Generators
LUFT	Leaking Underground Fuel Tank
LUST	Leaking Underground Storage Tank
MACT	Maximum Achievable Control Technology
MCL	Maximum Contaminant Level
MPRSA	Marine Protection, Research, and Sanctuaries Act
MSDS	Material Safety Data Sheets
NA	Nonattainment Area
NAAQS	National Ambient Air Quality Standards
NAPCTAC	National Air Pollution Control Techniques Advisory Committee

NCAPS	National Corrective Action Priority System (RCRA)
NCP	National Contingency Plan
NEPA	National Environmental Policy Act
NESHAP	National Emission Standard for Hazardous Air Pollutants
NIOSH	National Institute for Occupational Safety and Health
NOAA	National Oceanographic and Atmospheric Agency
NOV	Notice of Violation
NOx	Nitrogen Oxides
NPDES	National Pollutant Discharge Elimination System
NPL	National Priorities List
NPRM	Notice of Proposed Rulemaking
NRC	National Response Center *or* Nuclear Regulatory Commission
NRDC	Natural Resources Defense Council
NRT	Natural Resources Trustees
NSPS	New Source Performance Standards
NTP	National Toxicology Program
ORD	Office of Research and Development (EPA)
ORM	Other Regulated Materials
OSHA	Occupational Safety and Health Administration
OSHRC	Occupational Safety and Health Review Commission
OSTP	Office of Science and Technology Policy
OSW	Office of Solid Waste
OTA	Office of Technology Assessment
PA	Preliminary Investigation
PAH	Polynuclear Aromatic Hydrocarbons
PBR	Permit by Rule (California)
PCB	Polychlorinated Biphenyl
PCE	Perchloroethylene
PEC	Plant Environmental Coordinator
PEL	Personal Exposure Limit
PER	Process Emission Regulations
PIC	Production of Incomplete Combustion
PM	Particulate Matter
POM	Polycyclic Organic Matter
POTW	Publicly Owned Treatment Works

PRM	Proposed Rulemaking
PRP	Potentially Responsible Party
PSD	Prevent Significant Deterioration
PSD	Prevention of Significant Deterioration
PSES	Pretreatment Standards for Existing Sources
PSNS	Pretreatment Standards for New Sources
QA/QC	Quality Assurance/Quality Control
RA	Remedial Action
RACT	Reasonably Available Control Technology
RAP	Remedial Action Plan
RCRA	Resource Conservation and Recovery Act (the Solid Waste Disposal Act)
RD	Remedial Design
RFA	RCRA Facility Assessment
RFI	RCRA Facility Investigation
RI	Remedial Investigation
RI/FS	Remedial Investigation/Feasibility Study
RIA	Regulatory Impact Analysis
RMCL	Recommended Maximum Contaminant Level
RMPP	Risk Management and Prevention Plan
ROD	Record of Decision
ROSE	Remote Optical Sensing of Emissions
RQ	Reportable Quantity
RTECS	Registry of Toxic Effects of Controlled Substances
SAB	Science Advisory Board (EPA)
SARA	Superfund Amendments and Reauthorization Act
SCAQMD	South Coast Air Quality Management District (California)
SDWA	Safe Drinking Water Act
SEC	State Environmental Coordinator
SIC	Standard Industrial Classification
SIP	State (Air Quality) Implementation Plan
SNUR	Significant New Use Rule
SPCC	Spill Prevention Control and Countermeasure Plan
SQG	Small-Quantity Generator
SRF	State Revolving Funds
SSA	Sole-Source Aquifer

STAPPA	State and Territorial Air Pollution Program Administrators
STORET	Storage and Retrieval System
SWMU	Solid Waste Management Unit
TCLP	Toxic Characteristic Leaching Procedure
TLV	Threshold Limit Values
TMDL	Total Maximum Daily Loads
TQM	Total Quality Management
TRI	Toxic Release Inventory
TSCA	Toxic Substances Control Act
TSDF	Treatment, Storage, and Disposal Facility
TSP	Total Suspended Particulates
TSS	Total Suspended Solids
TWA	Time Weighted Average
UAO	Unilateral Administrative Order
UCR	Upper Confidence Range
UIC	Underground Injection Control
USDW	Underground Source of Drinking Water
UST	Underground Storage Tank
VHAP	Volatile Hazardous Air Pollutant
VOC	Volatile Organic Compound
VOL	Volatile Organic Liquid
WEF	Water Environment Federation
WQC	Water Quality Criteria
WQS	Water Quality Standard

Index

Accounting concepts, environmental costs and, 226–230
  capitalization of remedy assets, 229–230
  consistency, 227
  the going concern, 227
  insolvency, 227–228
  matching, 228
Administrative order on consent (*see* Consent order)
Advertising (*see* Communication)
Aerospace Industries Association, 116–118
Agencies, regulatory and enforcement:
  communicating with, 11–12, 54–59
  lead, 9, 11
  relations, tips for good, 59
  services provided by, 54–55
  state, typical divisions within, 54–58
  types of, 11–12
  (*See also* Regulation)
Air pollution
  indoor, 93
  mobile and stationary sources of, 91
  regulations, 90–93
  smog, 50–51
Air & Waste Management Association (AWMA), 118, 120–121
Air Force Material Command, U.S., 117
American Water Works Association (AWWA), 118–119
Acquisition and divestiture 2, 15
  (*See also* Liability, real estate transactions)
Army Corps of Engineers, U.S., 86, 90
Asbestos:
  in audits, 47
  and criminal liability, 36
  regulations, 94
Asbestos Hazard Emergency Response Act (AHERA), 94
Asbestos School Hazard Abatement Act, 93, 94

Ashland Oil Company, 191
Assembly Bill 646 (California), 180–182
Assessment (*see* Auditing; Site assessment)
Associations:
  benefits, 110–114
  benchmarking, 111–112
  current information, 110–111
  industry-specific studies, 111
  lobbying and regulatory interface, 111
  professional networking, 112
  cost, 106, 107, 109, 110
  levels of involvement, 112–114
  committee participation, 112
  mailing, 113–114
  meeting attendance, 113
  steering committee, 112
  profiles of representative, 9, 115–121
  structure, typical, 106–107
  types, 7, 105–110
  compared, 109
  formal and informal, 106–107
  general industry, 107–108
  industry-specific, 107–108
  industry- and environment-specific, 107, 110
Atomic Energy Commission, 62
Auditing:
  auditors, training of, 9
  benefits of, 39–41
  concerns about, 42
  conducting audits, 43–47
  for cost reduction, 42
  and legal counsel, 43–44
  prosecution, to deter, 41
  and risk reduction, 2, 39–42
  scope, 45–47

Bell Helicopter-Textron, 117

About the Contributors

Mark G. Busch Senior Environmental Control Engineer at Northrop Aircraft Division in Hawthorne, Calif. As the senior environmental engineer in Northrop's training group, Mr. Busch develops and presents training packages for management, salaried, and hourly personnel. He recently designed a program to train 5,600 employees in hazardous waste handling and spill and leak response. He serves on the curriculum advisory committee for hazardous materials technology at West Los Angeles College, and he is a member of the National Environmental Training Association.

John Cornelison Manager of Safety at America North, Inc. in Anchorage, Alaska. Mr. Cornelison coordinates all safety and training activities at the firm, which provides environmental consulting, engineering, and health and safety services to a wide range of clients. With 28 years of experience in environmental management and safety, he has managed projects costing up to $600 million both in the U.S. and overseas.

Paul B. Duff Director of Environmental Affairs at Textron Inc., in Providence, R.I. Mr. Duff has devoted 23 years to environmental matters. For the past seven years at Textron Inc., he has been involved in developing and implementing a comprehensive corporate environmental affairs program. The company's compliance program involves an annual self–survey at 140 manufacturing facilities throughout the U.S. and Canada. Trained as a chemical engineer, he has taught and lectured widely on environmental subjects.

Major John Gunderson   Attorney with the U.S. Air Force. He has served tours of duty in Korea, Spain, and throughout the United States. He holds an LL.M. in environmental law from George Washington University. Currently, Major Gunderson is chief of environmental law at Vandenberg Air Force Base in California.

Glenn Heyman   Environmental Scientist in the U.S. Environmental Protection Agency's Region IX head-quarters in San Francisco, Calif. He currently oversees corrective action activities under RCRA consent orders and serves as a technical consultant within the agency on hydrology issues. A registered geologist, he worked previously in environmental consulting and also in the oil and gas exploration industry, where he worked for ARCO Exploration Company in the Colorado Plateau area of Utah and Colorado.

Stephen T. Holzer, Esq.   Principal in the law firm of Parker, Milliken, Clark, O'Hara, and Samuelian in Los Angeles, Calif. With a background in general business litigation, Mr. Holzer has for the past seven years spe-cialized in environmental law. He advises major corpo-rations on regulatory compliance issues and has con-ducted environmental audits. He has lectured and advised clients on the rights of companies undergoing government environmental inspections, and has served as defense counsel in environmentally related misde-meanor and felony prosecutions.

Steven J. Jones   Supervising Air Quality Inspector at the South Coast Air Quality Management District head-quarters in Diamond Bar, Calif. The District is the lead agency for the enforcement of air pollution rules and regulations for five counties in southern California. He has 15 years of experience in environmental affairs, and has played a key role in some of the largest penalty set-tlements in the District's history. In addition to con-ducting inspections, he serves as a public speaker on the District's activities and operations. He holds an undergraduate degree in chemistry and a master's degree in environmental and occupational health.

Hank Martin Vice President and Managing Principal Engineer for McLaren-Hart Environmental Engineering in Warren, New Jersey. He is responsible for the development and implementation of air quality, regulatory compliance, and remedial action programs. Prior to joining McLaren-Hart, Mr. Martin was extensively involved in the legislative and regulatory process, first as environmental quality director for the California Manufacturers Association and later as an independent lobbyist specializing in environmental issues at the California State Legislature.

Gary A. Meyer, Esq. Principal in the law firm of Parker, Milliken, Clark, O'Hara, and Samuelian in Los Angeles, Calif., and cochair of the firm's Environmental Law Department. He represents clients in civil and criminal hazardous waste enforcement matters and is an expert in the environmental aspects of real estate and commercial transactions. He is a recent chairperson of the Environmental Law Section of a major southern California bar association, and also serves as an instructor in the Hazardous Materials Certification Program at the University of California, Los Angeles.

John E. Mullane Vice President and Director of the Division of Scientific, Technical, and Environmental Affairs at the public relations firm of Hill & Knowlton in New York City. His primary responsibilities are in the areas of environmental health, science, and medicine. Mr. Mullane consults with clients on sensitive issues such as facility siting, waste disposal, and product contamination. Experienced and trained in public relations crisis management, he has taught at Fordham University and is the author of numerous articles and papers on public relations topics.

Edward O. (Ned) Raynolds Senior Vice President at Hill & Knowlton in New York. His clients have included energy companies, public utilities, and a wide variety of other industrial and service enterprises. His past work includes supervising Hill & Knowlton's efforts in the Columbia Gas producer contract crisis. A recognized expert in crisis management, he is unit manager of Hill & Knowlton's Corporate Counseling Division.

Kenneth M. Ries Director, Environment and Energy, for The Dial Corp in Phoenix, Ariz. The Dial Corp manufactures chemicals, transportation equipment, and food, and provides diversified services to a wide variety of companies. He has more than 30 years of experience in addressing the broad range of issues arising in environmental and energy engineering. A registered professional engineer, he holds a bachelor's degree in civil engineering, a master's degree in sanitary engineering, and a Ph.D. in environmental engineering.

Kraig H. Scheyer Manager of the Safety, Health, and Environmental Affairs Department at TRW in Redondo Beach, Calif. Mr. Scheyer is a registered mechanical engineer with an M.B.A. from the University of California, Los Angeles. He is responsible for occupational and radiation safety, industrial hygiene, environmental compliance, and energy management for the Space and Defense Sector at TRW. The assistance he provides to space and defense facilities is directed at ensuring regulatory compliance and cost–effective energy use. Mr. Scheyer is also chairman of the California Aerospace Environmental Association.

Richard Varenchik Public Information Officer in the Department of Toxic Substances Control of the California Environmental Protection Agency. With 17 years of experience in journalism and public relations, he joined the California EPA. His prior experience included work as a newspaper reporter, news service manager, and magazine contributor. He also worked as a public information officer for the California State Legislature.

Norman L. Weiss Compliance Manager for EMCON Associates in Phoenix, Ariz. He has more than 15 years of experience in environmental compliance programs. Prior to his current assignment, he served as assistant director with the Arizona Department of Environmental Quality. He holds a bachelor of science degree in biological science and a master's degree in geography and land use studies.

W. Gordon Wood Vice President of Finance and Chief Financial Officer for the facilities division of a Fortune 100 company. Mr. Wood has more than 15 years of experience in financial operations management. He also has more than six years in financial analysis and auditing. As chief financial officer, his responsibilities include budgeting for potential environmental crises and ongoing environmental expenses, as well as providing financial advice and analysis to support major investment decisions.

Cathie Wright Member of the California State Senate with extensive experience in environmental legislation. In the Senate, she serves on the environmental safety and toxic materials legislative committees. She joined the Legislature in 1980 after holding positions in local government, where she gained direct experience in local environmental and waste management issues. As an assemblywoman she authored a number of environmental bills. In 1988, she was named Legislator of the Year.

Photo not available

Robert Young Manager of Environmental Services at Bell Helicopter in Forth Worth, Tex., prior to his retirement in 1992. In 25 years at this company, he held a variety of positions related to environmental affairs. Among his accomplishments are innovative energy conservation projects that won national awards. He also served on the environmental and energy committees of numerous industry and professional associations, and was involved in the early development of environmental industry groups in the State of Texas.

About the Editors

Betty J. Seldner   Environmental trainer, consultant, and educator in Santa Clarita, Calif. A former director of environmental management at a large aerospace company, she has devoted almost two decades to the environmental field. She currently operates her own consulting firm and serves as adjunct professor at West Coast University.

Joseph Cothrel   Writer and communications consultant specializing in environmental and energy issues, based in Chicago, Ill. His clients have included major companies in the electric, natural gas, and petroleum industries. He formerly served as senior technical editor at EMCON Associates, a national environmental engineering and consulting firm.